ORIGAMI OMNIBUS

ORIGAMI
OMNIBUS

Paper-folding for Everybody

Kunihiko Kasahara

Japan Publications, Inc.

© 1988 by Kunihiko Kasahara
Photographs by Kazuo Sugiyama

Published by Japan Publications, Inc., Tokyo

Distributors:
    UNITED STATES: Kodansha America, Inc. through Oxford University Press,
      198 Madison Avenue, New York, NY 10016.
    CANADA: Fitzhenry & Whiteside Ltd., 195 Allstate Parkway, Markham,
    Ontario, L3R 4T8.
    Australia and New Zealand: Bookwise International Pty Ltd.
      174 Cormack Road, Wingfield, SA   5013, Australia
    Asia and other countries: Japan Publications Trading Co., Ltd., 1-2-1,
    Sarugaku-cho,Chiyoda-ku, Tokyo 101-0064, Japan

First edition: January 1988
Fourteenth printing: February 2008

ISBN: 978-4-8170-9001-0

Printed in U.S.A.

Foreword

In late October, 1986, a large number of origamians gathered at the New York Origami Center to celebrate my eighty-eighth birthday. To my surprise, among them was Kunihiko Kasahara, who was on his way back to Japan after having delivered lectures on origami in Brazil and Chile. To my even greater surprise, he had changed little since the only other meeting I had with him, twenty years ago, when Alice Gray and I visited Japan.

When I asked how old he was, he evaded by asking my opinion of his age. "In your twenties, I'd say," was my reply. And he said, "Right." "Well then, you must have been an infant when we met the first time!" I retorted, to everyone's amusement.

Although he then frankly admitted to being forty-five—already middle-aged—he seemed much younger to me. And I suppose the reason is that being able to pursue origami enthusiastically and exclusively all these years has kept him happy and youthful. Time may move more slowly for him than for people in other, ordinary walks of life. Yes, I am convinced that origami can keep those who love it happy.

Origami Omnibus, his latest book, is, in his own words, a kind of graduate thesis devoted to the results of his twenty-five years of work in origami. Unlike some origamians, who close themselves up in their own creative world to the exclusion of all others, Kasahara is extremely open and, as *Origami for the Connoisseur*, which he co-authored with Toshie Takahama, makes clear, introduces good origami by other people with as much pride as he shows in introducing his own. Many younger origamians can learn something from his attitude in this respect.

Although *Origami Omnibus* is all in his style, ideas from many other origamians have happily come on board, as he points out, from place to place, in the text.

The youthful ardor with which he has filled this book is certain to open appealing vistas to many people, and it makes me happy to think how this will increase the number of happy origamians in the world.

October, 1987

Lillian Oppenheimer

Lillian Oppenheimer

Preface

It took more than a year to go over all the origami I have happily and enthusiastically worked on during the past twenty-five years and to select the ones I find successful. Because there were many that I wanted to include and because I have been loquacious in my explanations, this is the longest of all my origami books.

Nonetheless, since, as the very Japanese word indicates, actually folding paper accounts for the pleasure of origami. Indeed, most of my plentiful text pertains to the processes leading to the discovery of various origami works. I hope that, once the process is clear, the reader will understand the direction each origami pursues and will be stimulated to independent creative challenges.

I have tried to make the book more than sufficiently enjoyable to compensate for its size—and price. In its production, I have enjoyed the cooperation and good will of many people, including Iwao Yoshizaki, president of Japan Publications, Inc.; Yotsuko Watanabe, the editor; Richard L. Gage, the translator, Tatsundo Hayashi, the designer; and Kazuo Sugiyama, the photographer. I should like to express my heartfelt gratitude to all these people and suggest that the reader now move on to the text, where the quality of their work will immediately become apparent.

November, 1987
Kunihiko Kasahara

▲ Dove of Peace (p. 362)
   Rose (p. 338)

◄ Panorama Box with Four-seasonal
   Scenes, developed one after the
   other, beginning on the next page.

A Paper Wonderland

Boundless fantasy from a single, small sheet of paper. This is the pleasure and the miracle of the origami wonderland.

First eight small cubes from a single
large one.

▼

The Fun of Geometric Forms

The day when origami will be a highly valued educational tool in the mathematics classroom is just around the corner. I am delighted by anticipating its arrival.

Reversing and assembling 3 of the 8 small cubes create a beautiful geometric solid, or polyhedron. The complete development appears on the next page.

▼

Three developed polyhedrons are arranged to suggest a range of mountains. The remaining 5 compose seasonal scenes of—counterclockwise—spring, summer (early and full), autumn, and winter.

New Materials
In this scientific age, new materials are constantly being created and marketed.
These works make use of extremely popular plastic films and foil papers.

Contents

**Chapter 6: Viva Origami
    249**

The Future of a New Origami

Today at the mention of origami, everyone calls to mind the now world-famous small colored square sheets of paper everyone uses. Actually, however, the history of such paper employed in origami for amusement is fairly short. In the late nineteenth century, a paper dealer in the Yushima district of Tokyo imported colored papers from Europe, cut them into small squares, and sold them in sets called *origami*. And this was the origin of the kind of origami popular today.

Of course, origami itself is much older than the late nineteenth century. But unitl that time, it had been known by a variety of names—*kami-orimono, orisue, origata, tatamigami*, and so on—and had employed the kind of paper called *hanshi*, which is white on both sides and rectangular in shape.

It seems likely that the Yushima paper dealer decided to cut his paper square because many of the outstanding trditional origami folds—including the crane, the paper balloon, the so-called *yakko* serving man, and the ceremonial tray-stand called a *sambō* were all produced from squares of paper. No matter what his reasons, however, his idea was an excellent one that ensured great future development.

Frankly, it is difficult to explain why the square has been as importantas it has. Though it may not be an answer to the problem, my own impression is that the reason is to be found in the profound mystery inherent in the square. Observing a square piece of paper and experimenting the feel of limitless, pristine expanse it inspire awaken in me the desire to blaze my own trail in its spaces. Because they already represent preestablished ideas, such other forms as rectangles and triangles inspire this feeling to a much lesser extent.

In saying this, I have no intention of rejecting these forms. Indeed, I deal with them extensively as the outcomes of deliberate operations. But I shall go into all of this in detail in the body of the text.

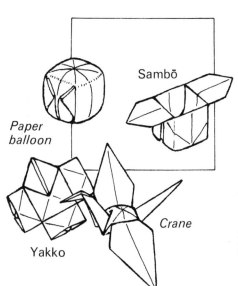

Sambō

Paper balloon

Yakko

Crane

In this book I intend to go beyond the appeal of finished folds and hope to examine the fascination of origami from various viewpoints. In keeping with what I said in the preceding paragraphs, I will use square paper as the basis and attempt to discover what happens to it with the initial one or two folds.

First, examine *A* and imagine folding corner *P* upward to a series of locations along the edge connecting corners *a* and *b*. Producing *B* by folding *P* divides the square in half into two equal rectangles. Producing *D* by folding *P* to *b* divides the square in half into two equal triangles. Neither of these ordinary results arouses any interest.

Effects of adopting different viewpoints

How much more challenging it is to attempt to fold so that, as is the case in *B* and *D*, the areas are equal and are half of the original sheet, though the forms produced are squares or pentagons. Can you do it?

No doubt, when you turn the page and see the answers, you will say, "Oh! So that's what you're talking about." *C*, which is midway between *B* and *D*, employs what is called the Haga Theorem and divides side *bc* into three equal parts. As astonishing as it might seem, serial folding, like the kind shown in *E*, generates a parabola.

A

B

C
Part of the truth of the Haga Theorem

D

E

I hit upon this phenomenon in *E* myself but then later found solid scientific explanation for it in a book entitled *Shakai-jin no Sugaku* (Mathematics for the working man), by Kazuo Takano.

Parabola

Folding corner *P* to various positions along side *ab*—moving from *a* to *b*—produces a line or crease describing a parabola, of which *P* is the focal point.

I think you should now understand how a few simple folds in a square piece of paper can be very significant. Repeated discoveries of this kind made from novel standpoints will make origami very effective in the teaching of geometry and mathematics.

When judged solely on the basis of the forms it can produce, origami may be either praised as art or condemned as mere imitation. The point I wish to make here is that, when one's viewpoint is altered, origami is seen as including many possibilities extending far beyond mere completed figures.

I must point out, however, that this book is intended for the general origami fan. Consequently, I have neither the intention nor the capability of delving profoundly into mathematical and scientific issues. Nonetheless, I have included a number of works—especially in Chapters 2 and 5—incorporating the discoveries and viewpoints of outstanding mathematically-minded origami researchers.

At present origami is going through a stage of transition from a lyrical handicraft to an intellectual hobby. We are witnessing what might be called the birth of modern origami. But in these rapidly changing times, how long the modernity represented by this book will continue to be modern is debatable.

The outstanding work on the facing page, the *tatō* was discovered by Kōji Fushimi and his wife Mitsué. At about the same time, I evolved a fold that is very similar. The difference between my version and the Fushimi one led Hisashi Abè to discover his Tripartite Fold at an Arbitrary Angle, which I shall deal with later.

Various ways to fold a square in half

(The answer to the problem posed on the preceding page)

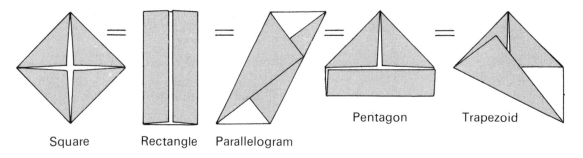

Square   Rectangle   Parallelogram   Pentagon   Trapezoid

Hiroshi Noguchi, *Kodansha Gendai Shinsho*
Zukei Asobi no Sekai (The world of playing with geometric figures). First edition, 1981. A detailed report appears in this book.

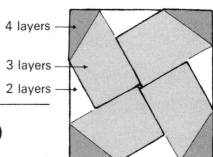

4 layers

3 layers

2 layers

Kōji Fushimi *tatō* (variant fold)

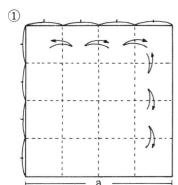

①

1 : 1/3

Area

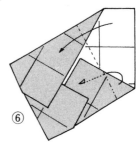

⑦

$a : b = 1 : \dfrac{1}{\sqrt{3}} = \sqrt{3} : 1$

b

If it is folded of thin paper, light will shine through this figure, clearly indicating by means of light and dark the areas in which there are more and less layers. The areas of 2 and 4 layers have geometrically similar configurations. Bringing the 4-layer area on top of the 2-layer areas results in an overall figure consistently 3 layers thick. Mitsué Fushimi explains that it is possible to ascertain visually 1/3 of the area.

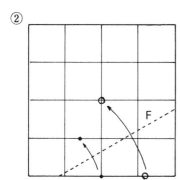

②

F

In this fold, crease *F* must make it possible for the pairs of points to align. In the original Fushimi version, this was explained as 2 processes.

⑥

③

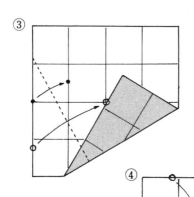

⑤

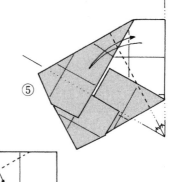

④

Reference
Origami no Kikagaku (The geometry of origami) by Kōji and Mitsué Fushimi, Nihon Hyoron-sha; first edition, July, 1979.
A milestone work in origami mathematics.

A

Crab folded from 2 sheets of paper. By Toshio Chino

Now to discuss a few of the major points of this book. One is the ideal origami should strive to attain. In the past, one of those ideals was the production of forms from a single sheet of paper without resorting to cutting. It was always assumed that work employing no cutting and avoiding assembling elements folded from more than one sheet was superior.

Many origamians still feel that this attitude is correct. Certainly it is justifiable in terms of level of technical folding skill. But abiding by these restrictions does not always necessarily produce the best origami work.

If we assume that origami's appeal derives solely from the forms of finished works, the objective characteristics of such works are rectilinear sharpness and rich symbolism.

As concrete examples, the crab in Fig. A, the work of the late Toshio Chino, is breathtaking in the cleanliness of its form.

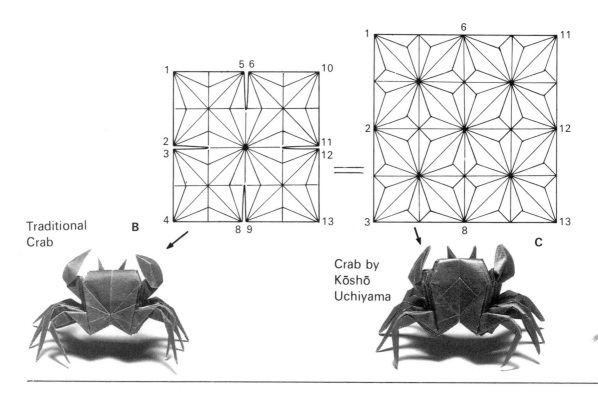

Traditional Crab **B**

Crab by Kōshō Uchiyama **C**

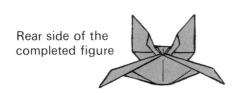

Rear side of the completed figure

D

Complete by adjusting points *a*, *b*, and *c* so that the figure stands.

a   b   ⑦   c

⑥

⑤

④

The two crab folds in *B* and *C*, on the opposite page, elicit exclamations of wonder. But the source of the admiration is less the forms themselves than the intuitively perceived skill required to produce such complicated work from a single sheet of paper.

Which of the works is more outstanding? From the traditional standpoint, the one that uses no cutting and is produced from a single sheet of paper must be judged superior. But this judgment clearly takes into consideration primarily technical considerations.

In the final analysis, judgments of this kind depend largely on emotion and personal preference. The true ideal is on the higher plane of understanding of the diversity of the human imagination. My crab (*D*) is based on Mr. Chino's and was inspired solely by my respect for him.

③   This is called the balloon base.

Crab

②

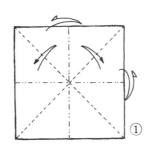

①

Whirling top

A small version of the ornament in the illustration at bottom left.

Although the somewhat rigid discussion up to this point might seem to suggest otherwise, the main aim of this book is to develop understanding of the diversity of the human imagination by clearly showing that the possibilities of a single sheet of paper are without limit and embrace such things as producing delightful origami forms, illustrating mathematical truths, and demonstrating rich functional variation. I hope that the many origami examples presented in the text will help achieve this aim. In concluding the introduction, I should like to offer some products of imaginative combination.

Robert Neal has combined six of the so-called balloon bases to produce a splendid ornament. Combining three of these bases represents imagination applied in three dimensions. The combination of the three is tantamount to folding from a single rectangular sheet.

Now, let us proceed to the main text and, working together, start the upward climb to new levels opening on still wider vistas of origami enjoyment.

Ornament by Robert Neal

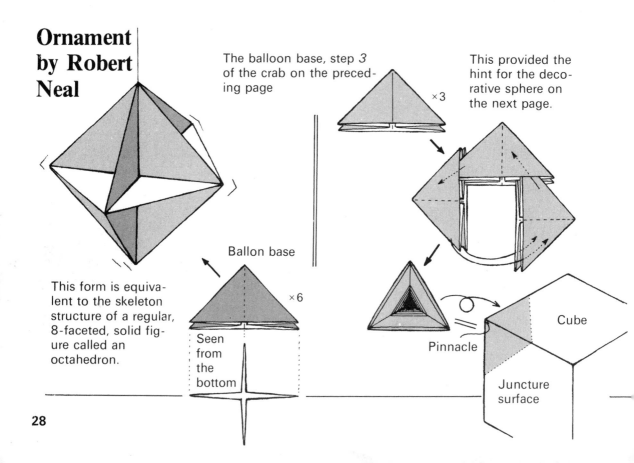

The balloon base, step *3* of the crab on the preceding page

This provided the hint for the decorative sphere on the next page.

×3

This form is equivalent to the skeleton structure of a regular, 8-faceted, solid figure called an octahedron.

Ballon base

×6

Seen from the bottom

Pinnacle

Cube

Juncture surface

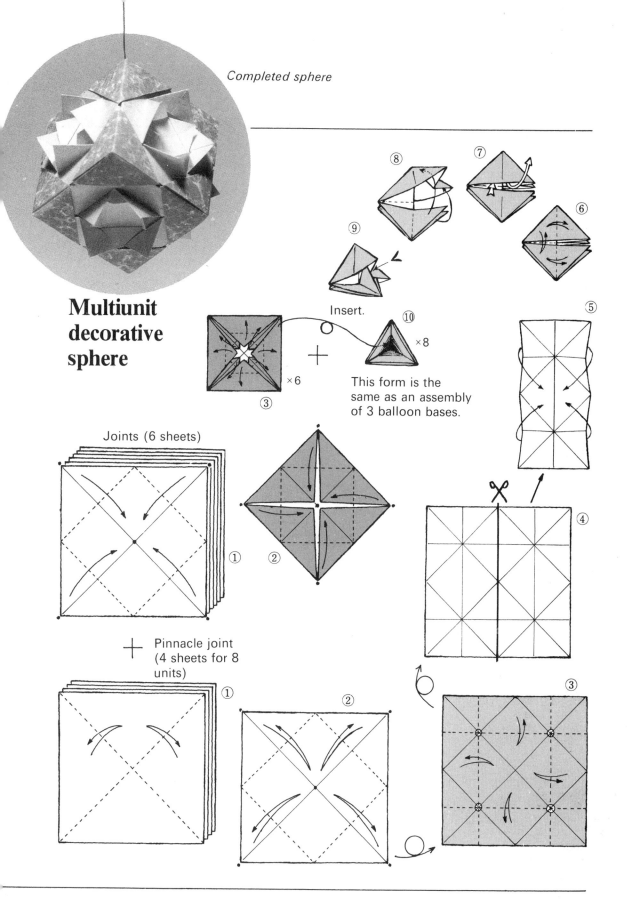

Completed sphere

Multiunit decorative sphere

Insert.

This form is the same as an assembly of 3 balloon bases.

Joints (6 sheets)

Pinnacle joint (4 sheets for 8 units)

Symbols and Folding Techniques

- - - - - - - - -   Valley fold

_ .. _ .. _ .. _ ...   Mountain fold

————————▶   Move paper in this direction.

————————▷   Fold under.

══════════▷   Pull or open out.

Figure enlargement

Pleat.

Turn the model over.

Crease by first folding and then unfolding.

❯   Push inward.

Spread layers then squash.

Inside reverse fold

Outside reverse fold

Folding sequence indicator
Supplemental explanations

.............,..........   X-ray view

⬧▶   Continued on next page.

Chapter 1

Expressions Unlimited

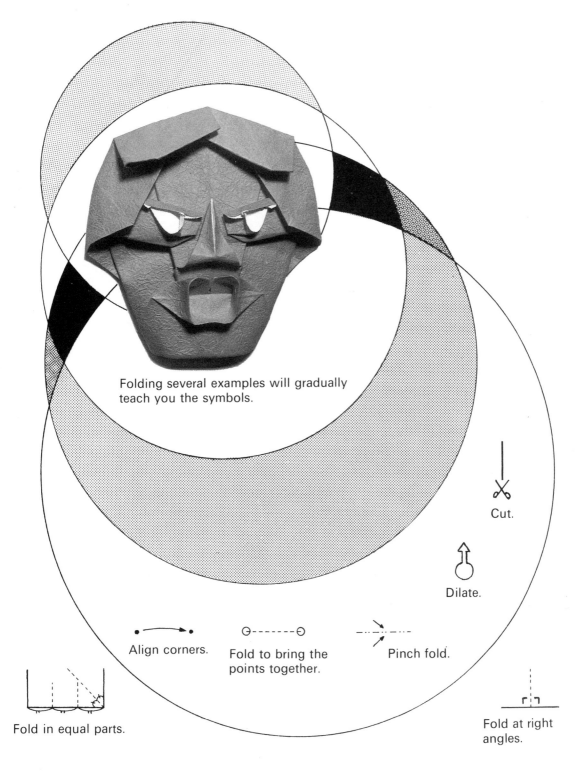

Folding several examples will gradually teach you the symbols.

Cut.

Dilate.

Align corners.

Fold to bring the points together.

Pinch fold.

Fold in equal parts.

Fold at right angles.

Masks for All Seasons

Simply folding a plain sheet of paper generates infinitely variable expressions that can be used in producing human facial emotional displays as well as in suggesting the forms of various birds and animals. To start out the book, I have assembled a collection of masks that give an excellent idea of the boundless wonder of origami.

Grinning Old Man

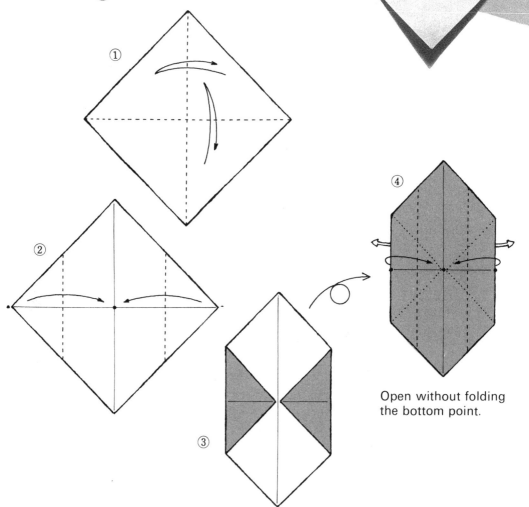

Open without folding the bottom point.

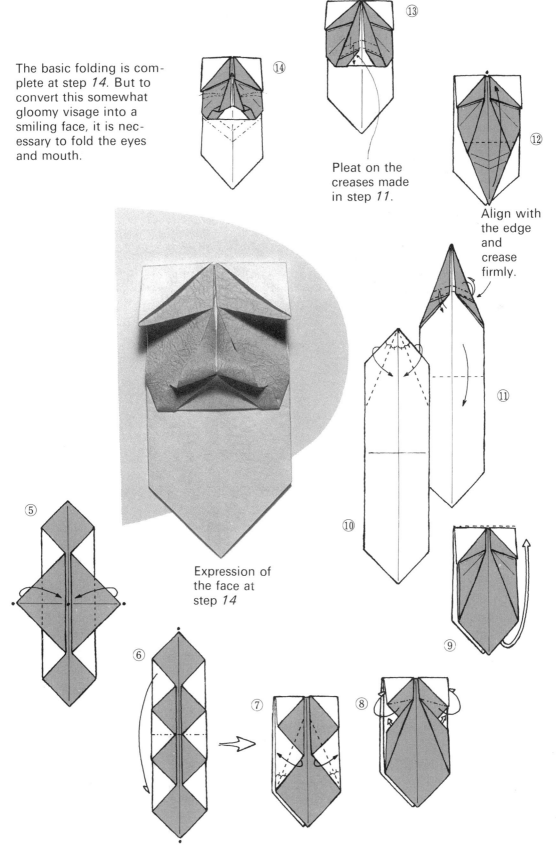

The basic folding is complete at step *14*. But to convert this somewhat gloomy visage into a smiling face, it is necessary to fold the eyes and mouth.

⑭

⑬

Pleat on the creases made in step *11*.

⑫

Align with the edge and crease firmly.

⑪

⑩

Expression of the face at step *14*

⑤

⑨

⑥

⑦

⑧

Celestial General

This mask is based on the faces of the twelve Celestial Generals whose statues often accompany those of the Buddha of Healing Bhaishaja-guru (known as Yakushi in Japanese). The folding is easy, but it is important to judge size and paper quality to suggest the strength and dignity of so austere a being as a celestial general.

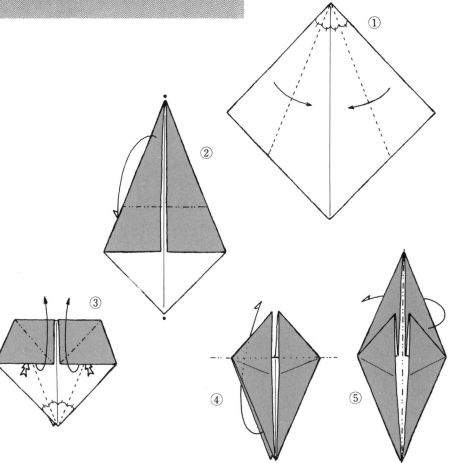

Steps *4* and *5* constitute what is known as the fish base, the origins of which may be traced to the fish-shaped banners called *koinobori* displayed in Japan on Boys' Day, May 5.

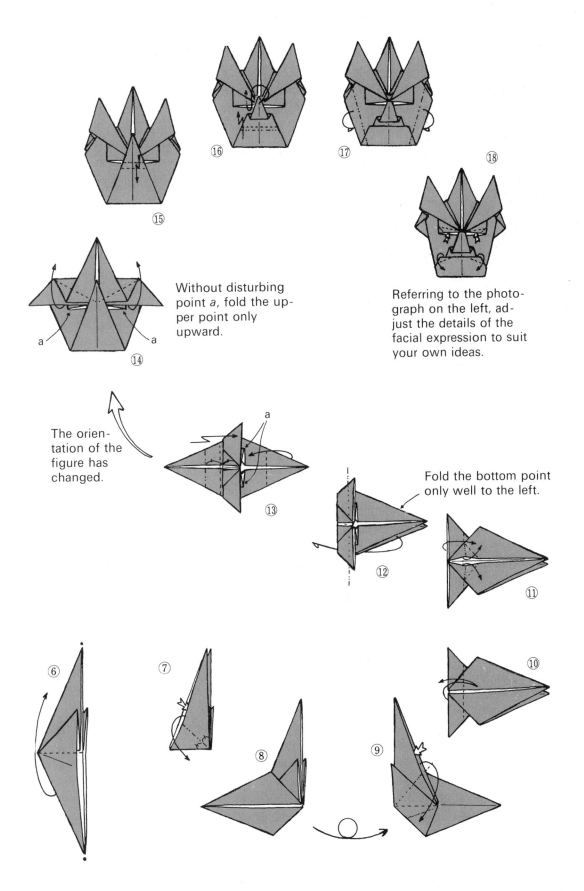

⑯

⑰

⑱

⑮

Without disturbing point *a*, fold the upper point only upward.

⑭

Referring to the photograph on the left, adjust the details of the facial expression to suit your own ideas.

The orientation of the figure has changed.

a

⑬

Fold the bottom point only well to the left.

⑫

⑪

⑥

⑦

⑧

⑨

⑩

Demon Mask

This example demonstrates how changes in folding at the finishing stage can completely alter the expression.

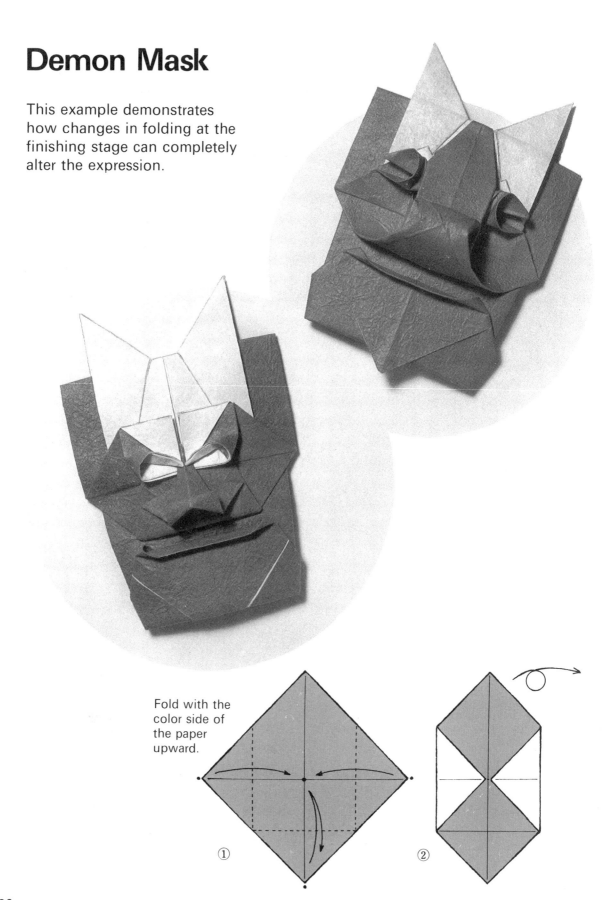

Fold with the color side of the paper upward.

①

②

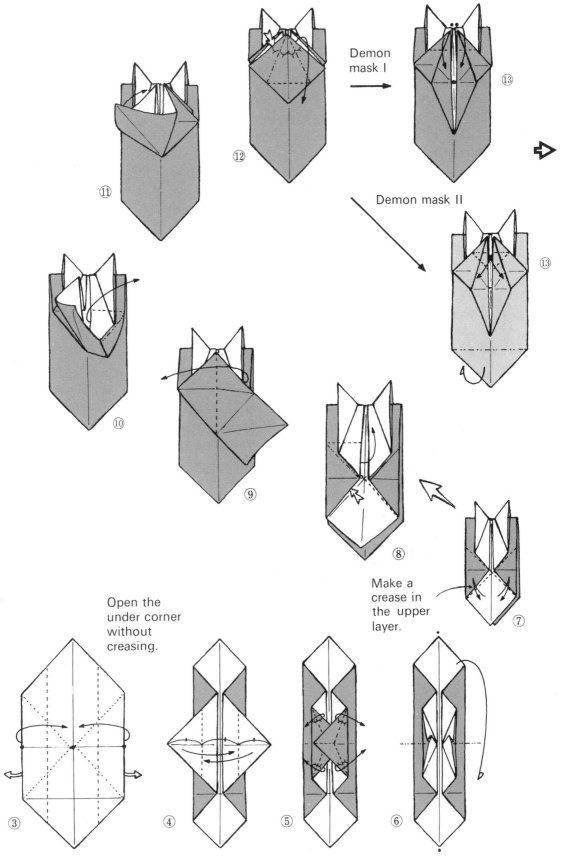

Demon mask I

⑬

Demon mask II

⑬

⑫

⑪

⑩

⑨

⑧

Make a crease in the upper layer.

⑦

Open the under corner without creasing.

③

④

⑤

⑥

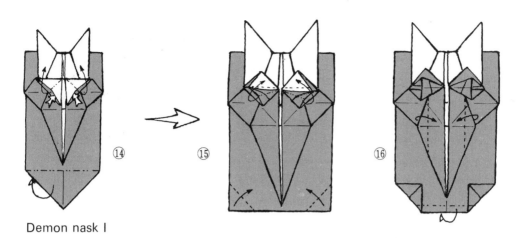

⑭ ⑮ ⑯

Demon nask I

Demon mask II

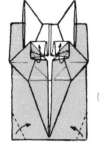

⑭

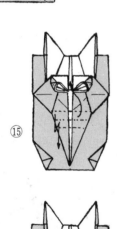

⑮

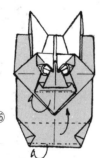

⑯

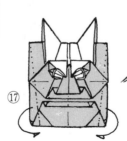

⑰

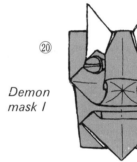

⑳

Demon
mask I

The completed mask

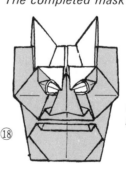

⑱

Demon
mask II

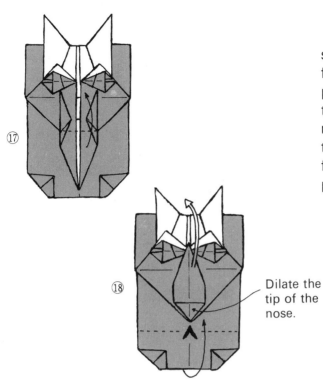

⑰

Although the mask theme shows how minor changes in folding lines greatly alter expression, in masks such features as eyes, nose, and mouth tend to become stereotyped. That is why I strove for a highly individual expression in Demon Mask I.

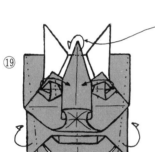

⑱

Dilate the tip of the nose.

⑲

It is a good idea to use a little glue to fix this point behind the mask.

Devil

Minor changes make the mask much more frightening.

Tengu Mask

The *Tengu* is a long-nosed goblin of Japanese folklore.

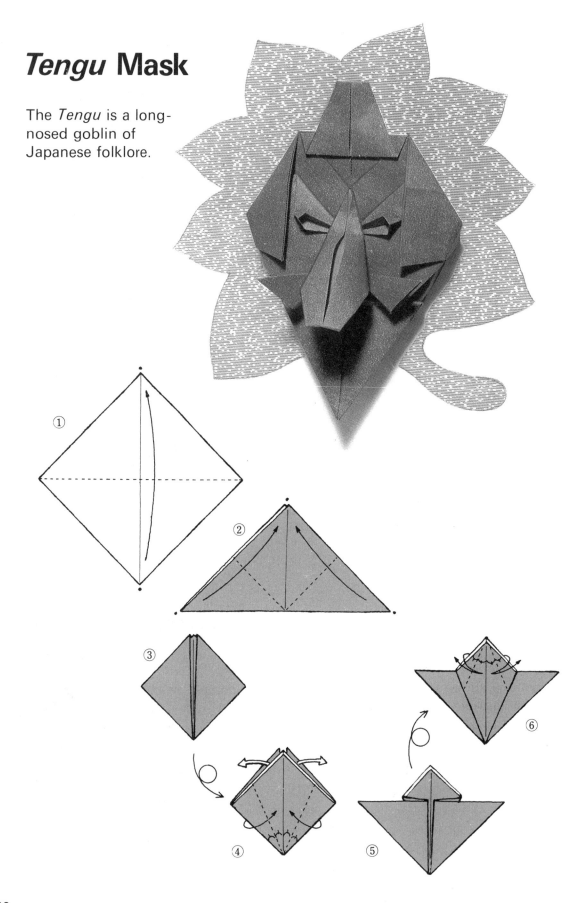

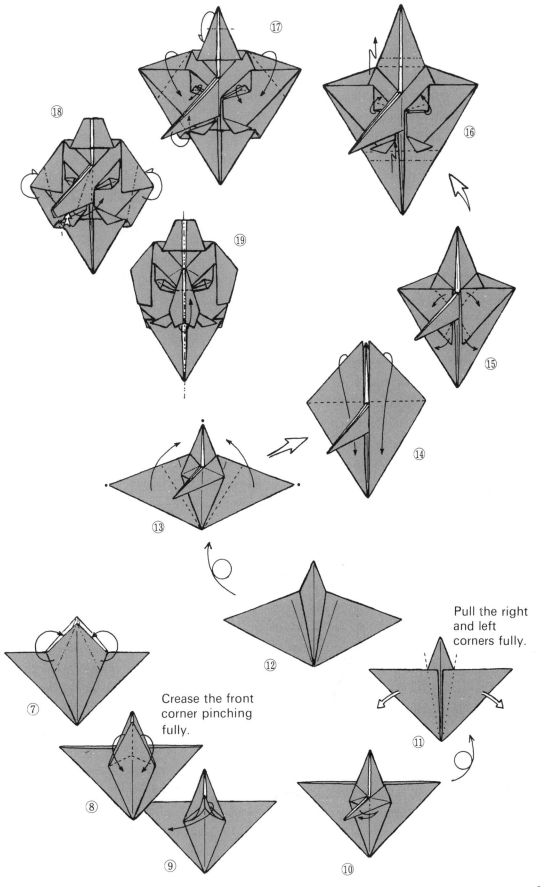

Crease the front corner pinching fully.

Pull the right and left corners fully.

Pinocchio Mask

From the long nose mask, we move to a mask representing the face of the puppet Pinocchio, from the famous story of the same name by Collodi. As you will remember, each time Pinocchio told a lie his nose grew longer. Since folding them produces too rigid an impression, I have painted in the eyes.

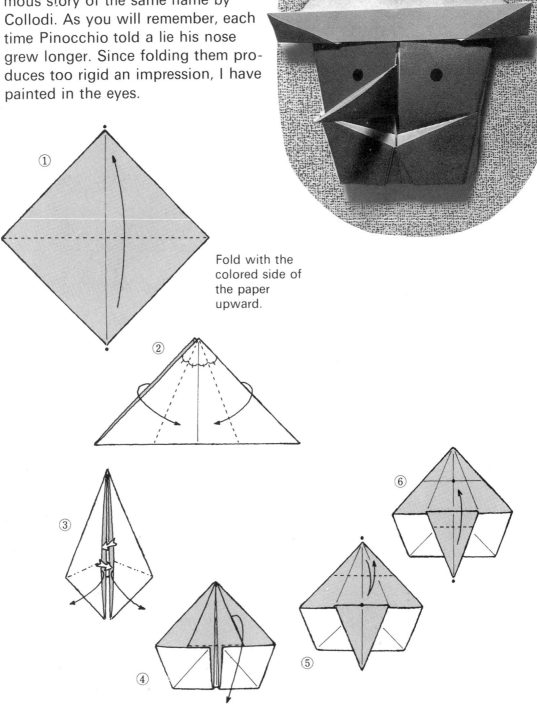

①

Fold with the colored side of the paper upward.

②

③

④

⑤

⑥

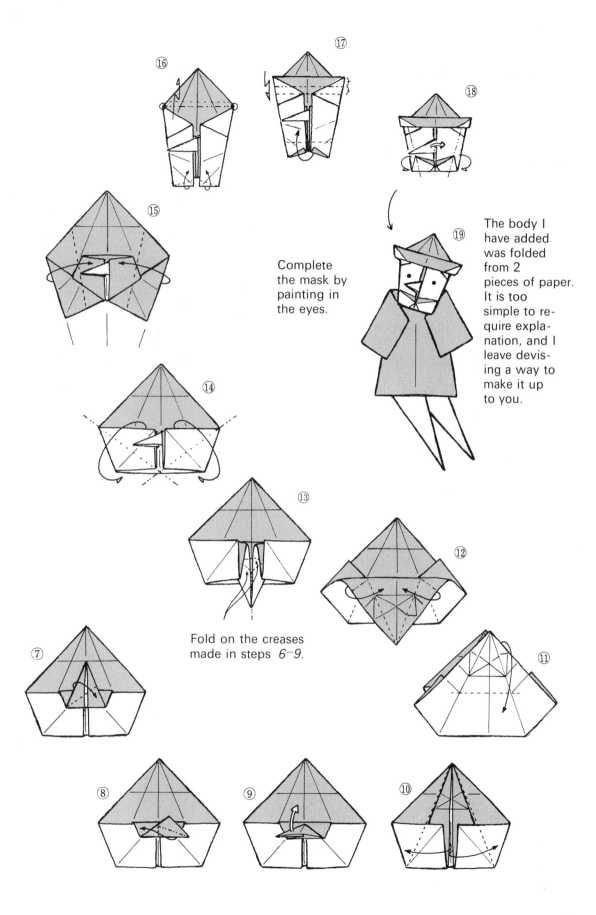

Complete
the mask by
painting in
the eyes.

The body I
have added
was folded
from 2
pieces of paper.
It is too
simple to re-
quire expla-
nation, and I
leave devis-
ing a way to
make it up
to you.

Fold on the creases
made in steps 6-9.

Monster from the Arabian Nights

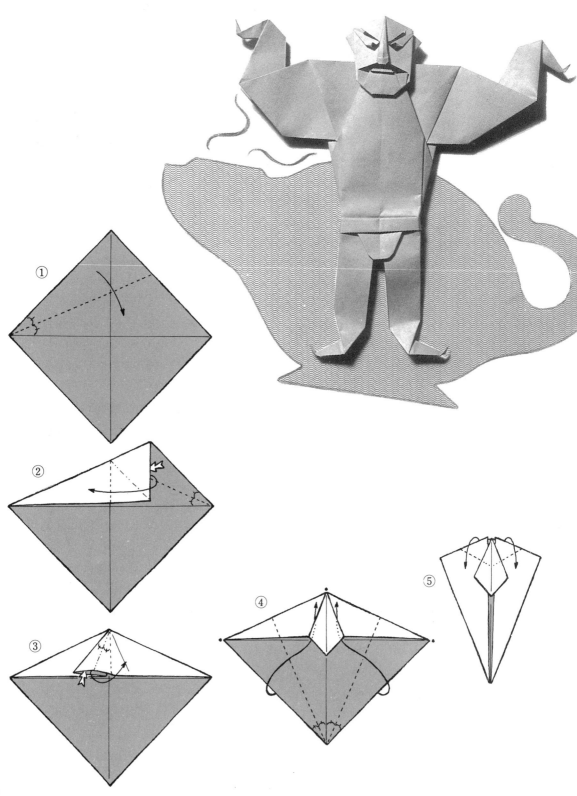

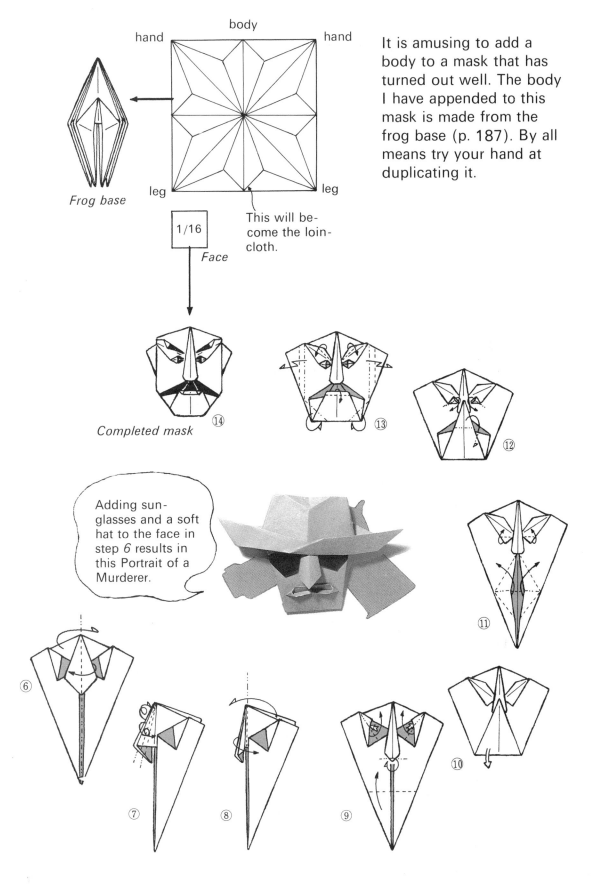

body

hand · hand

Frog base

This will become the loin-cloth.

leg · leg

1/16

Face

It is amusing to add a body to a mask that has turned out well. The body I have appended to this mask is made from the frog base (p. 187). By all means try your hand at duplicating it.

Completed mask ⑭

⑬

⑫

Adding sunglasses and a soft hat to the face in step 6 results in this Portrait of a Murderer.

⑪

⑥

⑦

⑧

⑨

⑩

Singer of Antiwar Songs

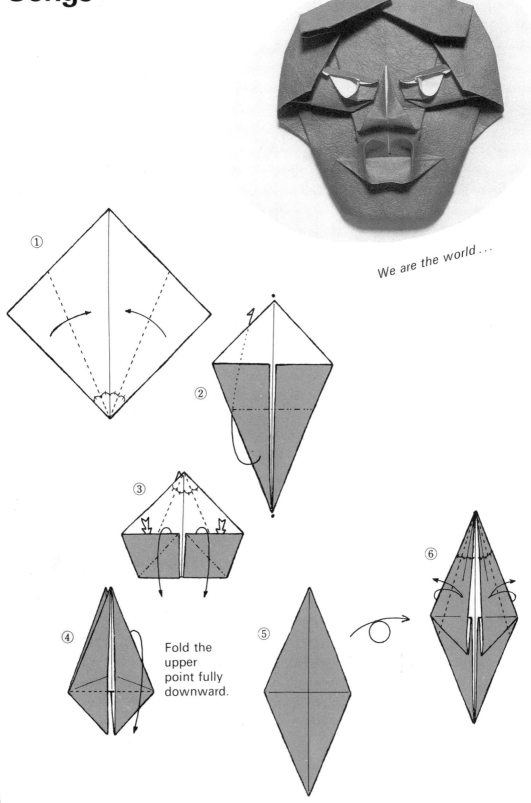

We are the world...

①

②

③

④ Fold the upper point fully downward.

⑤

⑥

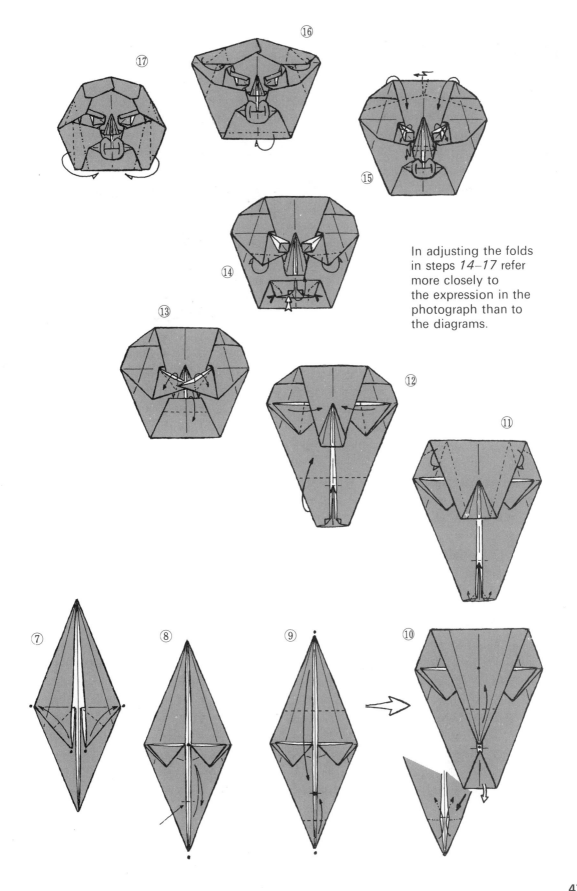

In adjusting the folds
in steps *14–17* refer
more closely to
the expression in the
photograph than to
the diagrams.

Kamui Mask

Interest in the archaeology of the Ainu people of northern Japan led me to devise this face of *Kamui*, which means God in the Ainu language.

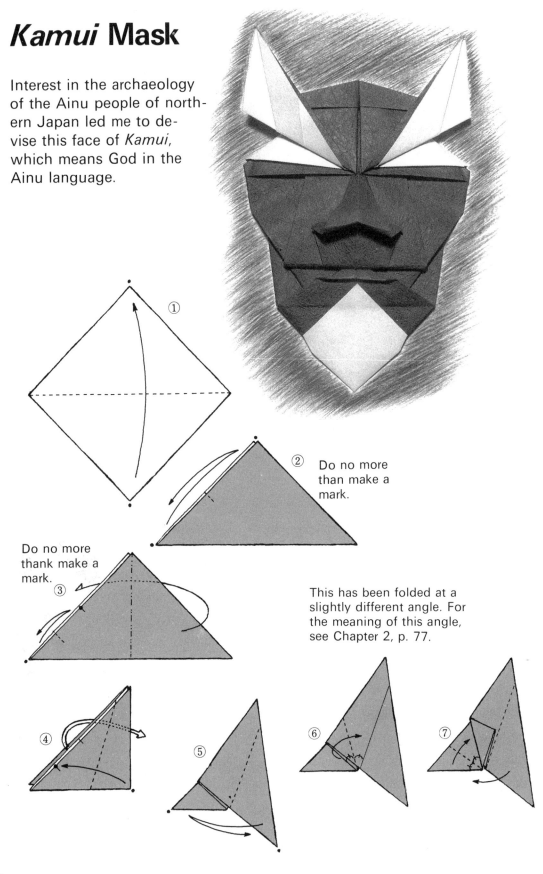

①

② Do no more than make a mark.

Do no more thank make a mark.

③

This has been folded at a slightly different angle. For the meaning of this angle, see Chapter 2, p. 77.

④

⑤

⑥

⑦

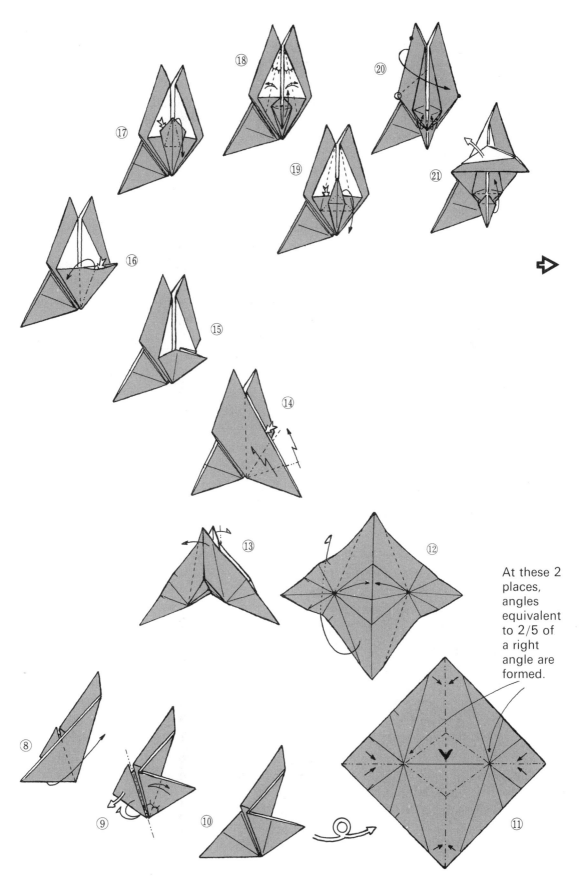

At these 2 places, angles equivalent to 2/5 of a right angle are formed.

49

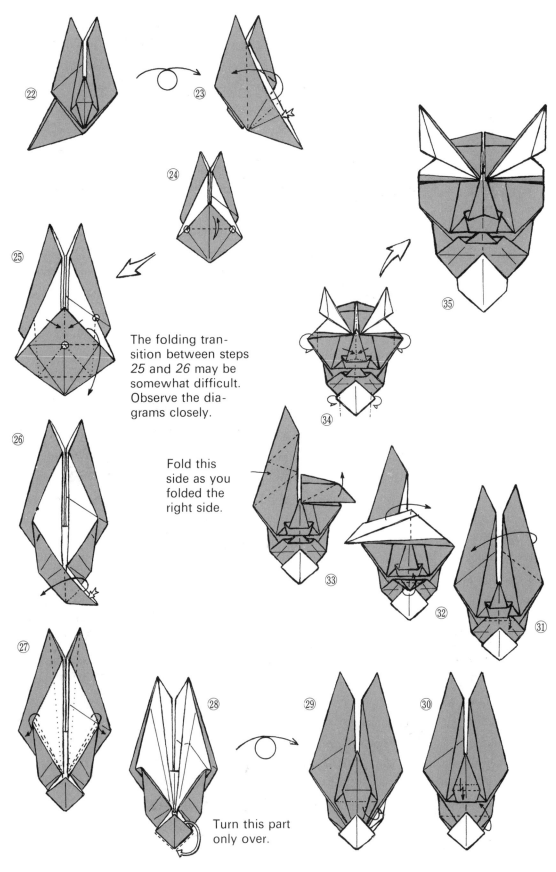

The folding tran-
sition between steps
25 and *26* may be
somewhat difficult.
Observe the dia-
grams closely.

Fold this
side as you
folded the
right side.

Turn this part
only over.

Lion

Now that we have worked with expressions in human and humanlike faces, let us conclude this chapter with a few funny animal faces. Full animal forms, which are more common in origami, are treated in Chapter 4. Folding methods are given for only two of the animal faces shown below.

Funny animal faces

Gorilla

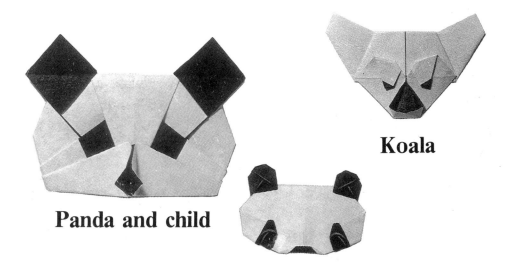

Koala

Panda and child

Lion (Male) Mane

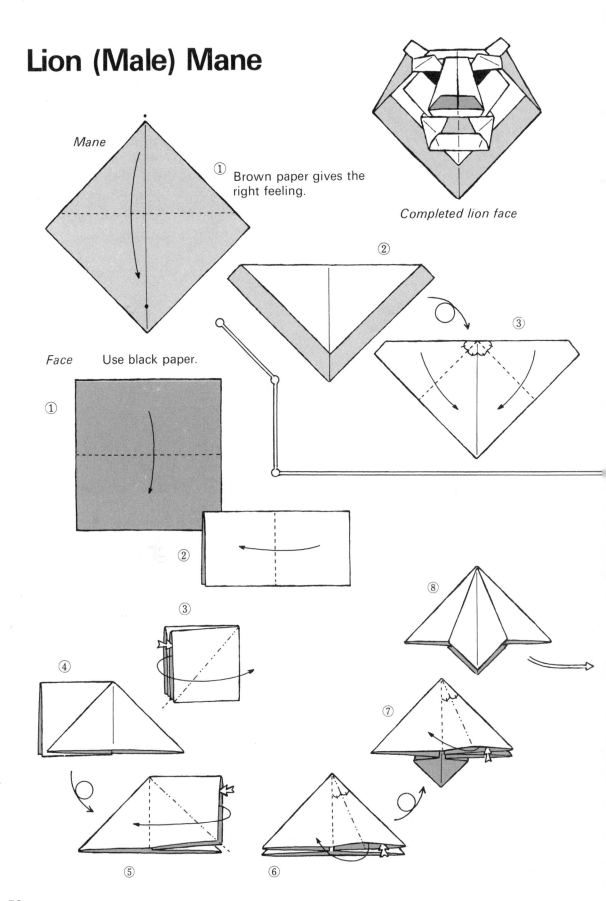

Mane

① Brown paper gives the right feeling.

Completed lion face

②

③

Face Use black paper.

①

②

③

④

⑤

⑥

⑦

⑧

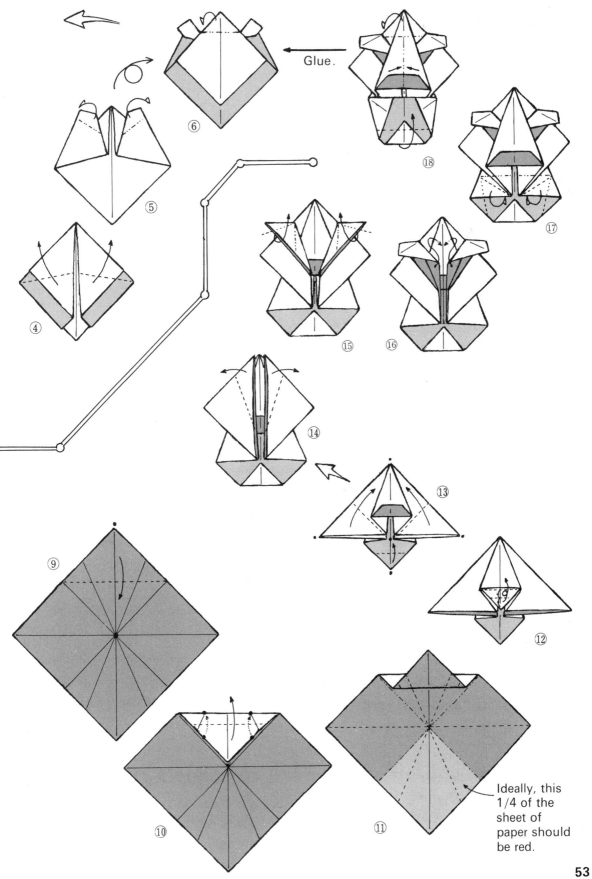

Glue.

Ideally, this
1/4 of the
sheet of
paper should
be red.

Gorilla

My version is a reworking of an idea by my senior in the field Atsushi Miyashita. Try your own hand at making a body to suit this gorilla head.

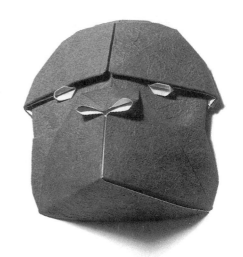

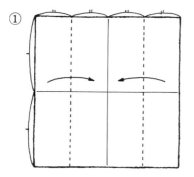

Referring to the photograph, strive to create a feeling of power and humorousness.

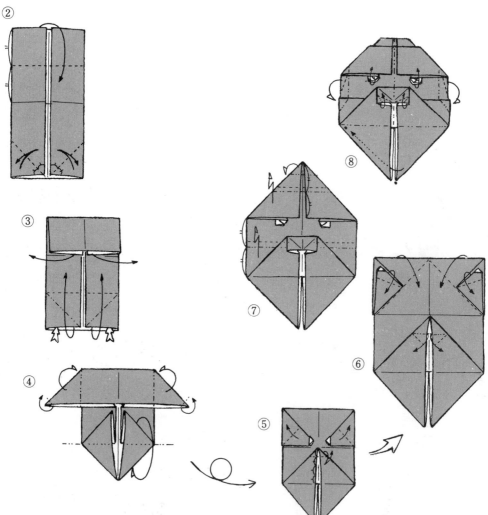

Chapter 2

Origami to Make You Think

A New Path

The well-established origami pursuit of beautiful static forms will no doubt continue long into the future. Producing birds, other animals, flowers, insects, and other creatures from single sheets of paper and reproducing the kinds of facial expressions represented by the masks in the preceding chapter are easy and fun and therefore remain among origami's greatest appeals. Consequently, many such forms are included in this book.

But modern origami has added to this appeal the stimulation and interest of investigating functionality, posing and solving puzzles, and pursuing geometric qualities through folding paper. And this has had an elevating effect on the quality of origami in general.

To demonstrate my meaning, I shall explain as we examine an actual example. The Rouge Container shown on the right is a practical piece of packaging said to have been devised for the Maeda family, extremely wealthy feudal lords of what was once called Kaga (modern Ishikawa Prefecture). But, if practical function were the sole consideration in its design, there would be no need in folding steps 5 through 9, whose only significance is aesthetic.

In addition, though the original deviser of the package may not have intended it, the ratio of exposed red and white surfaces of the paper is 1 : 1. This may seem like a very minor discovery, but it makes possible the creation of the form shown in *B* on the next page and the amusing puzzle associated with it. That puzzle is as follows: at stage *6*, the ratio between the colored and white surfaces is 4 : 3; the problem is to make that ratio 3 : 3 by performing only 1 fold. New viewpoints of this kind open fresh paths to still greater origami interest.

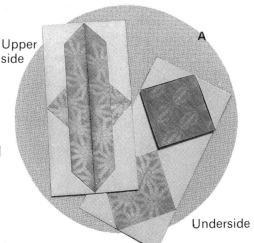

Upper side

Underside

A

Rouge container

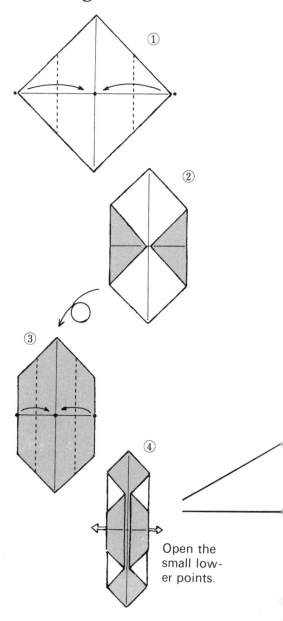

① ② ③ ④

Open the small lower points.

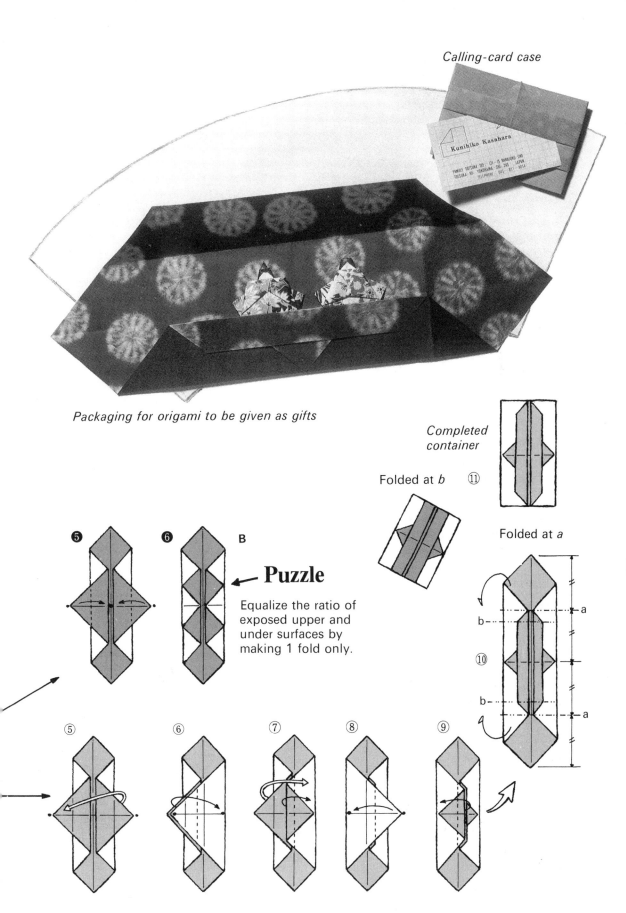

Calling-card case

Packaging for origami to be given as gifts

Completed container

Folded at *b*   ⑪

Folded at *a*

⑤   ⑥   B

Puzzle

Equalize the ratio of exposed upper and under surfaces by making 1 fold only.

⑤   ⑥   ⑦   ⑧   ⑨   ⑩

b — — a
b — — a

The Pleasure of Thinking

A

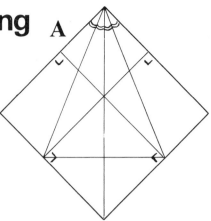

How many isosceles triangle can you find?

Now that you understand that, in addition to the beauty of form, the stimuli of its functional, geometric, and puzzle-like attributes account for much of the charm of origami, I shall examine a number of other examples from this new vantage point.

Though not a work but only a piece of paper creased in six lines, the square in *A* poses an interesting question: how many isosceles triangles can you find in it?

The answer is not as easy as might seem. It is seventeen. But this is less than a puzzle than a purely geometric problem demanding proof. Providing proof posits knowledge of the following three fundamental geomeric theorems:
(1) The sum of the angles of a triangle must be two right angles.
(2) The two base angles of an isosceles triangle are equal.
(3) Alternate angles are equal.
I leave the proof of these theorems to algebra books. What I am attempting to demonstrate here is that viewing forms and creases, not solely from the aesthetic, but from other vantage points as well opens up whole new vistas of possibilities and interest.

Incidentally, the origami in *B* and *C* too are more than visually interesting. Inherent in them are arresting geometric discoveries.

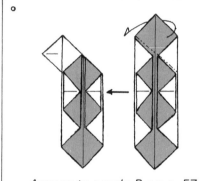

Answer to puzzle B on p. 57

There are other possible correct answers; but this one, shown to me by Atsumi Funaoka, of Hyogo Prefecture, is the most elegant I have encountered.

B. Crow

$\angle\alpha : \angle\beta : \angle\delta$
$= 1 : 2 : 3$

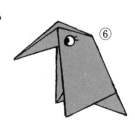

C. Grass

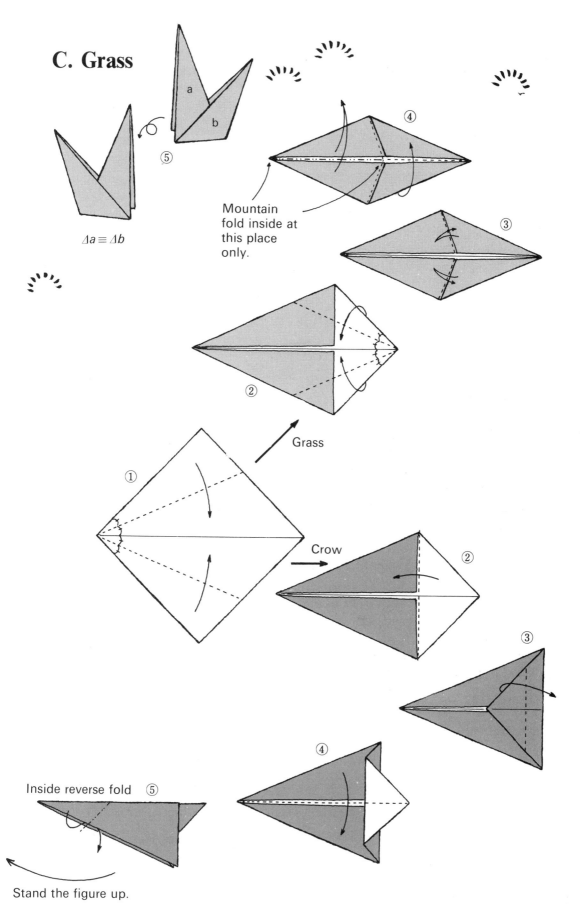

$\Delta a \equiv \Delta b$

Mountain fold inside at this place only.

Grass

Crow

Inside reverse fold

Stand the figure up.

59

The Assembly Technique

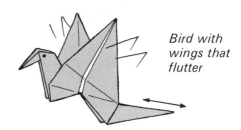

The many practically functional traditional Japanese origami folds demonstrate great variety. Aside from numerous containers, like the one already discussed, several of these serve surprising functions. I introduce a few of them here in drawings only. Since they turn up repeatedly in introductory books, I have reluctantly omitted instructions on their production. Still I hope more people will apply their ingenuity energetically to the pursuit of origami that actually work in these delightful ways.

Moving on from the topic of function, I should like to discuss the technique of assembling units to produce single works like the traditional *menko*, the dirk used by the *ninja* spies of the past, and an old-fashioned mat to put under a teapot.

Though from the purist view, compound works of this kind may seem to represent retrogression, as has recently been proved, they are actually related to the important development of unit origami. Though this topic is more fully treated in Chapter 5, a few examples of this kind of work are shown here: for instance, the origami on the next page, which is a reworking of the traditional cut fold.

Traditional masterpieces that actually work in amusing ways

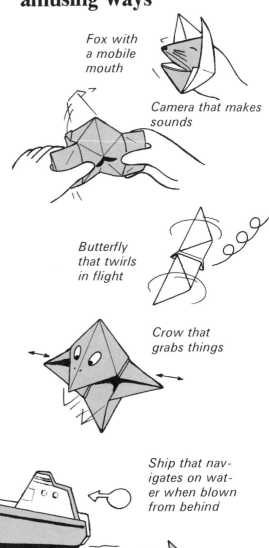

Bird with wings that flutter

Fox with a mobile mouth

Camera that makes sounds

Butterfly that twirls in flight

Crow that grabs things

Ship that navigates on water when blown from behind

Double-firing paper noisemaker

Jumping frog

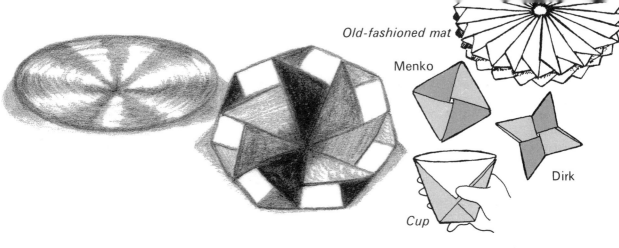

Old-fashioned mat

Menko

Dirk

Cup

Jumbo unit spinning top

Fold 7 sheets of paper according to steps *1–5* to make 7 units.

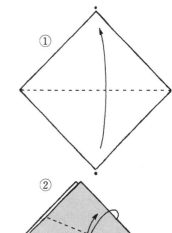

①

②

Crease the upper layer.

③

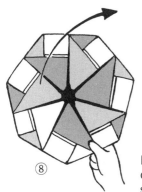

⑧

It can be spun across the top of a table or other smooth, flat surface.

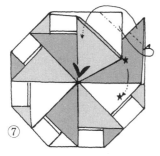

⑦

Make 7 units as in steps *5* and *6* and assemble them. A dishlike form results when the last and first units are joined.

④

Insert the upper layer in the forward slot.

⑥

1

2

Insert 1 point in the slot of the unit below and the other 2 points in the slots in the forward triangular slot.

Completed unit

⑤

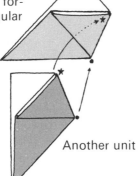

Another unit

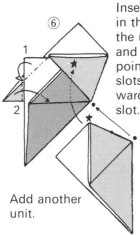

Add another unit.

Solid Forms Made Easy

A

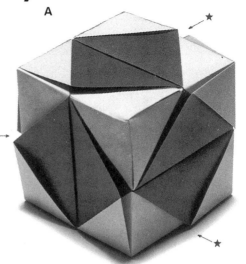

Since, as you will have learned by now, assembly is an extremely simple idea, it is equally as extremely useful.

Certainly, even within the limitations of the traditionalist ideal of origami from a single, uncut sheet of paper, various innovations and developments were forthcoming. But stubborn adherence to that ideal entailed considerable technical difficulty and made it hard to produce multidimensional solid-geometric forms that were neat and clean in appearance. Unit assembly solves this problem. In addition, it provides unexpected pleasure and makes possible complex variations.

Here I present a unit-assembly version of Rouge Container shown in the opening of this chapter. Fold it yourself to experience what I mean.

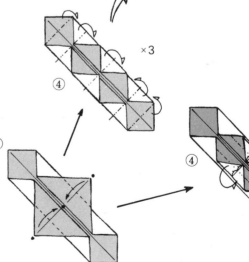

Assembly method

Unit origami — cube: four variations

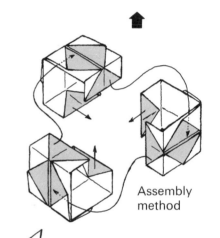

①

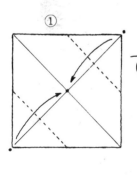

②

③

④

×3

④

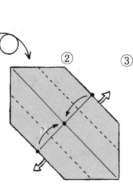

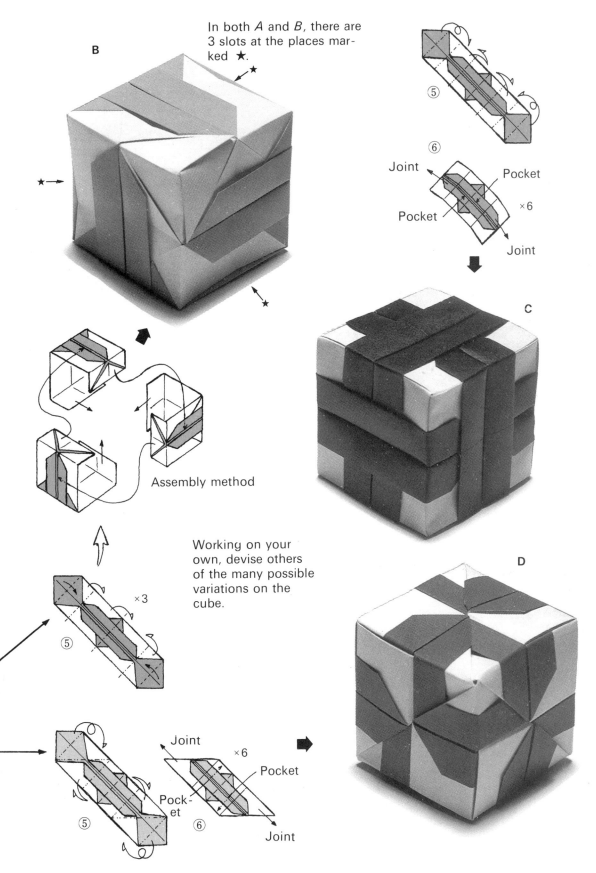

In both *A* and *B*, there are 3 slots at the places marked ★.

B

⑤

⑥

Joint

Pocket

Pocket

×6

Joint

Assembly method

Working on your own, devise others of the many possible variations on the cube.

×3

⑤

⑤

Joint

Pocket

×6

Pocket

⑥

Joint

C

D

More Than Expected

In the preceding section, three- and six-unit assemblies were used to produce Rouge Containers of four different patterns, exactly according to plan. On this page, I present the way I attempted to make use of the colored upper and white under sides of origami paper to produce the cubes in the right column as representations of the numbers of dots on the faces of a dice, shown in the left column. I did not think the plan would go as well as it did. Still a more pleasant surprise, the cubes fulfill the dice requirement that the sum of the dots on the top and bottom faces always equal seven. Though I may seem to be praising my own efforts, I am happy that this project was so splendidly successful. Being able to encounter fascinating works of this kind depends on taking a broad view of all possibilities.

Dice (2-unit assembly)

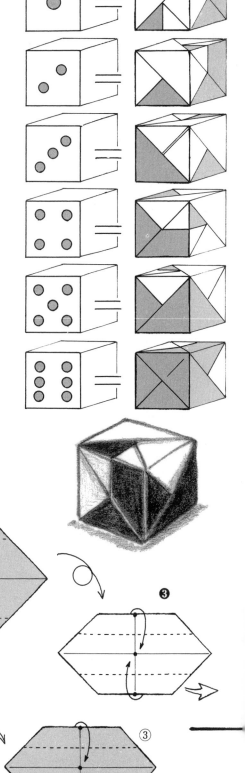

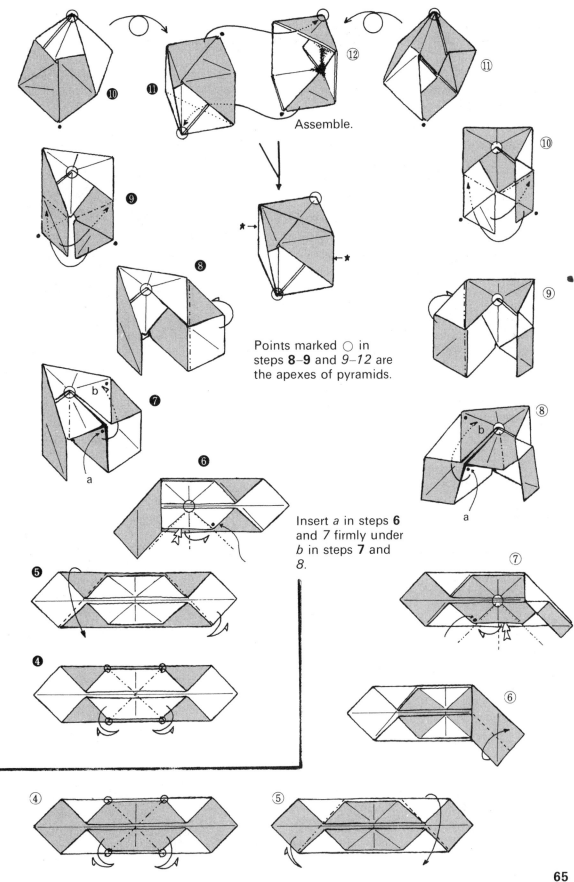

Assemble.

⑫ ⑪ ⑩

⑨ ⑩

⑧ ⑨

Points marked ○ in
steps **8**–**9** and *9–12* are
the apexes of pyramids.

⑦ ⑧

a

⑥

Insert *a* in steps **6**
and *7* firmly under
b in steps **7** and
8.

a

⑤ ⑦

④ ⑥

④ ⑤

Cube with a Pierrot Face

If a dice that always turns up a six seemed beyond expectation, this work was completely unanticipated. This six-unit inflated structure was the starting point for all of the unit origami already presented (see explanation on p. 208). The slightest folding alteration in six-unit structures of this kind changes the pattern of the finished form totally and always with surprising results. Viewed in the position shown in the drawings on p. 67, this work suddenly reveals its amusing expression.

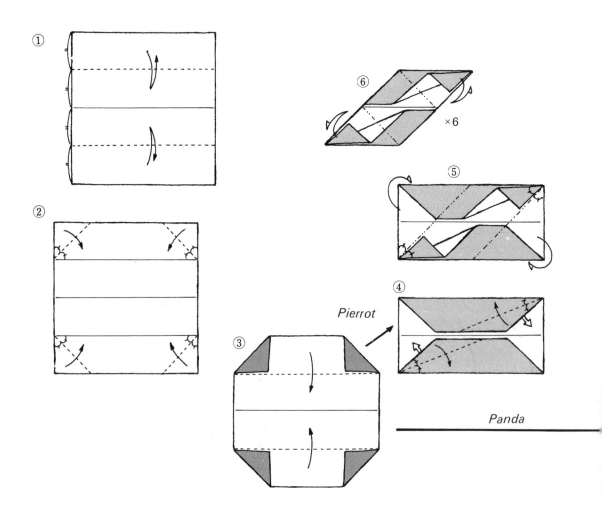

①

⑥ ×6

②

⑤

③

④

Pierrot

Panda

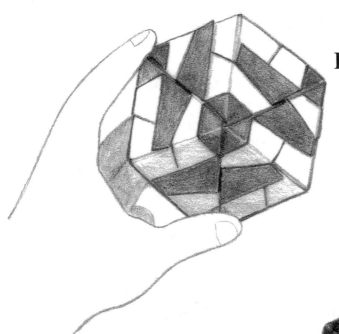

Pierrot face

Panda face

For the Pierrot use paper that
is red on one side and white
on the other; for the Panda,
use paper that is white on one
side and black on the other.
Then, the right face becomes
apparent when the cubes are
viewed in the positions shown
in the drawings.

Cube with a Panda Face

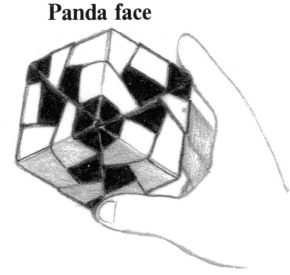

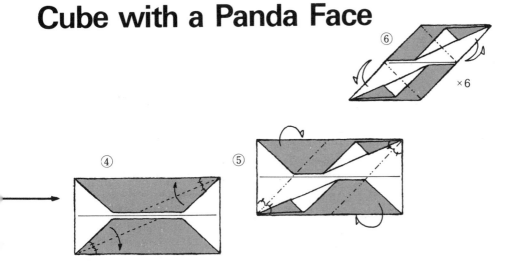

Paper Shapes

As is by now obvious, most origami paper is square. This shape was naturally selected because it is easiest to use and because it does not necessitate establishing troublesome conventions.

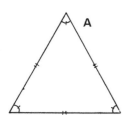 A

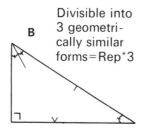 B Divisible into 3 geometrically similar forms = Rep*3

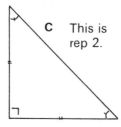 C This is rep 2.

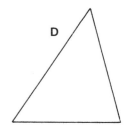 D

Although the triangle might seem to be suitable, as the diagrams above indicate, it is troublesome to deal with because it comes in a number of different varieties, each with its own characteristics. The same thing can be said of the rectangle. As has been remarked in the introduction, I do not reject all shapes other than the square. But it is better to work from the square in devising shapes that suit the conditions of the form you want to produce.

Round and oval papers are unsuitable because folding produces straight lines on their surfaces. It is true that round origami was popular for a while. But it was closer to collage than to true origami; and the need to make numerous folds gradually obliterated the round lines of the original paper. Of course, some origami involving few folds and making good use of curved lines are possible; but they are, at best, few in number.

Nonetheless, it is important to understand characteristics thoroughly before using other than square paper. The shapes on p. 69 represent some of the possibilities. Let us examine them to discover which lend themselves fairly readily to origami use.

* The word, derived from "repeating tiles," represents a concept for filling plane areas and relates to the idea of the minimum unit. The triangle in *B*, which can be divided into three identical triangles that are geometrically similar to the original triangle is said to be rep 3.

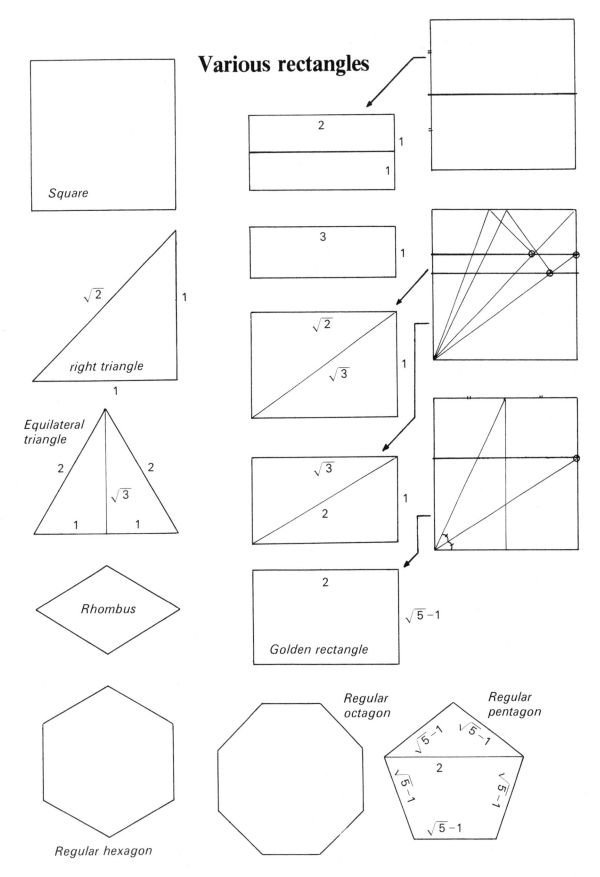

Various rectangles

Square

right triangle

Equilateral triangle

Rhombus

Regular hexagon

Regular octagon

Regular pentagon

Golden rectangle

Producing Major Paper Shapes

The term on p. 68 refers to dividing forms into forms that are geometrically similar to and congruent with each other. A form that produces such geometrically similar forms when halved is called rep 2; one that does so when divided into three equal parts, rep 3; one that does so when equally quartered, rep 4; and so on. Though most triangles are rep 4, the one in *B* on p. 68 is rep 3; and the one in *C* is rep 2.

The forms in *B* below, which turn up constantly in origami, are the only ones that are rep 2. Rectangles whose side proportion is $\sqrt{2}:1$ demonstrate the commonly observed proportions found in such familiar things as writing paper and books. This is an economical rectangle because it requires no extensive cutting or trimming. *A* helps make clear its nature in terms of mathematical principles. It is possible to ascertain whether paper and other daily materials demonstrate these proportions in the manner shown in *C*.

Examine and learn the ways of producing such paper shapes as the equilateral triangle, the rhombus, and the regular hexagon on p. 71. Mastering the production of the origami triangular measure is extremely convenient.

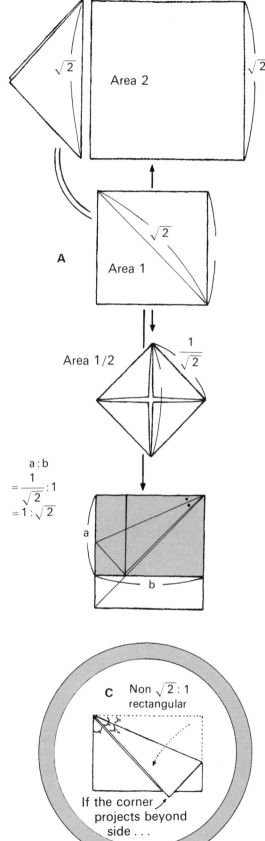

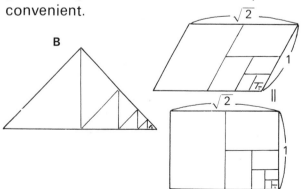

70

Origami triangular measure

With a very few folds it is possible to make a triangular measure that is useful in mathematical study. Learn to do this for yourself.

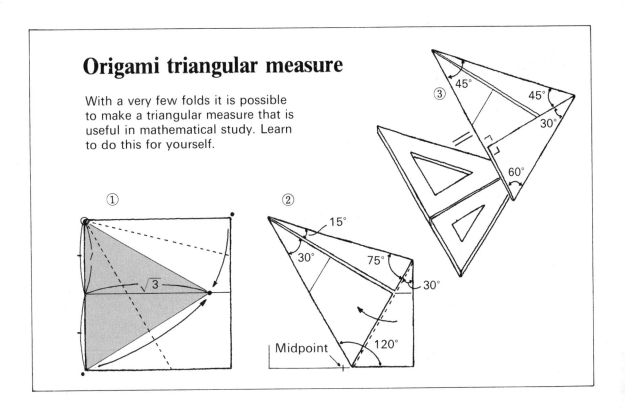

Folding for angles of 30 and 60 degrees

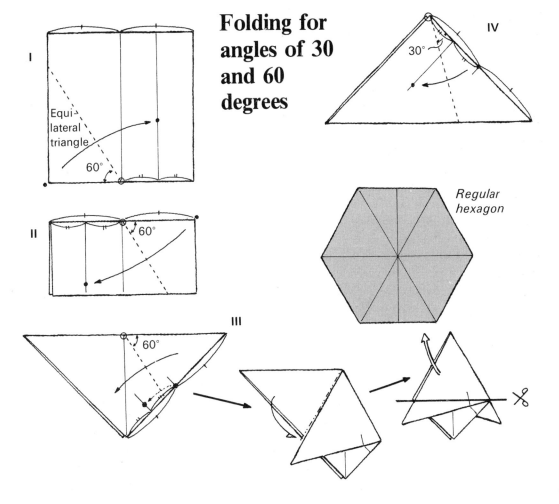

The Golden Rectangle

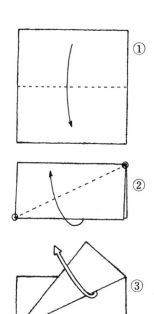

①

All of the other forms on p. 69 have already been explained, but the Golden Rectangle and the regular pentagon are so difficult to deal with that, until fairly recently, even origami researchers with outstanding mathematical talents have struggled—happily—with the problem. At present, the method illustrated on the right seems the best way to generate the Golden Rectangle. Tokushige Terada, one of the people who helped enlighten me on this topic, discovered this method in a book entitled *Kōzu o tsukuru tame ni* (Composing) by Sadao Matsumura. Since then, he has discovered various ways of generating the regular pentagon too.

② ③

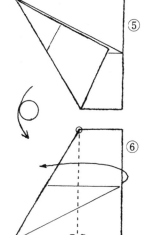

④ ⑤

The ratio of the short side to the long side (the Golden Ratio) of the Golden Rectangle is the same as the ratio of a side of a regular pentagon to its diagonal line. In other words, the Golden Rectangle and the regular pentagon are the same form. It must be remembered, however, that these two forms have captured great attention solely for the sake of satisfactorily producing such origami forms as the gentian or cherry blossom or the five-pointed star.

Folding the Golden Rectangle

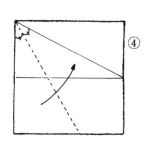

⑥

Although the diagram shows 8 steps, the golden rectangle can be produced successfully with only 4 creases.

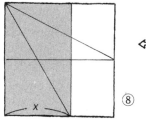

⑧

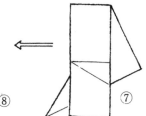

⑦

72

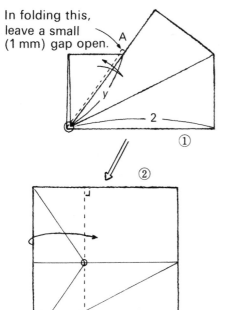

In folding this, leave a small (1 mm) gap open.

① ② ③

Approximate folding of a regular pentagon

At step *3* in the folding for the Golden Rectangle (p. 72), in attempting to determine the length of *y* (when the length of a side is taken as 2), we saw that $y=5/4=1.25$. This gives such approximate decimal fractions as $x=\sqrt{5}-1 \fallingdotseq 1.236$.

Slightly shifting the position of *A* in step *1* on this page produced the highly useful regular pentagon shown in step *4*.

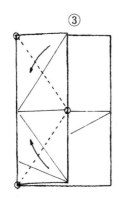

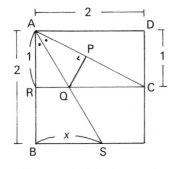

Intermediate steps not shown.

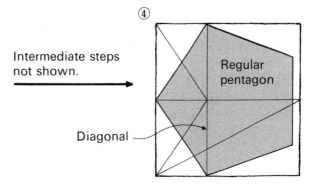

Regular pentagon

Diagonal

One vertical is dropped from point *Q* in step *8* on p. 72.

Proof

According to the Pythagorean theorem, if the side of a square is 2, $\overline{AC}=\sqrt{5}$. Consequently, $\overline{PC}=\sqrt{5}-1$.

$\triangle ADC \sim \triangle CPQ$,

$$\therefore \overline{PQ}=\frac{\sqrt{5}-1}{2}=\overline{QR}.$$

$\triangle ARQ \sim \triangle ABC$,
$\therefore x=\sqrt{5}-1$.

(Proofed by Hisashi Abé.)

Regular-pentagonal Knot

It is an attractive tradition in many old-fashioned Japanese inns to prepare cotton sleeping robes for guests and to arrange on top of the robe a sash tied in a pentagonal knot. No doubt, some practice is needed to master the technique of producing such a knot.

I have already explained that enthusiastic attention to folding the Golden Rectangle and the regular pentagon is based on the desire to produce origami. Here I offer proof in the form of a fold based on the pentagonal knot in which some inns tie guests sashes. In this instance, however, no mastery is demanded. Simply follow the diagrams faithfully.

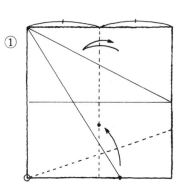

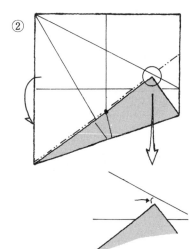

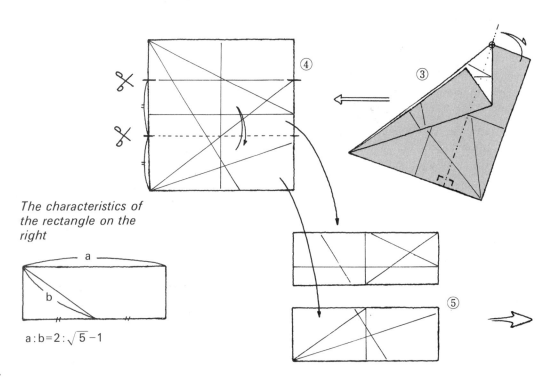

The characteristics of the rectangle on the right

$a : b = 2 : \sqrt{5} - 1$

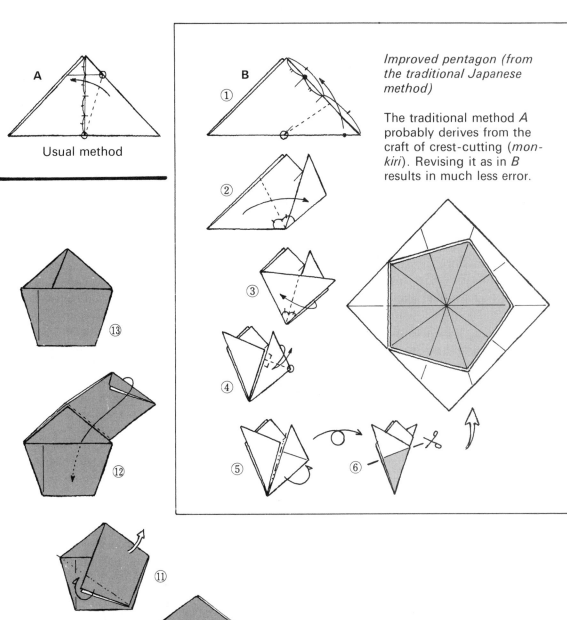

A

Usual method

B

Improved pentagon (from the traditional Japanese method)

The traditional method *A* probably derives from the craft of crest-cutting (*mon-kiri*). Revising it as in *B* results in much less error.

① ② ③ ④ ⑤ ⑥

⑬ ⑫ ⑪ ⑩ ⑨ ⑧ ⑦

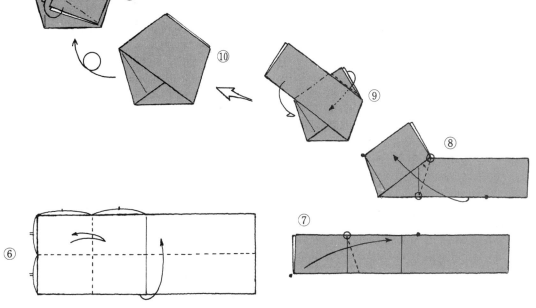

⑥

The Importance of Perceiving

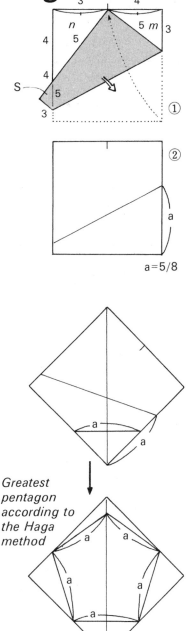

① ②

a=5/8

Greatest pentagon according to the Haga method

Here we see how precisely aligning corner and corner or corner and side leads to the discovery of wonderful mathematical truths. Oddly, and unfortunately, some origami specialists who failed to understand its significance have branded such precision of folding as reprehensible, copying, and mere discipline. Today, however, I am encouraged to notice that many scholars affectionately understand the importance of preciseness. One of them is Kazuo Haga, who, shortly after developing an interest in origami, made a wonderful discovery as the result of one fold and a half (the half fold consisted of merely making a mark). In the introduction I touched on this discovery, which Kōji Fushimi has named the Haga Theorem.

One application of the theorem was the production of the three triangles (Δn, Δm, and Δs) shown in the figure in the upper right. They are geometrically similar figures, all of which have sides proportioned $3:4:5$. Since, according to the Pythagorean theorem, the square on the hypotenuse is equal to the sum of the squares on the other two sides $5^2=4^2+3^2$. Therefore $a=5/8$.

Making immediate use of this discovery, Mr. Haga devised the pentagon shown here, which is highly useful and effective. As a matter of fact, however, he had long been in possession of the values on which the pentagon is based.

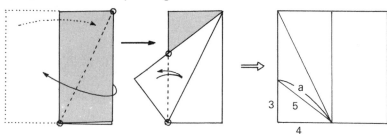

Whether we discover or overlook such things depends on the important power of perception. I hope all of you will be perceptive enough to make discoveries of your own.

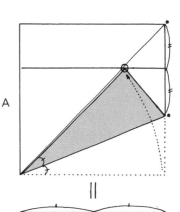

A on the right is for producing the rectangle whose proportions are $\sqrt{2}$ to 1. You are already familiar with it. But the considerably different folding method in B produces the same kind of rectangle. Folding it in half, as in C, too is interesting. From the standpoint of the importance of logic, A must be given pride of place. Still the other gives the kind of pleasure in mathematical agreement suggested by the triangles on the preceding page.

Method for folding a rectangle whose proportions are $\sqrt{2}$: 1

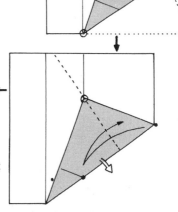

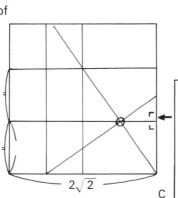

$2\sqrt{2}$

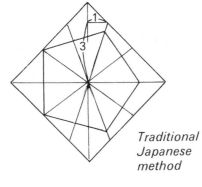

Traditional Japanese method

The American system is less effective because the pentagon it produces is small, but it is pleasing to fold and results in minimum aberration.

American method

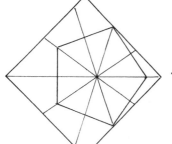

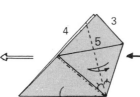

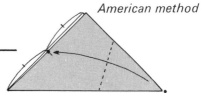

Alice Gray, editor in chief of *The Origamian*, taught me taught me the American system.

Skeleton Structures of Regular Polyhedrons

The skeleton of the regular octahedron appears in the forms of Mr. Neal's Ornament on p. 20. Here I have attempted to produce five different regular polyhedrons (see p. 205) with a uniform style.

Skeleton of a regular tetrahedron

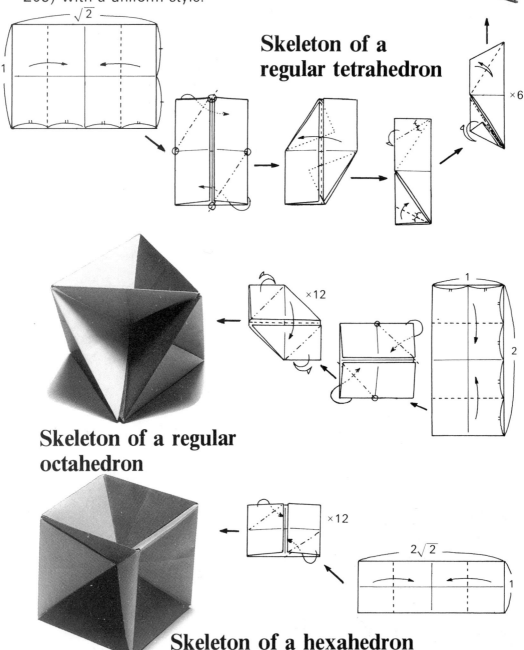

Skeleton of a regular octahedron

Skeleton of a hexahedron

Skeleton of a regular dodecahedron

An example of applying the
folding method for the
Golden Rectangle (p. 72).

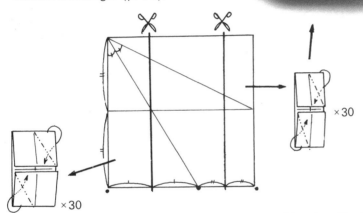

×30

×30

No detailed instructions are
given. But people who are interested can regard the assembly of these solid figures
as fascinating puzzles to solve.
The figures will be more sturdy if a little glue is applied to
the insertions at junction
points.

Skeleton of a regular icosahedron

Several Beautiful Containers

To allay the disappointment of people who, having followed the explanations of ways to produce paper in various regular polygonal forms, now read that, throughout the rest of the book, we will use only square or rectangular paper, I include these beautiful containers. They are all folded in the same way, but using paper of various shapes results in dramatically different finished appearances. This kind of thing is part of the pleasure of origami. Mitsué Nakano, a fellow origamian, has published the container made from regular-octagonal paper.

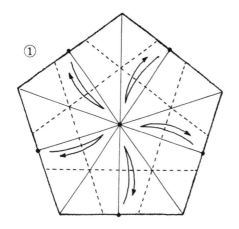

To expand the fold to full-dimensional form from step *6*, insert your right index finger into the part marked with a white arrow. Then grip the bottom, baglike corner between the thumb and index finger of your left hand. Continuing this all the way round will complete the container.

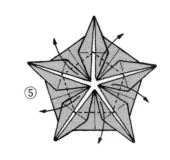

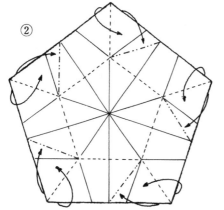

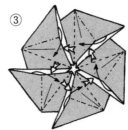

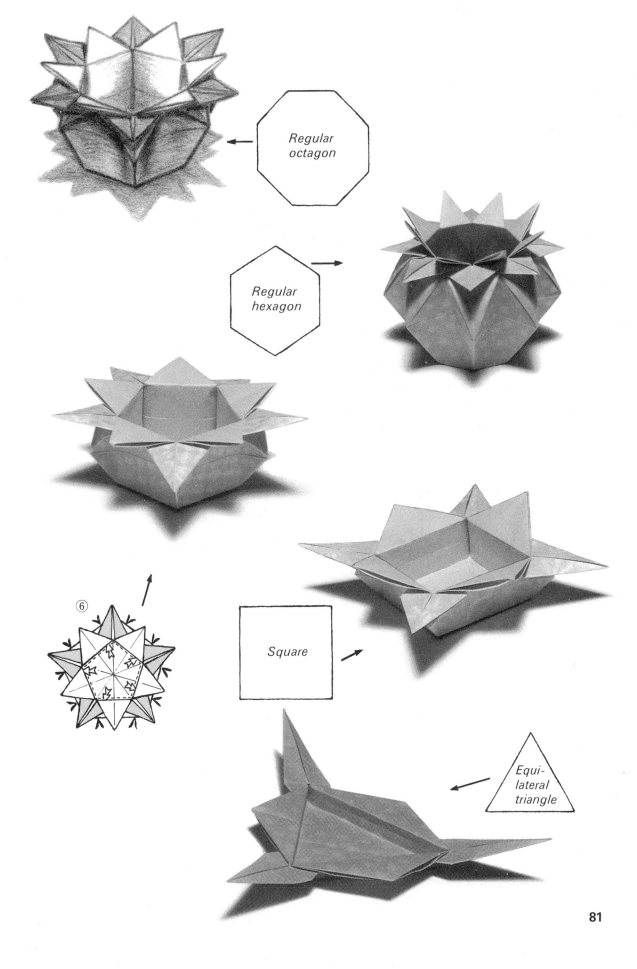

Regular octagon

Regular hexagon

⑥

Square

Equilateral triangle

81

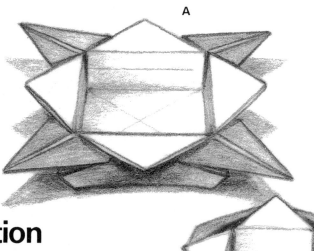

A

B

Form Variation

On the preceding pages, we saw how using paper of different shapes produces different final results. Now we shall see how altering folding immediately before the final finishing steps has the same effect. *A* is from p. 81.

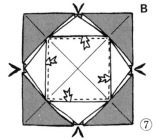

B

⑦

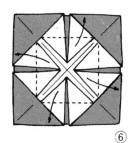

⑥

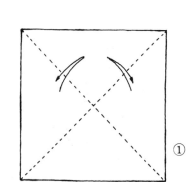

①

②

③

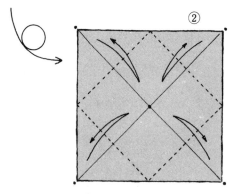

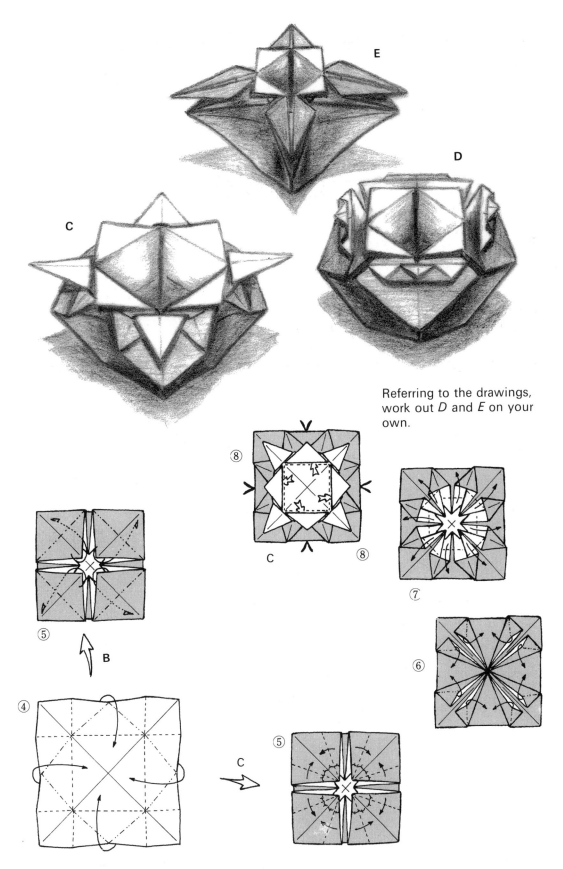

E

D

C

Referring to the drawings,
work out *D* and *E* on your
own.

⑧

C

⑧

⑦

⑥

⑤

B

④

C

⑤

Odd-number Even Divisions

Having demonstrated the production of equilateral triangles and regular pentagons, now I shall explain how to divide the length of a piece of paper into odd-numbered equal divisions. In actual origami, we frequently need to divide paper into three or five equal parts. Having to divide it into seven, nine, or more equal parts is rarely necessary.

The best way to produce the often re-quired tripartite equal division is to round the paper, without creasing it, and adjust it, hit or miss, until equal thirds are established (*A*). Then the creases can be made.

Since this rough system will not work for dividing a length of paper into five equal parts, we have devised an entertaining, puzzlelike method. First divide both sides of the square into quarters by folding six crease lines as shown in step *1*. Then fold on a line connecting points *a* and *c* (step *2*). This will give values of 3 for *A* and 4 for *B*. Points *P* are on lines dividing the width of the paper into thirds.

If, in the right triangle created by folding to connect *a* and *c*, *A* is 3 and *B* is 4, on the basis of the Pythagorean theorem, we can see that the hypotenuse *C* is 5. Folding as in step *3* will divide the length into five equal parts, as seen in step *4*. In that step, point *m* is the center of the side. One fold and a half as in step *5* brings the corner to a point on a line exactly 1/5 across the

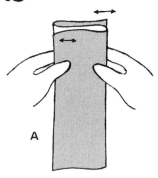

A

The Pythagorean theorem: $A^2 + B^2 = C^2$.

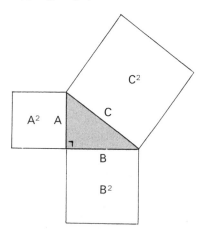

When $A=3$ and $B=4$, on the basis of the Pythagorean theorem, $C=5$.

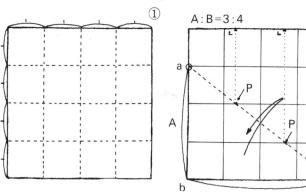

①   A : B = 3 : 4   ②

③

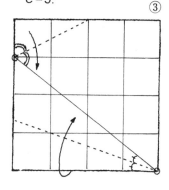

84

① Gauge sheet diagram

2/7

5 equal parts
6 equal parts
7 equal parts

②

8 7 6 5 4 3 2 1

7 6 5 4 3 2 1

Simplified way of making divisions

Although it is not as elegant as things associated with origami usually are, I offer the division method shown in the chart on the left because it is rational and theoretically sound.

Prepare a gauge sheet in the following way. Fold a sheet of origami paper into an even number of equal parts—let us say, eight. Using this, you can divide other sheets of paper into any number of parts by positioning them on the gauge sheet as shown in the drawing. A still faster way, is to make similar use of the parallel lines on notebook paper. In Japan, primary-school children are taught this system. Though schools have their practical aims in explaining how this system works in making even divisions, understanding mathematical truths like the one shown below in step *5* is much more thrilling.

width of the paper. The noteworthy element is this: point *m* in step *4* is the center of the base. In other words, in step *5*, which is half the fold, five equal parts have already been determined.

One and a half folds
The second is called half a fold because point *m* need be no more than a mark.

P=point of 5 equal divisions

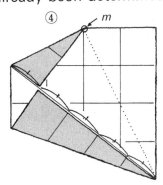

④ *m*

Steps *1–4* are for the sake of explaining step *5*.

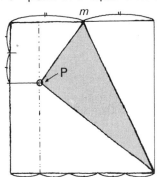

⑤ *m*

P

Applying Five-part Equal Folding: Two Solid Figures

Let us immediately apply the system just presented for dividing a side into five equal parts in these two solid figures. They may seem less expressive and interesting than the solid figures we made earlier, but they can stimulate your ingenuity in interesting ways.

As is clear from the drawings, the first evolved from a solid representation of the traditional *menko*. Interestingly, step *1* of the *menko* fits exactly into step *2* of the solid form.

The second of the solid forms is nearly one half the volume of the solid forms on pp. 62 and 66. Mathematically insignificant, this point makes the work interesting by attracting attention to the topic of volume.

Solid figure I

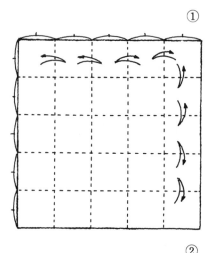

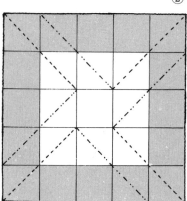

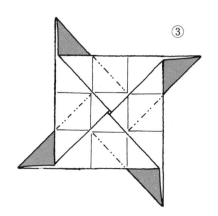

Traditional *menko*

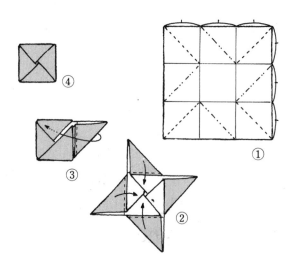

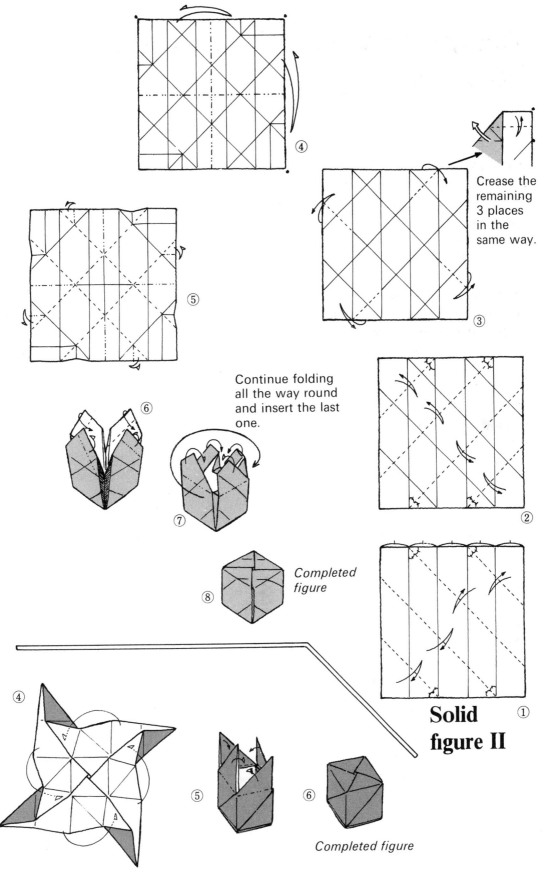

④

③

Crease the
remaining
3 places
in the
same way.

⑤

②

Continue folding
all the way round
and insert the last
one.

⑥

⑦

①

**Solid
figure II**

⑧ *Completed
figure*

④

⑤

⑥

Completed figure

Meaning of the Origami Bases

Pattern basic fold

The so-called basic forms or bases have been of the greatest importance to representational origami in its attempts to produce figures of birds and animals. We are indebted to such of our predecessors as Michirō Uchiyama, Kōshō Uchiyama, Akira Yoshizawa, James Sakoda, and Kōya Ohashi for organizing and popularizing these forms. But today, as origami extends its horizons, we find that none of the previously established systems covers everything.

Developmental drawing

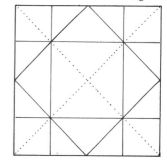

Developmental drawing

For instance, it is not certain whether the Pattern Fold and the Pinwheel Fold shown on the right should be made from the same base or from different bases or whether the base from which the Table Fold is produced is a compound of crane bases or a development of the Pattern Fold. Even the very popular bases shown on p. 89 occur in *A* and *B* versions. Possibly lack of attention to apparently minor matters of this kind derives from a failure to take into consideration relations with the mathematics of origami.

Jun Maekawa has brought order to the picture; but, since it is difficult to explain verbally, I shall attempt to cultivate understanding of his theory by applying it in a few actual origami later.

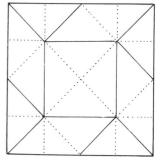

Pinwheel

Developmental drawing

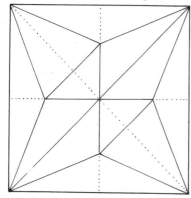

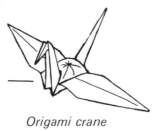

Origami crane

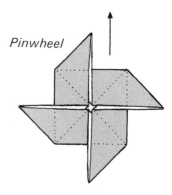

Table basic fold

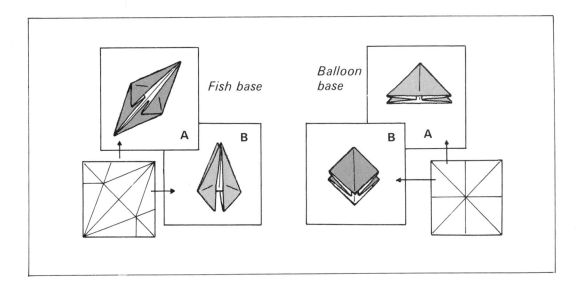

Fish base

A

B

Balloon base

B

A

The Maekawa theory

Determining the minimal compositional unit of the basic form on the basis of the number of equal parts into which angles are divided.

$$\angle \alpha = 1/n \angle R \ (n = 2, 3, 4, 5 \cdots)$$

When $n = 2$, 1 form as in a on the left
When $n = 4$, 2 forms as in a and b on the left
When $n = 3$, 1 form as in c below

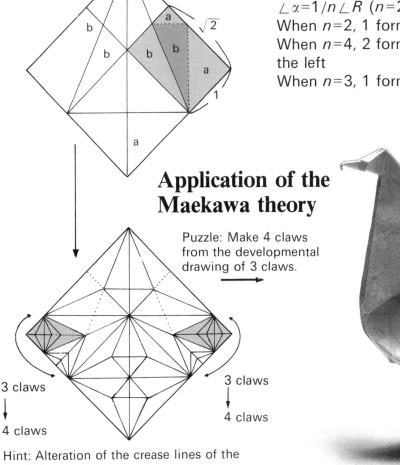

Application of the Maekawa theory

Puzzle: Make 4 claws from the developmental drawing of 3 claws. →

3 claws
↓
4 claws

3 claws
↓
4 claws

Hint: Alteration of the crease lines of the shaded area.

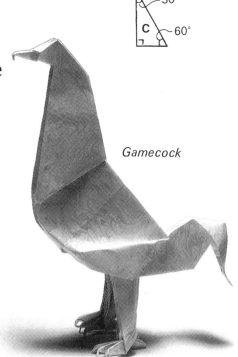

Gamecock

Tyrannosaurus— Application of the Maekawa Theory

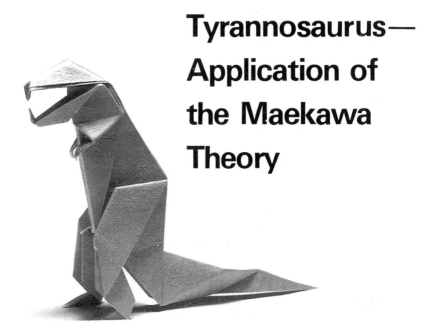

This work is found in the section called "The World of the Dinosaurs" (pp. 182–198), in Chapter 4.

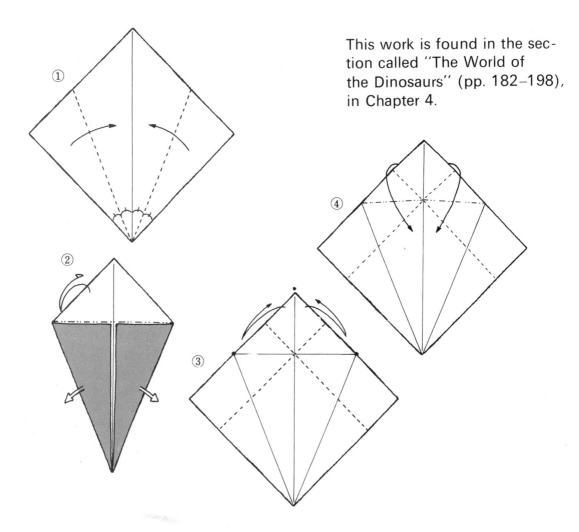

Unlike that of painting or sculpture, the appeal of origami always includes an element of return to the original state and consists of the dualities of representational expression and geometric forms and of the equal pleasures of the completed figure and of the process whereby it comes into being. We must always be on the lookout for possible discoveries in the intermediate shapes appearing during this process.

For instance, in step *4* we might ask ourselves again how many isosceles triangles the figure contains. Or it might be interesting to consider *a*, *b*, and *c* in step *5* in terms of mathematical significance. Thinking this way can greatly enhance the pleasure origami gives.

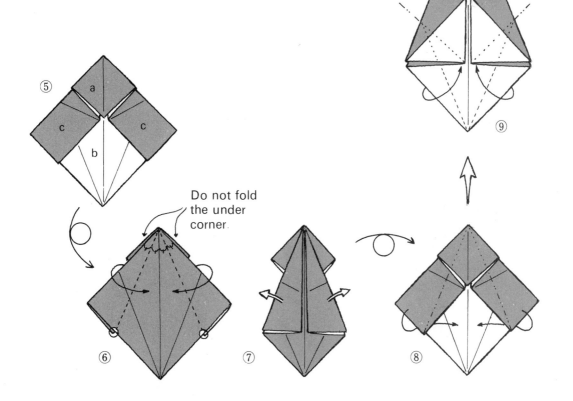

Fold this side too as in steps *9* and *10*.

Do not fold the under corner.

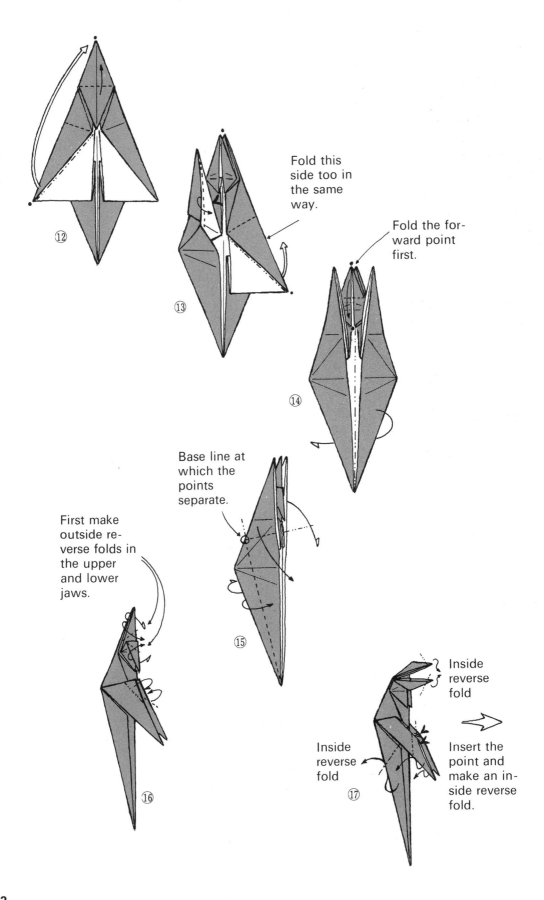

Fold this
side too in
the same
way.

Fold the for-
ward point
first.

⑫

⑬

⑭

Base line at
which the
points
separate.

First make
outside re-
verse folds in
the upper
and lower
jaws.

⑮

Inside
reverse
fold

Inside
reverse
fold

Insert the
point and
make an in-
side reverse
fold.

⑯

⑰

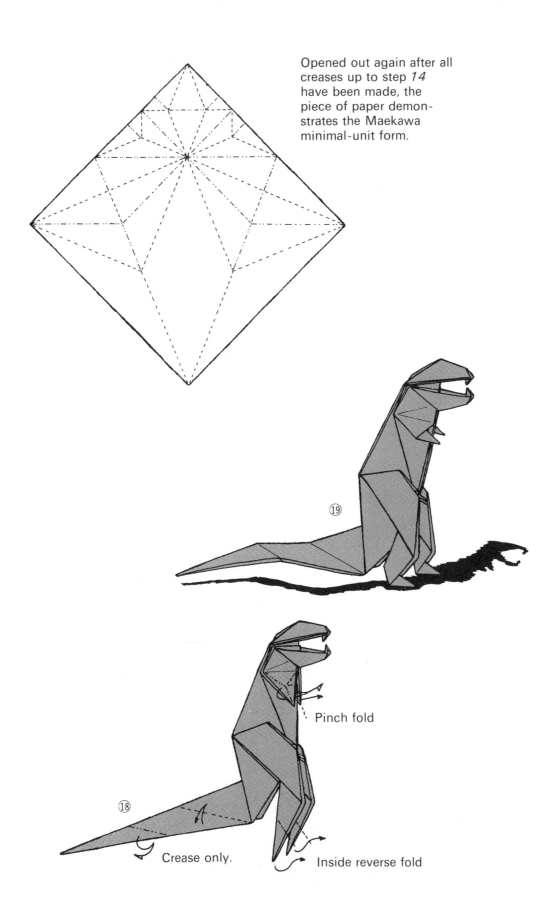

Opened out again after all creases up to step *14* have been made, the piece of paper demonstrates the Maekawa minimal-unit form.

⑲

⑱

Pinch fold

Crease only.

Inside reverse fold

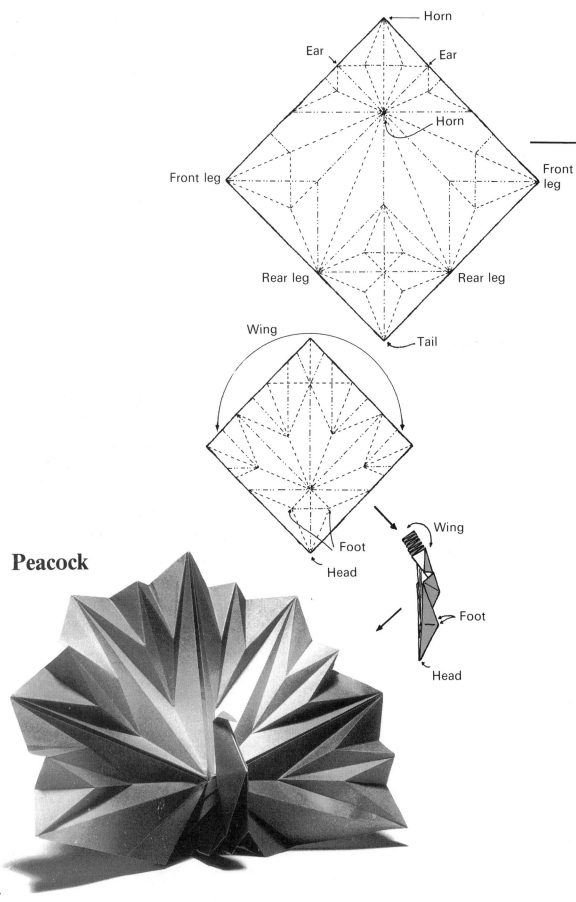

Horn

Ear   Ear

Horn

Front leg   Front leg

Rear leg   Rear leg

Tail

Wing

Foot

Head

Wing

Foot

Head

Peacock

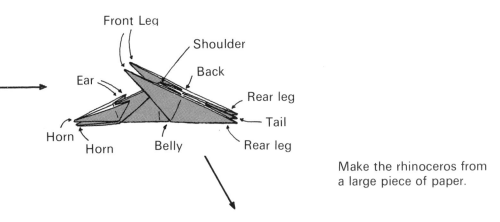

Front Leg

Shoulder

Back

Ear

Rear leg

Tail

Horn

Horn

Belly

Rear leg

Make the rhinoceros from
a large piece of paper.

Rhinoceros

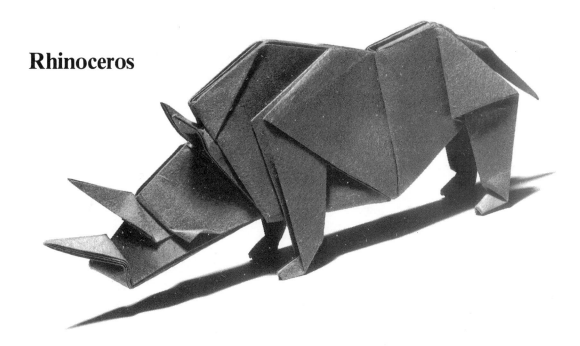

Those of you who are interested should try folding these two works
from the developmental drawings, the sketches, and the photographs
of the finished origami. You will find they are much easier than you
thought. This is a convenient way of recording new works.

Iso-area Folding
(The Kawasaki Theory)

Like Jun Maekawa, a man of original ideas, Toshikazu Kawasaki has developed the idea of iso-area folding by means of which obverse and reverse of a piece of paper are exposed to equal extents. Though difficult to explain verbally, his theory is easily understood when presented in actual origami. You will see what I mean if you learn as you make the folds shown on the right. *A* is the traditional pinwheel. Converting its valley folds to mountain folds and its mountain folds to valley folds results in the inversion form. In the case of *B* (a work published by Akira Yoshizawa), however, a slight rotation results in identical front and back sides in which the obverse and reverse of the paper are exposed to equal extents.

A

Inversion form

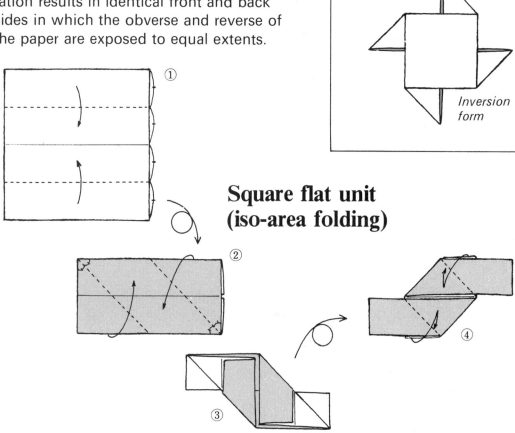

Square flat unit
(iso-area folding)

①

②

③

④

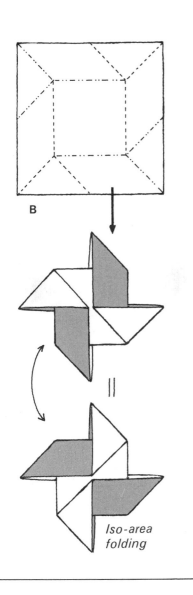

B

Iso-area folding

In the completed figure there is a pocket in each side of the square.

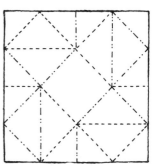

Square flat unit— developmental drawing

This will produce a fold exactly like the one in step *12* even if all its mountain folds are converted to valley folds and its valley folds converted to mountain folds.

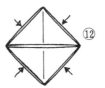

⑫

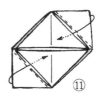

⑪

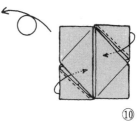

⑩

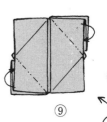

⑨

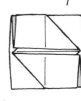

⑧

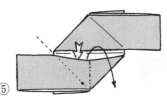

⑤

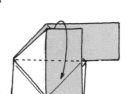

⑥

Fold here as in steps *5* and *6*.

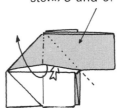

⑦

97

Puzzle Cube I

In this figure, instead of a square flat unit like the one on the preceding page, we will make Right-triangular Flat Units. The degree of absolute similarity in them, however, is less than in the case of the square.

Without worrying about this, having made two kinds of flat units, we can proceed to the construction of an amusing puzzle figure. Assembled as shown in Figs. *I* through *III* on the opposite page, the flat units can be converted into a solid figure with a single touch. Furthermore, inverting them changes the color of the figure. Takenao Handa taught me how to do this.

Do not attempt to force the units in inverting them.

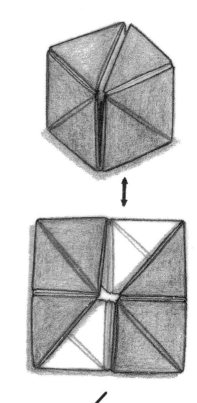

Right-triangular Flat Unit

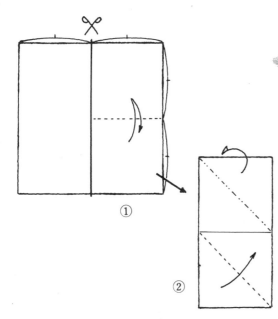

① ②

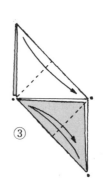

③ ④

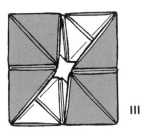

III

II

A and *b* are practically completely iso-area.

a

b

Ensure stability by putting a dab of glue on each tab. Do the same with the final step *a*.

I

a

×4

The joining tabs are 1/16 the size of the square.

×8

×4

⑤

⑥

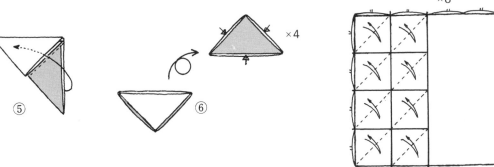

A Convenient Rectangle

In the explanation of paper shapes on p. 68 I have already mentioned deliberate use of rectangles in this book. And, indeed there is a rectangle that works perfectly to achieve certain aims. For example, a rectangle with 1:2 proportions makes it possible to produce the same figure that took three balloon bases to make in the introduction.

The figures below show how it is possible to use a rectangle with proportions of 1:3 to make a five-pointed star, which usually requires five sheets of square paper. On the opposite page, you will see how it is possible to produce from one rectangular sheet the figure that took 16, including what was necessary for joining tabs on p. 99.

Five-pointed star

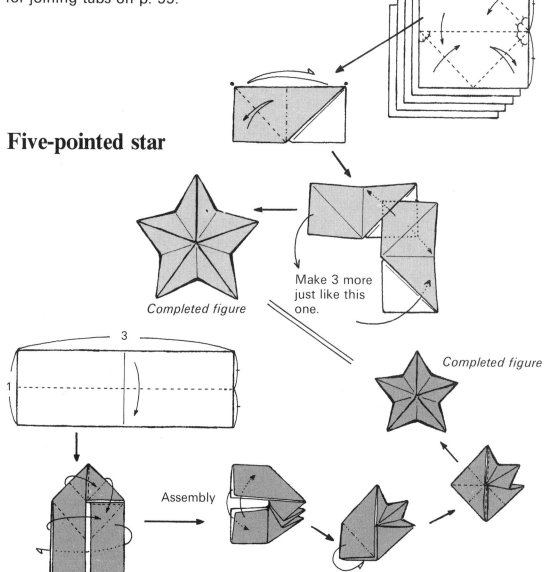

Completed figure

Make 3 more just like this one.

Completed figure

Assembly

Making Puzzle Cube I from one sheet of paper demands a special, long rectangle, which can be easily produced according to the method shown in steps *1* and *2*. The Haga-Fushimi Theorem (Mr. Fushimi's expansion of the Haga Theorem) makes possible dividing the side of a square into nine equal parts. A rectangle with a side made up of four of those nine equal parts is what is required for the Puzzle Cube. Nonetheless, since the paper needed for this rectangle must be fairly large, it is probably still more fun to break the cube down into units.

Puzzle cube (one rectangular sheet)

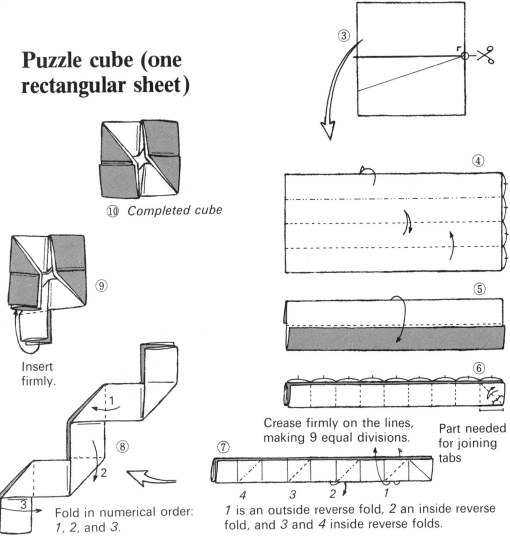

①

② 4/9

Division on the basis of the Haga-Fushimi Theorem

③

④

⑤

⑥ Part needed for joining tabs

Crease firmly on the lines, making 9 equal divisions.

⑦ 4 3 2 1

1 is an outside reverse fold, *2* an inside reverse fold, and *3* and *4* inside reverse folds.

⑩ *Completed cube*

⑨

Insert firmly.

⑧ 1 2 3

Fold in numerical order: *1*, *2*, and *3*.

Puzzle Cube II

For the next twenty pages, I will explain a puzzle consisting of a single cube, like the one shown below, into which are fitted five other cubes. All of the cubes, except *F*, are made of two sheets of paper. Paper sizes, which decrease at regular intervals, are shown on p. 103. Cube *F* fits inside Cube *E*, Cube *E* inside Cube *D*, and so on until all are contained in Cube *A*.

When the set is complete, get together a group of friends and make the presentation shown on p. 103 until you reach the last box and the essential puzzle. It is more effective if all thirteen sheets of paper are of different colors.

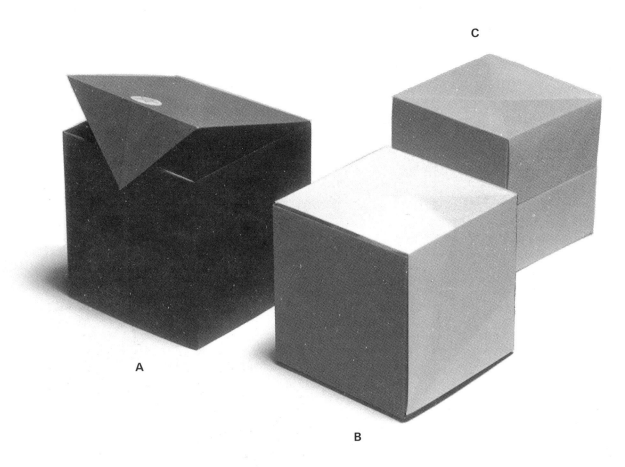

1. The six faces of this cube have been divided in half. (Take out Cube *B*.)

2. It is possible to think of another kind of cube, like this one, in which the six faces are divided in half. These are the only two kinds.

3. But, if the method is changed slightly, it is possible to devise four ways of producing geometrically similar figures by bisecting through the centers or points of rhombuses on a given surface. (Take out Cube *C*.)

4. This is cut along the color boundary. Think of some other way to cut.

   (Let your friends tell you which cube to remove. Generally they will select either *D* or *E*.)

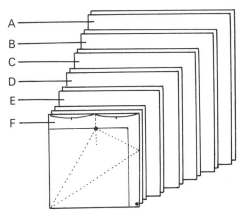

Paper sizes decrease at a decrement of 1 cm; that is, *A* is 15 cm to a side, *B* is 14 cm to a side, *C* is 13 cm to a side, and so on. One of the 3 sheets for *F* is still 1 cm smaller than the other 2 (see p. 118).

5. Now you know three ways of bisecting. The final one is a regular hexagon. (Then take out cube *F*.)

6. Now, to make things interesting, I intend to make one incision in the final cube to produce a polyhedron. Do you understand what I am going to do?

Since the outermost cube must be sturdy to serve as a container for the others, use a little glue on all but one of its joint tabs. No glue is used in any of the other cubes.

Cube *A* — Bisecting I

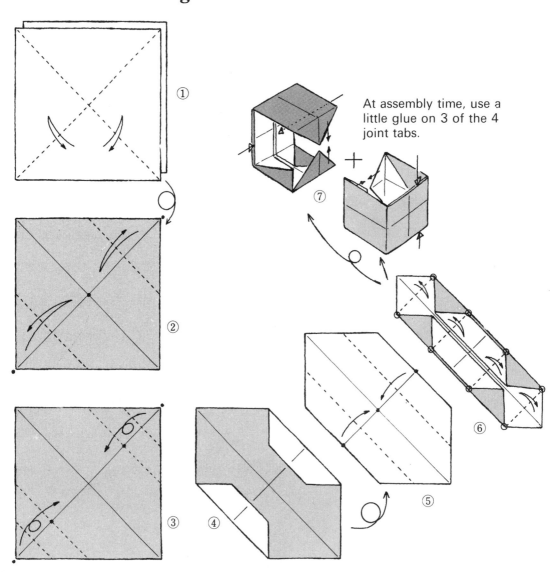

At assembly time, use a little glue on 3 of the 4 joint tabs.

Cube B—
Bisecting II

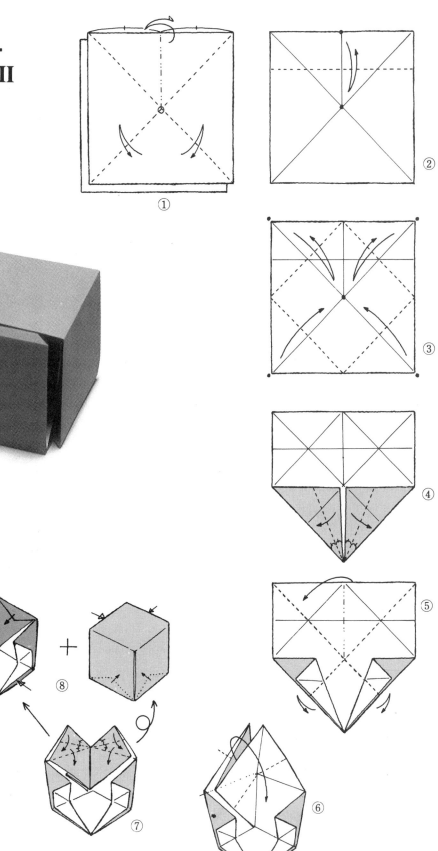

①
②
③
④
⑤
⑥
⑦
⑧

This cube makes good use of the traditional origami master-piece called the *masu* measuring box. Making a nest of these boxes, in diminishing sizes, from the same size of paper is explained on p. 276.

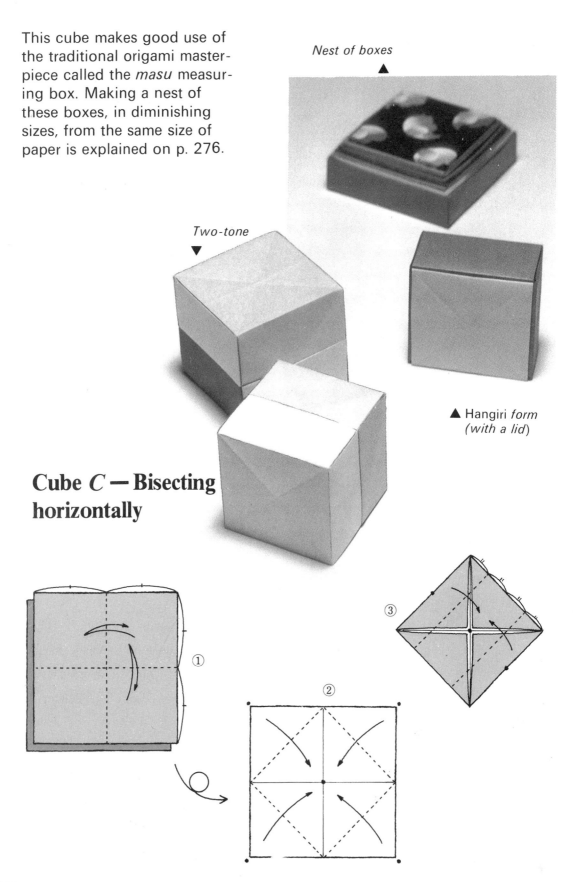

Nest of boxes
▲

Two-tone
▼

▲ Hangiri *form (with a lid)*

Cube *C* — Bisecting horizontally

①

②

③

Two-tone treatment

As a detour, try your hand at making these houses. The 2-story house and the tree are explained in Chapter 6.

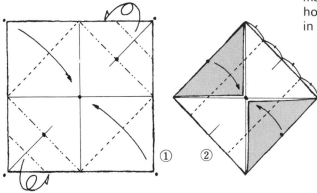

From this point, fold as in steps *4–8*.

Traditional masu *measuring box*

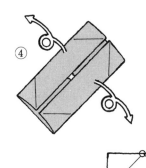

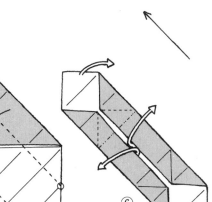

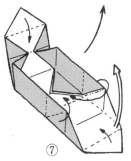

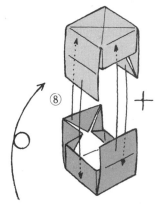

Cube *D*—Bisecting on the diagonal

In combination, these geometrically similar figures produce a cube. In isolation, they serve as the roofs for houses made from the individual elements making up diagonally bisected cubes. Try your hand at them; they are used again in Chapter 6.

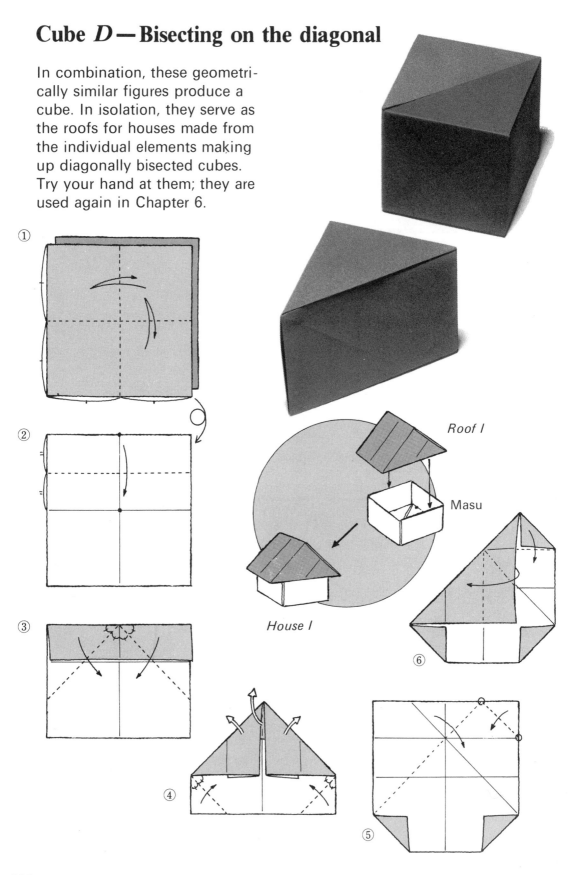

Roof I

Masu

House I

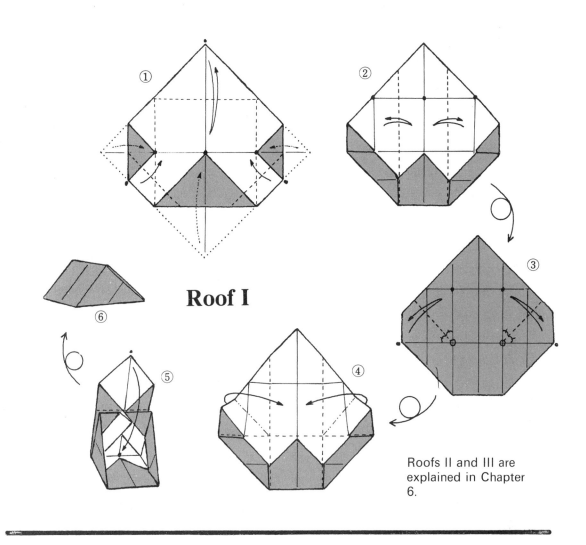

Roof I

Roofs II and III are explained in Chapter 6.

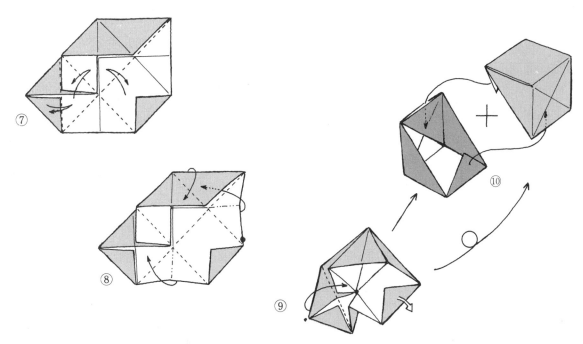

Lids for Elements

This too is only indirectly related to the puzzle, but the elements into which the cubes are divided may be fitted with lids.

Rectangular lid for cube *D*

Square lid for cube *C*

Begin with step *6* on p. 107.

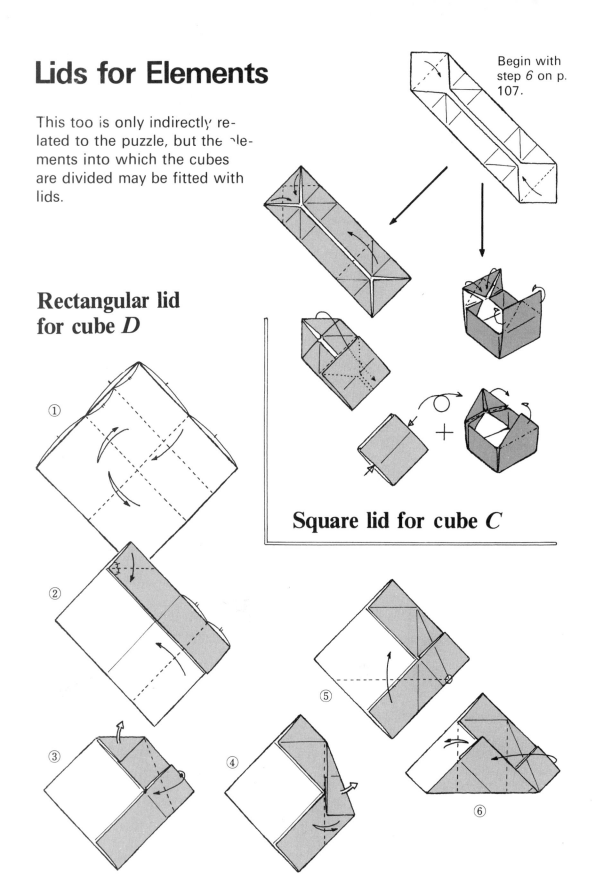

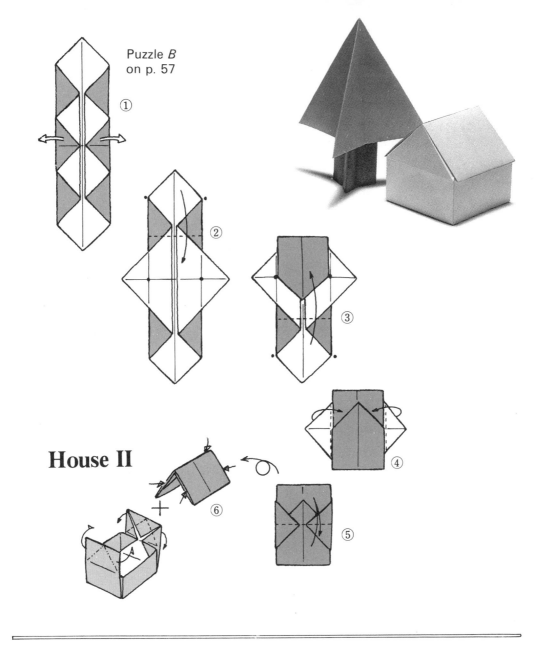

Puzzle *B*
on p. 57

① ② ③ ④ ⑤

House II

⑥

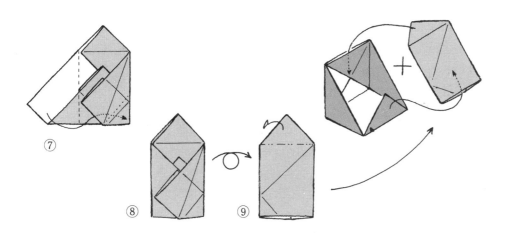

⑦ ⑧ ⑨

Cube *E*—Bisecting III

What shepe may the cross
section be assumed to take in
this case?

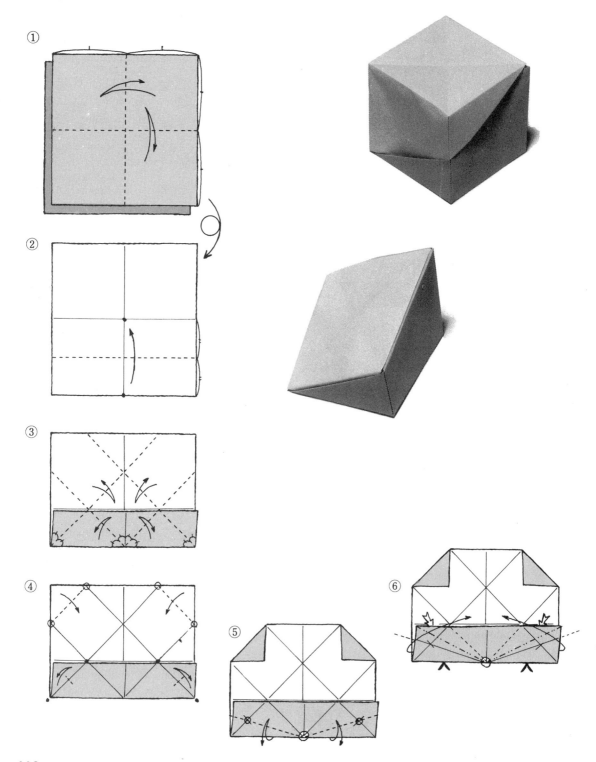

① ② ③ ④ ⑤ ⑥

Handmade teaching materials

When completed, the lidded versions of the four bisected cubes all have different sections. These cannot be used in the puzzle, since they cannot be fitted inside each other. Consequently, they are all made of the same size paper. Models of this kind make good handmade teaching materials for posing such mathematical problems as ascertaining which of the four cross sections has the greatest area.

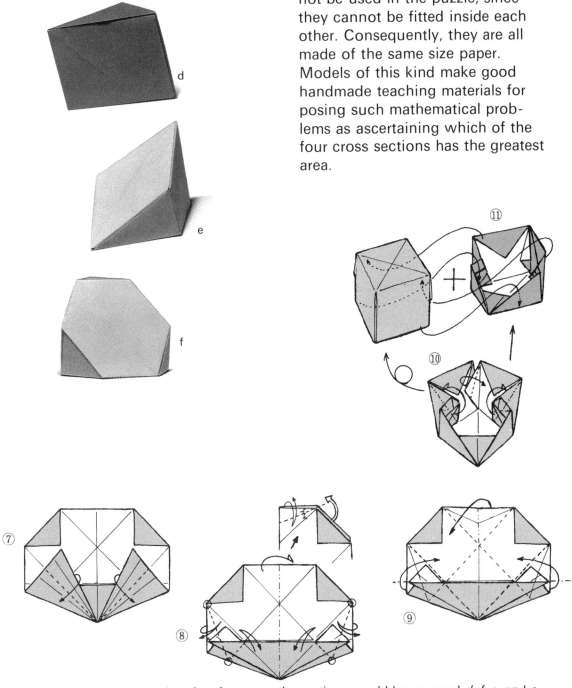

● In decreasing order of surface area, the sections would be arranged *d*, *f*, *e*, and *c*.

Rhombic lid for Cube *E*

This is the most elaborate of the cube folds from *D* through *F*. I leave working out the improvements no doubt needed in the folding method up to the readers' ingenuity.

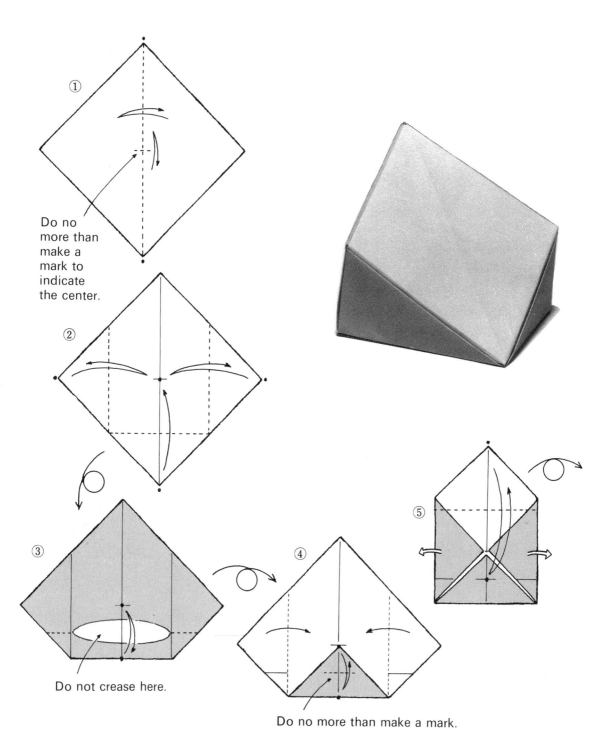

① Do no more than make a mark to indicate the center.

②

③ Do not crease here.

④

⑤

Do no more than make a mark.

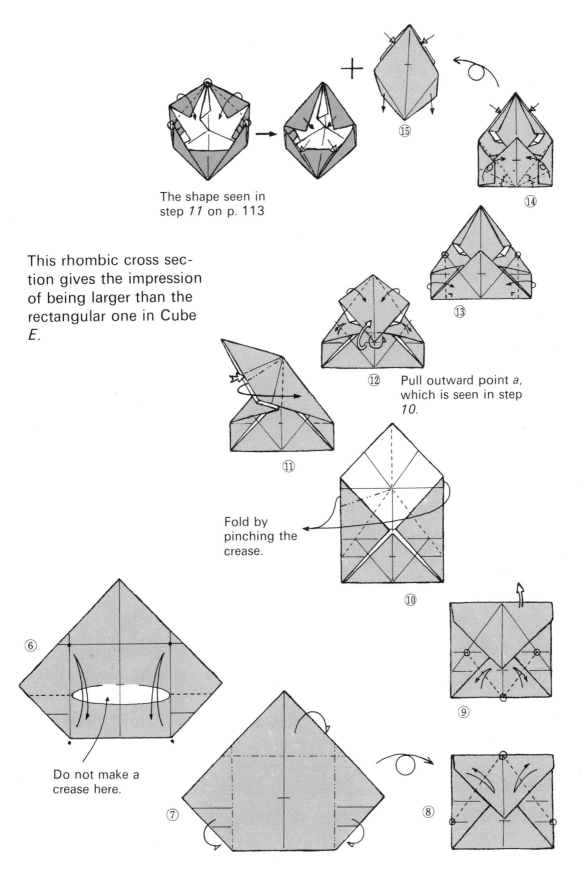

The shape seen in step *11* on p. 113

This rhombic cross section gives the impression of being larger than the rectangular one in Cube *E*.

⑮

⑭

⑬

⑫ Pull outward point *a*, which is seen in step *10*.

⑪

Fold by pinching the crease.

⑩

⑥

Do not make a crease here.

⑦

⑨

⑧

115

Building-block Bisection

On the right you see an assembly of four of the eight small cubes into which the larger cube was equally divided. Undeniably this is a bisecting form of the cube. Although not directly related to the bisected-cube puzzle, this is an interesting detour.

Make 2 and combine them.

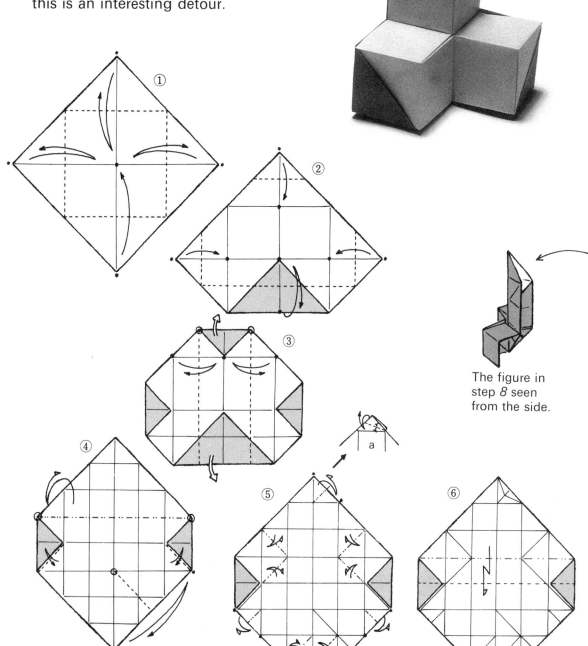

The figure in step 8 seen from the side.

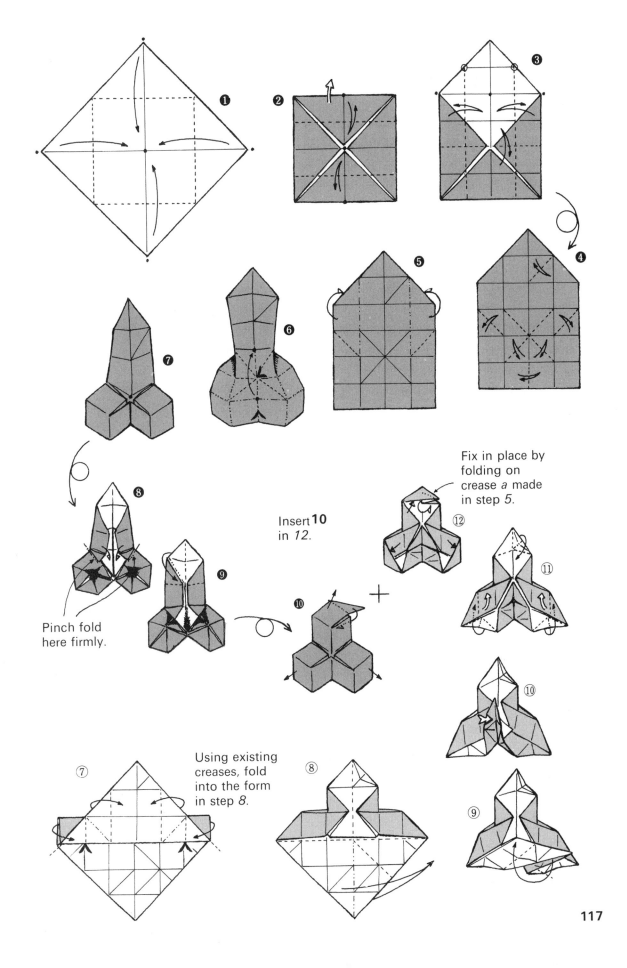

❶ ❷ ❸ ❹ ❺ ❻ ❼

Fix in place by folding on crease *a* made in step *5*.

⑫

Insert **10** in *12*.

⑪

Pinch fold here firmly.

❽ ❾ ❿

⑩

Using existing creases, fold into the form in step *8*.

⑦ ⑧ ⑨

117

Making a Cube from a Cube with a Single Cut

As is seen in the photograph on p. 119, making three creases in a regular-hexagonal plane makes it resemble a cube.

①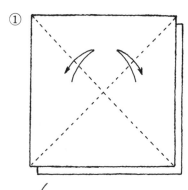

Cube _F_

②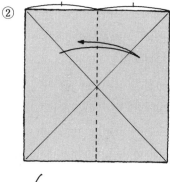

③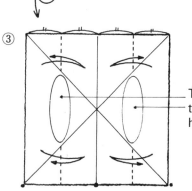

Take care not to make crease here.

The same size paper will fit if this is a Regular-hexagonal Flat Unit made as shown on p. 224, in Chapter 5.

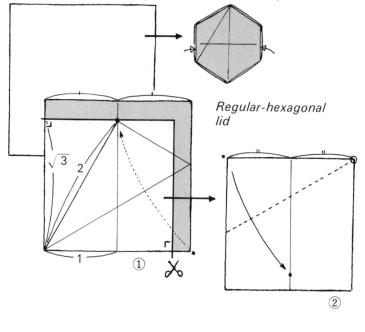

Regular-hexagonal lid

① ②

④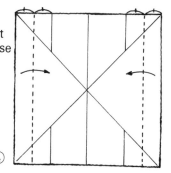

⑤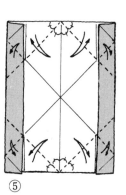

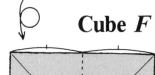

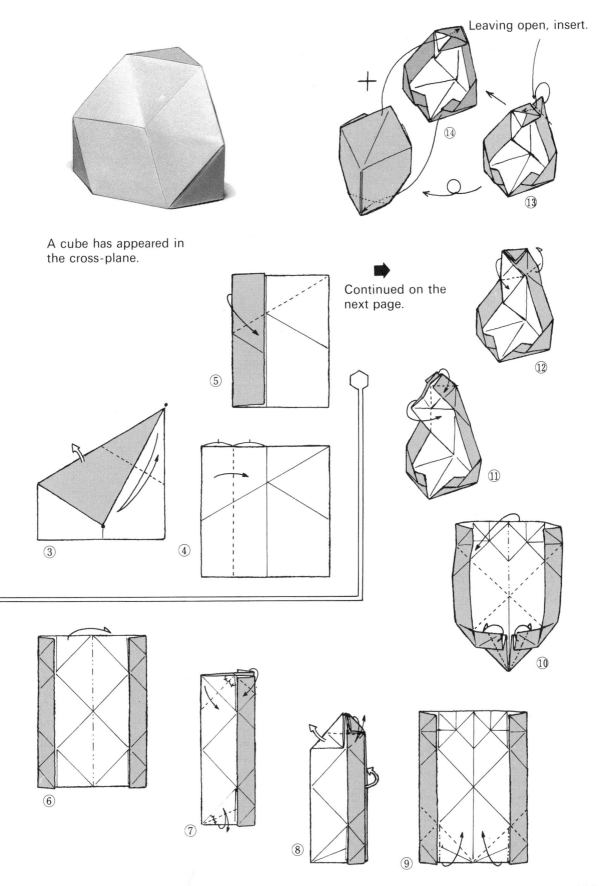

Leaving open, insert.

+

⑭

⑬

A cube has appeared in
the cross-plane.

Continued on the
next page.

⑫

⑪

⑩

⑤

④

③

⑥

⑦

⑧

⑨

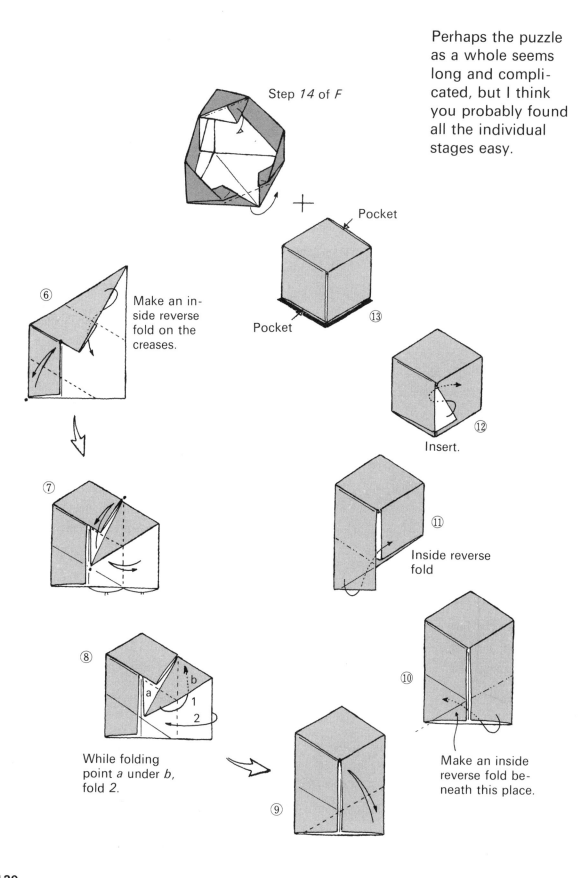

Step *14* of *F*

Perhaps the puzzle as a whole seems long and complicated, but I think you probably found all the individual stages easy.

Pocket

Pocket

⑬

⑫ Insert.

⑪ Inside reverse fold

⑥ Make an inside reverse fold on the creases.

⑦

⑩ Make an inside reverse fold beneath this place.

⑧ While folding point *a* under *b*, fold *2*.

a   b   1   2

⑨

Chapter 3

Fly, Crane, Fly!

Challenging the Eternally Fascinating Origami Crane

Challenge I

Red-crested white crane

The immortal origami classic, the crane, has maintained its appeal and beauty throughout the ages. For the devoted origamian, it is an object of affection and, at the same time, a stimulus to the spirit of challenge. The challenges presented here are offered, not with the intention of supplanting the traditional fold, but in the hope of further amplifying its charm through the application of original variations on the basic theme.

For many years people have amused themselves in this way, to the extent, indeed, that a very thick book could be made of nothing but the results of attempts to vary the traditional crane origami. From examining the results of their efforts, I have come to the conclusion that the challenges all fall into one of three major categories. The oldest is représented by the double connected crane called *Imose-yama* by a certain Rokōan. The fold is found in a book on folding thousand-crane amulets (1797). The aim of the design is to produce two identical cranes that are exactly like the traditional one in all respects except that they are joined. Various people, including Michiaki Katō, Kazunobu Kijima, Kazuo Kodama, Hiroshi Yamagata, Kazuyoshi Tanaka, and Shizuka Nakamura have produced splendid works in this category. The original and practical chopsticks envelope by Sachiko Kawahata, though not two connected cranes, belongs in this category because it uses part of the paper to fold the crane (actually half a crane) and the rest of the same piece of paper to produce the envelope.

Imose-yama by Rokōan, found in the 1797 edition of Semba-zuru Orikata (*Folding thousand-crane amulets*)

"Begging for favors" by Kazunobu Kijima

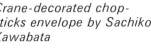

Crane-decorated chopsticks envelope by Sachiko Kawabata

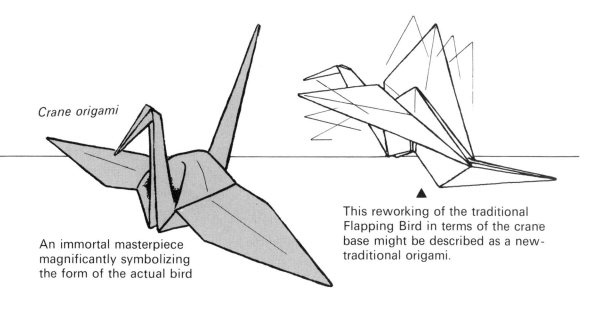

Crane origami

An immortal masterpiece magnificantly symbolizing the form of the actual bird

This reworking of the traditional Flapping Bird in terms of the crane base might be described as a new-traditional origami.

Challenge II

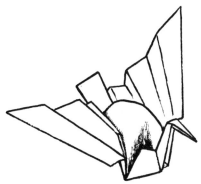

New Year's Crane, by Toshio Chino

Although it might appear indistinguishable from other more general approaches, altering part of the form of the crane while following the folding method of the traditional crane base and using the word *crane* in the name of the new work offer clear proof of willingness to make a challenge. This is the second of my three categories. There are many examples of the use of this approach, which begins with the classical origami crane. In the preface to his book *Henka Orizuru* (Crane origami variations; 1971), Eiji Nakamura treats the topic most ambitiously by speaking of "a thousand variations." Although not a crane at all, the phoenix, which I discovered in a book on folk origami entitled *Denshō Origami III* (1984), by Masurō Tsujimura, belongs in this category.

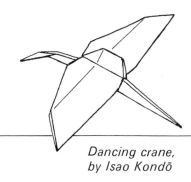

Dancing crane, by Isao Kondō

Traditional phoenix

This is made from a square sheet. But the paper must be thin for good results. Perhaps this accounts for the fold's failure to gain wide popularity.

New Enthusiasm

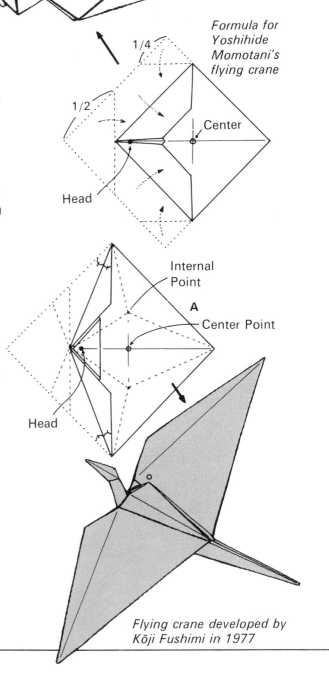

The face is roundish because of the many layers of paper.

The flying crane

Challenge III

In the first two challenges, interest is concentrated on lyrical expressiveness, although the connected cranes include an element of mathematical puzzle and Miss Kawahata's chopsticks envelope is practically functional. In this third challenge, interest shifts to the element of motion and the production of a crane with mobile wings. Of course, in this case too, lyrical beauty is very important.

With a new kind of enthusiasm, Professor and Mrs. Kōji Fushimi have produced a whole series of origami as a highly valuable teaching means for the cultivation of intuitive powers in geometry. Central in the series is the flying crane. Sky-flying Crane by Yoshihide Momotani, included in a 1976 supplement edition of *Kodomo no Kagaku* (Science for children), ignited Professor Fushimi's enthusiasm for this kind of origami. As the drawing above shows, this is a clear and simple fold. It is the idea of folding a crane actually capable of flying that deserves praise for originality. Because of several overlapping layers, the head tends to be slightly round.

Formula for Yoshihide Momotani's flying crane

1/4

1/2

Center

Head

Internal Point

A

Center Point

Head

Flying crane developed by Kōji Fushimi in 1977

124

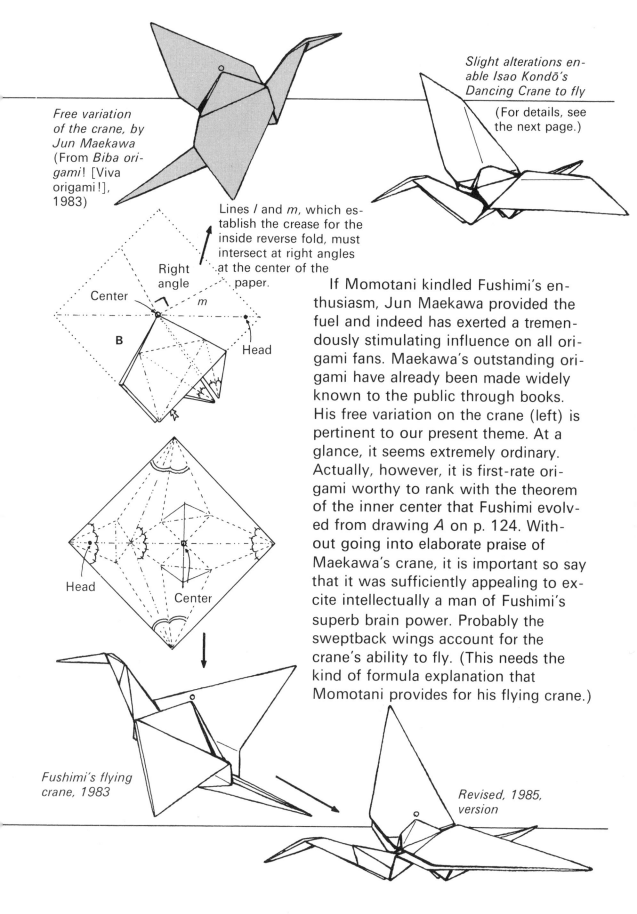

Free variation of the crane, by Jun Maekawa (From Biba origami! [Viva origami!], 1983)

Slight alterations enable Isao Kondō's Dancing Crane to fly

(For details, see the next page.)

Lines *l* and *m*, which establish the crease for the inside reverse fold, must intersect at right angles at the center of the paper.

Right angle

Center

B

m

Head

Head

Center

Fushimi's flying crane, 1983

Revised, 1985, version

If Momotani kindled Fushimi's enthusiasm, Jun Maekawa provided the fuel and indeed has exerted a tremendously stimulating influence on all origami fans. Maekawa's outstanding origami have already been made widely known to the public through books. His free variation on the crane (left) is pertinent to our present theme. At a glance, it seems extremely ordinary. Actually, however, it is first-rate origami worthy to rank with the theorem of the inner center that Fushimi evolved from drawing *A* on p. 124. Without going into elaborate praise of Maekawa's crane, it is important so say that it was sufficiently appealing to excite intellectually a man of Fushimi's superb brain power. Probably the sweptback wings account for the crane's ability to fly. (This needs the kind of formula explanation that Momotani provides for his flying crane.)

Challenging the Challengers

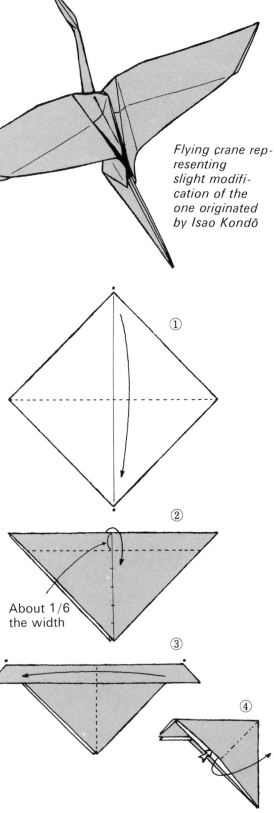

Flying crane No. 1

After having introduced some excellent works by people who have challenged the classical origami crane, I now propose challenging those challengers by allowing them to pit their works against each other. It is difficult to establish superiority among works like Rokōan's *Imose-yama*, Kijima's Begging for Favors, Chino's New Year's Crane, or Kondō's Dancing Crane. But competition among them is important as long as the idea of a flying crane alone is the criterion. In the competition, points could be given for flying performance, realism of completed form, rhythm in folding production process, and new geometric discoveries. Skillfully setting up competitions of this kind could have a very stimulating effect on origami development.

Realizing the closeness of the race among the competitors, however, I decided to do no more than develop one of the cranes already devised and selected the one by Isao Kondō.

Flying crane representing slight modification of the one originated by Isao Kondō

①

②

About 1/6 the width

③

④

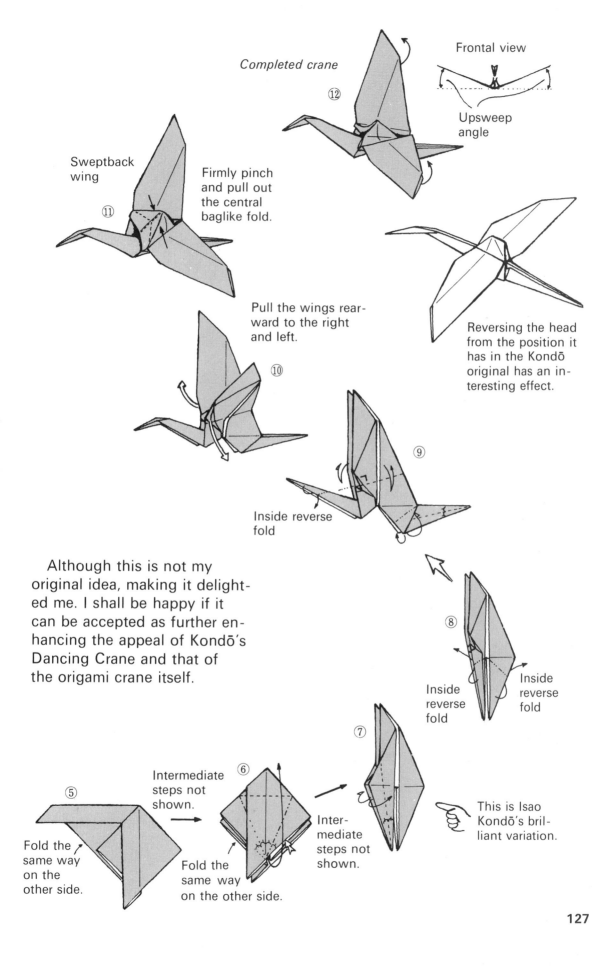

Completed crane

Frontal view

⑫

Upsweep angle

Sweptback wing

Firmly pinch and pull out the central baglike fold.

⑪

Reversing the head from the position it has in the Kondō original has an interesting effect.

Pull the wings rearward to the right and left.

⑩

Inside reverse fold

⑨

Although this is not my original idea, making it delighted me. I shall be happy if it can be accepted as further enhancing the appeal of Kondō's Dancing Crane and that of the origami crane itself.

⑧

Inside reverse fold

Inside reverse fold

⑦

Intermediate steps not shown.

⑥

⑤

This is Isao Kondō's brilliant variation.

Fold the same way on the other side.

Fold the same way on the other side.

Intermediate steps not shown.

127

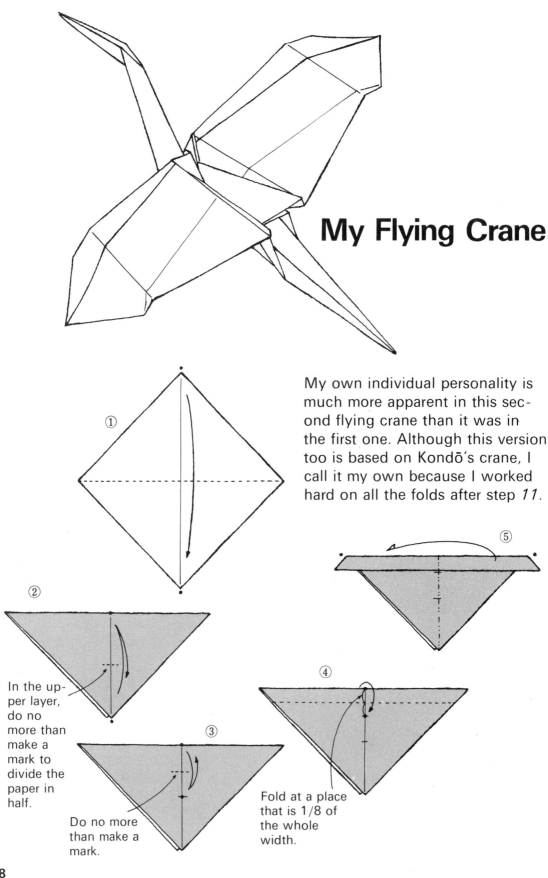

My Flying Crane

My own individual personality is much more apparent in this second flying crane than it was in the first one. Although this version too is based on Kondō's crane, I call it my own because I worked hard on all the folds after step *11*.

①

②

In the upper layer, do no more than make a mark to divide the paper in half.

③

Do no more than make a mark.

④

Fold at a place that is 1/8 of the whole width.

⑤

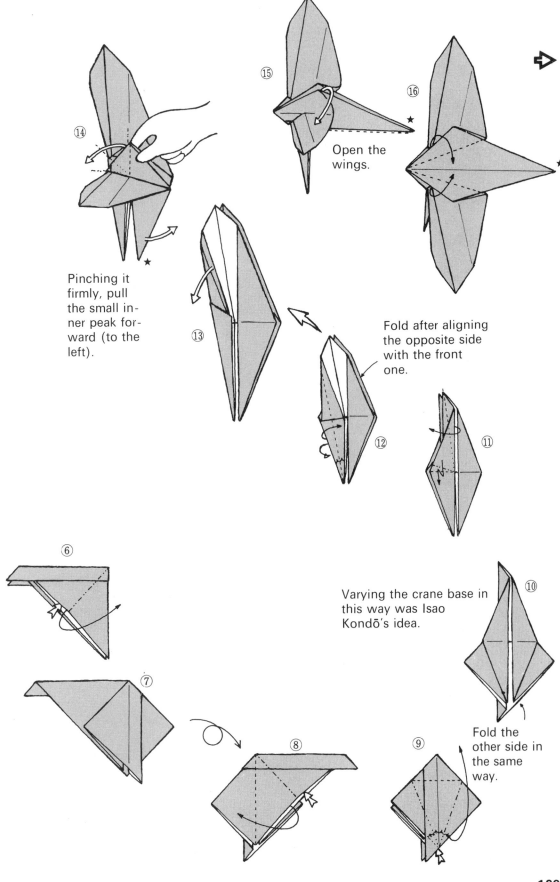

⑮

Open the wings.

⑯

⑭

Pinching it firmly, pull the small inner peak forward (to the left).

⑬

Fold after aligning the opposite side with the front one.

⑫

⑪

⑥

⑦

⑧

Varying the crane base in this way was Isao Kondō's idea.

⑩

Fold the other side in the same way.

⑨

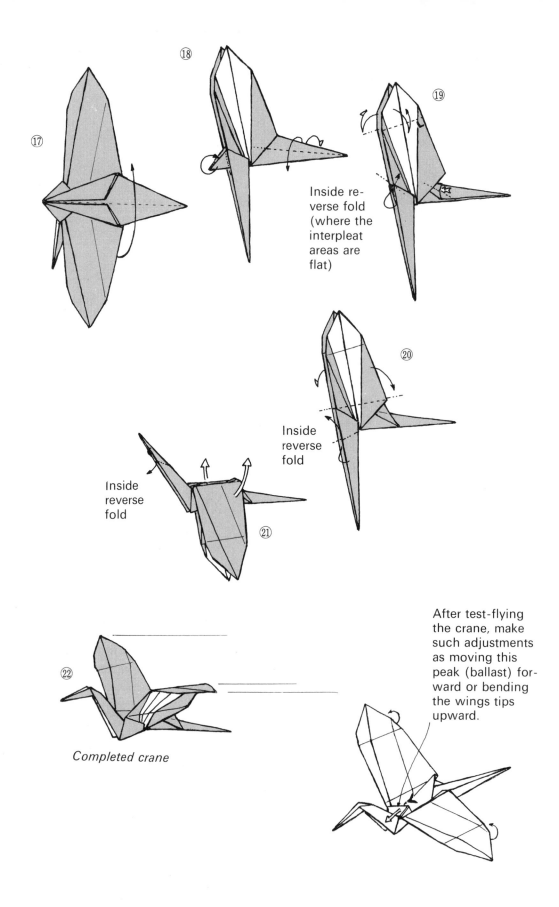

⑰

⑱

⑲ Inside re-
verse fold
(where the
interpleat
areas are
flat)

⑳ Inside
reverse
fold

Inside
reverse
fold

㉑

㉒ Completed crane

After test-flying
the crane, make
such adjustments
as moving this
peak (ballast) for-
ward or bending
the wings tips
upward.

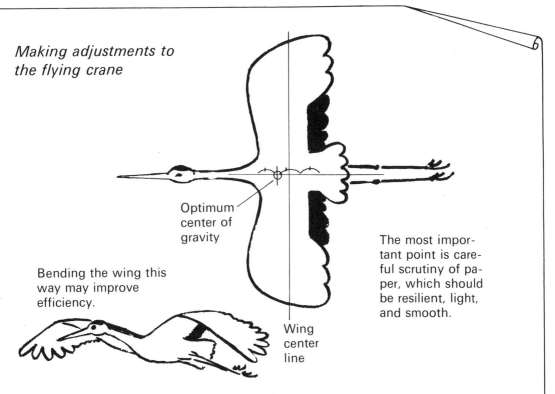

Making adjustments to the flying crane

Optimum
center of
gravity

Bending the wing this
way may improve
efficiency.

The most impor-
tant point is care-
ful scrutiny of pa-
per, which should
be resilient, light,
and smooth.

Wing
center
line

Making a bend in the center of the wings produces an interesting
effect.

In the case of the crane and of all other flying birds, the center of
gravity should be forward of the wing center line. In origami terms,
two ways of achieving this end are conceivable.

1. Creating ballast in the head and the wing tips by means of several
layers of paper.

2. Throwing the center of gravity forward by sweeping the wings
back.

Smooth flying requires attention to more than center of gravity.
But, bearing these two methods in mind as guidelines, launch your
crane time and time again, making the necessary alterations each time,
until it flies as you want it to. Altering the wing elevation angle and
devising wing flaps for control are good ways to improve flight
performance.

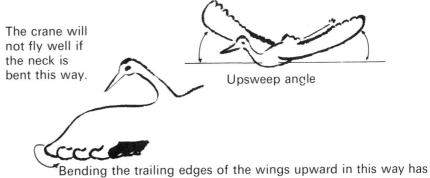

The crane will
not fly well if
the neck is
bent this way.

Upsweep angle

Bending the trailing edges of the wings upward in this way has
an effect like that of adjusting the flaps of an aircraft.

Flying White Heron

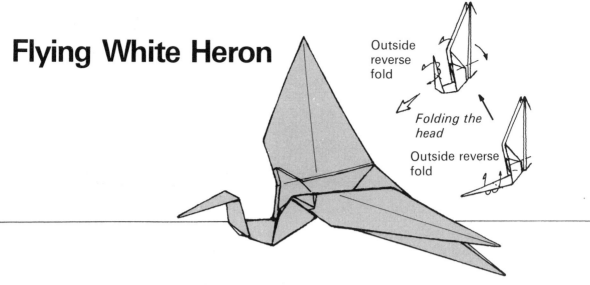

Outside reverse fold

Folding the head

Outside reverse fold

I am especially pround of steps *14* and *15* in My Flying Crane, which, as I have said, is based on Kondō's version, the realistic appearance of the wings in which I found especially striking. This third variation on the origami crane, my own version of a flying white heron, incorporates those folding steps of which I am proud. In other words, this is a conversion of the traditional origami crane into an origami white heron.

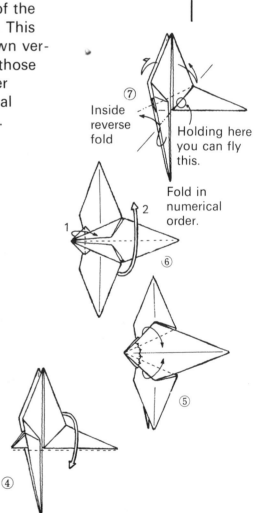

⑦

Inside reverse fold

Holding here you can fly this.

Fold in numerical order.

1   2

⑥

⑤

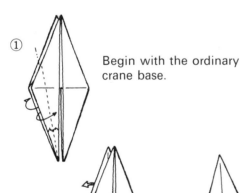

①   Begin with the ordinary crane base.

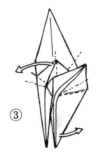

②   ③   ④

Crane in flight

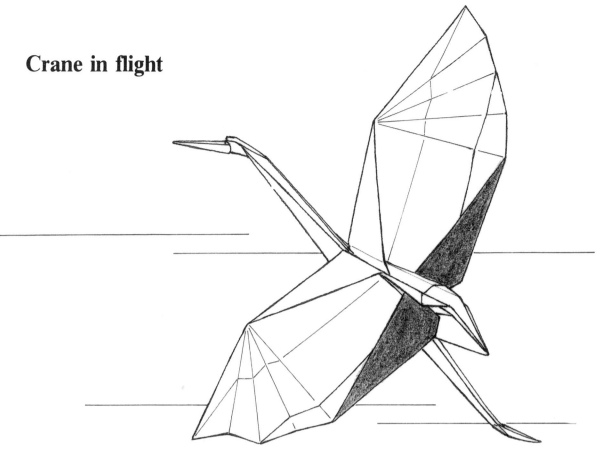

The emphasis in this work is on realism of appearance. The impression made on me by Kondō's Dancing Crane led me to devise this version. Three years intervene between it and the Flying Crane, which is comparatively recent.

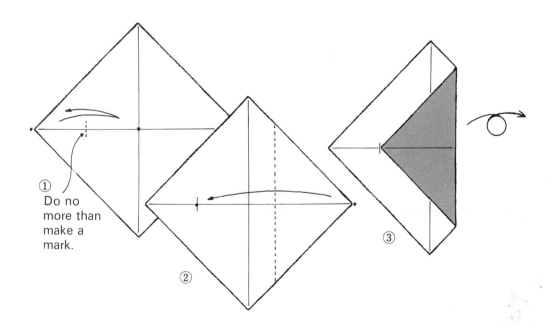

① Do no more than make a mark.

②

③

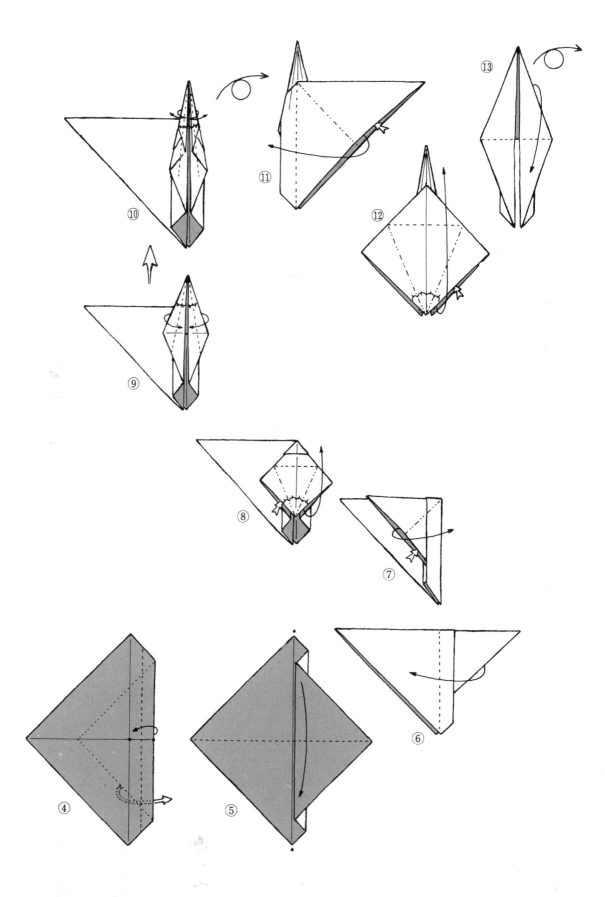

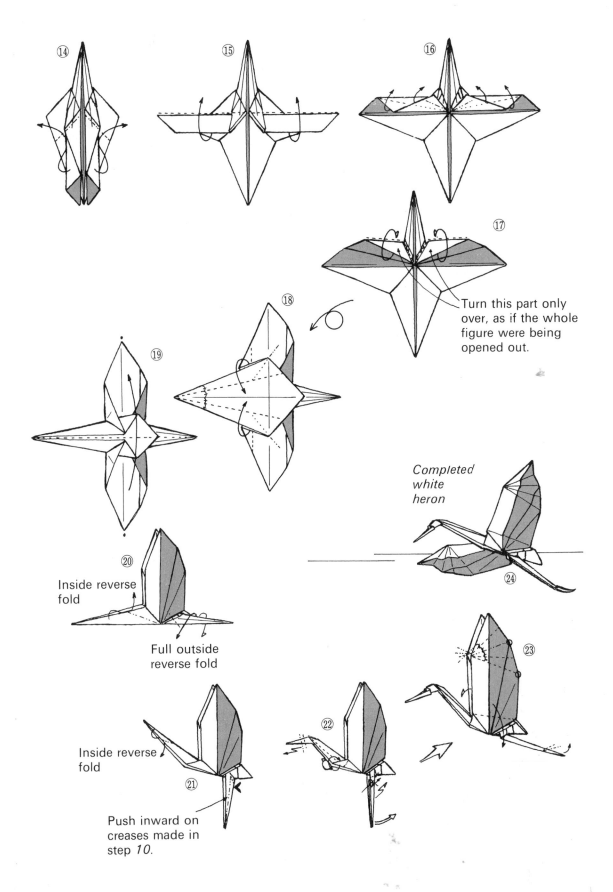

⑭

⑮

⑯

⑰ Turn this part only over, as if the whole figure were being opened out.

⑱

⑲

⑳ Inside reverse fold

Full outside reverse fold

㉑ Inside reverse fold

Push inward on creases made in step 10.

㉒

㉓

Completed white heron

㉔

Variations on the Flying White Heron

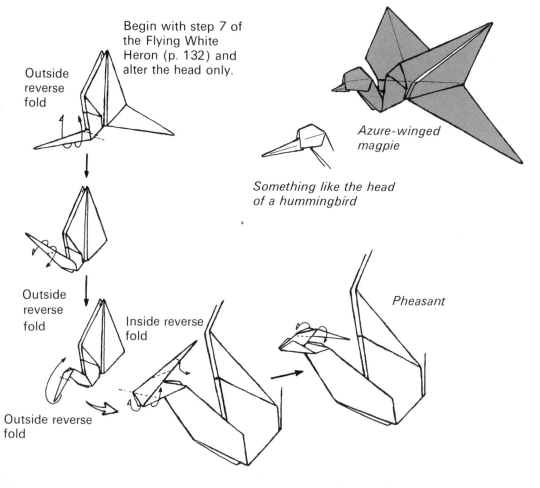

Flying common pheasant

We have about come to the end of my challenges to the classical origami crane. In trying to devise realistic-looking versions that actually fly, we may well be biting off more than we can chew. No matter how good they are, the folds can never match the performance of airplanes. Nonetheless, this origami white heron flies well enough to warrant making slight alterations to create other kinds of birds from it.

(*Note:* Please remember to make such adjustments as angling the wings upward or folding flaps in the trailing edges of the wings.)

Begin with step 7 of the Flying White Heron (p. 132) and alter the head only.

Outside reverse fold

Outside reverse fold

Outside reverse fold

Inside reverse fold

Azure-winged magpie

Something like the head of a hummingbird

Pheasant

El Condor Pasa — The Condor Passes

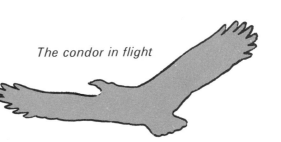

The condor in flight

To round out Chapter 3, I offer this old origami, in which emphasis is placed on flight performance. I used to call it Glider *Tombi* (the *tombi* is a bird called the Siberian black kite). But ever since I developed a taste for South American music, I always hum the famous Peruvian song *El Condor Pasa* whenever I fly one of these. And this led me to change the name.

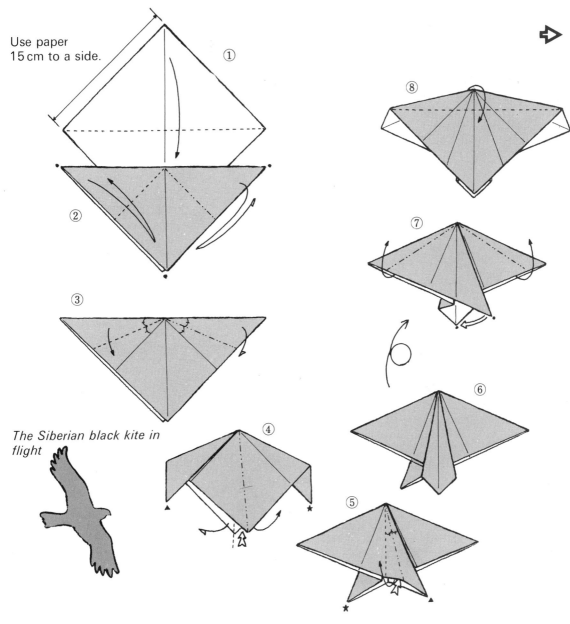

Use paper 15 cm to a side.

The Siberian black kite in flight

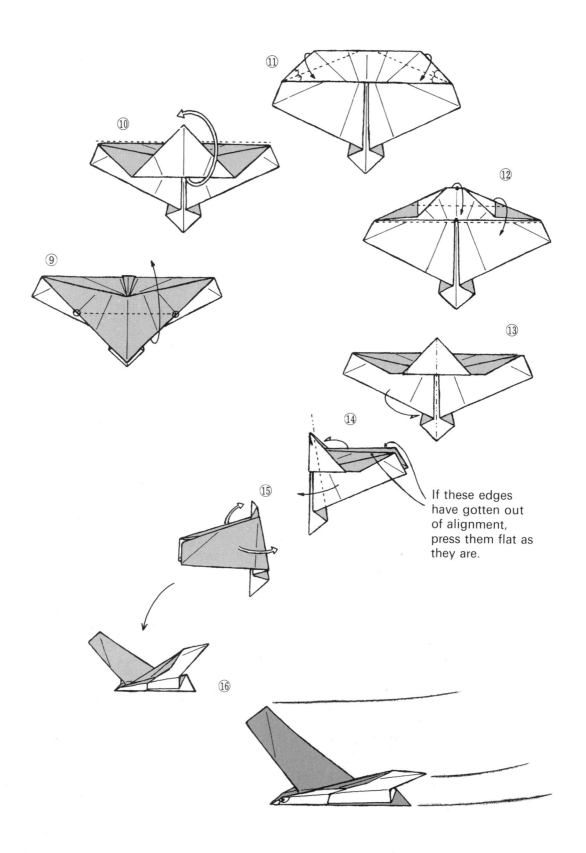

If these edges
have gotten out
of alignment,
press them flat as
they are.

138

Starting the Animals

Koala

Animal figures are an ever-popular origami theme transcending all age and nationality boundaries and requiring no explanation to enjoy. This chapter shows how to produce, by folding square sheets of paper, many of the animals that have become stars of fairy tales, motion pictures, and television. The latter part of the chapter includes mythical beasts like the dragons plus dinosaurs, now to be seen only in the world of fossils.

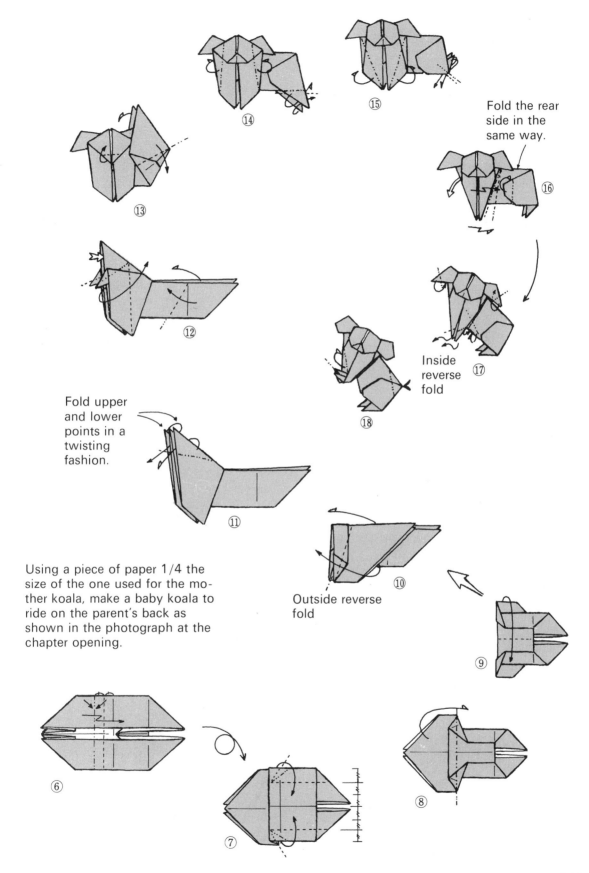

⑬

⑭

⑮

Fold the rear
side in the
same way.

⑯

Inside
reverse
fold ⑰

⑱

⑫

Fold upper
and lower
points in a
twisting
fashion.

⑪

Using a piece of paper 1/4 the
size of the one used for the mo-
ther koala, make a baby koala to
ride on the parent's back as
shown in the photograph at the
chapter opening.

⑩

Outside reverse
fold

⑨

⑥

⑦

⑧

The Smart Way to Read the Chart: Stay One Step Ahead

Readers who have breezed through the folds to this point may not need this hint. Still I should like remind you of the importance of always glancing ahead a step farther than the one you are performing at the given moment. Because they understand this, children generally have no trouble with folding. The Llama (p. 144) has been devised as an effective test of skill at reading the diagrams.

Persian Cat

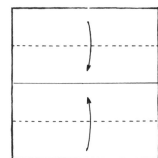

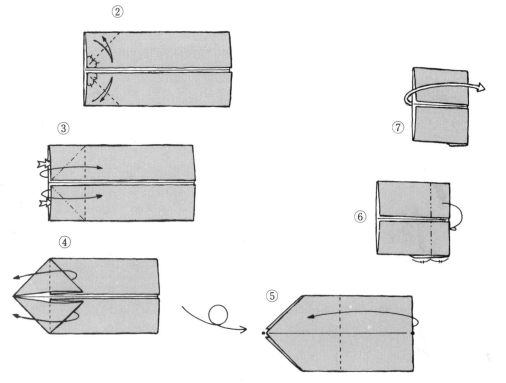

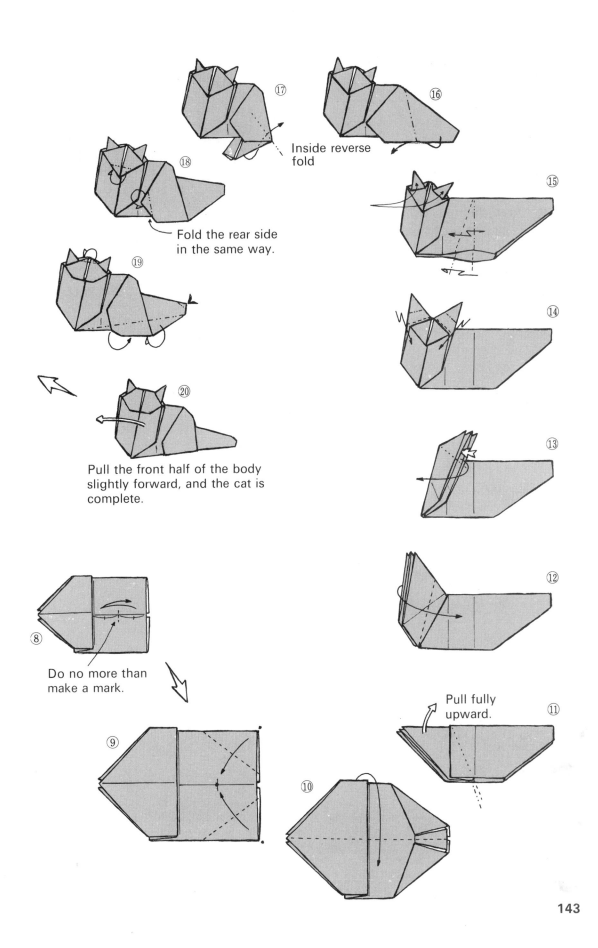

⑰

⑯

Inside reverse fold

⑱

Fold the rear side in the same way.

⑮

⑲

⑭

⑳

Pull the front half of the body slightly forward, and the cat is complete.

⑬

⑧

Do no more than make a mark.

⑫

⑨

Pull fully upward.

⑪

⑩

143

Llama

The llama is an animal of the greatest importance to the people who live high in the Andes Mountains of South America. Since the multiple layers make the camel-like face somewhat thick, it is good to use thin paper.

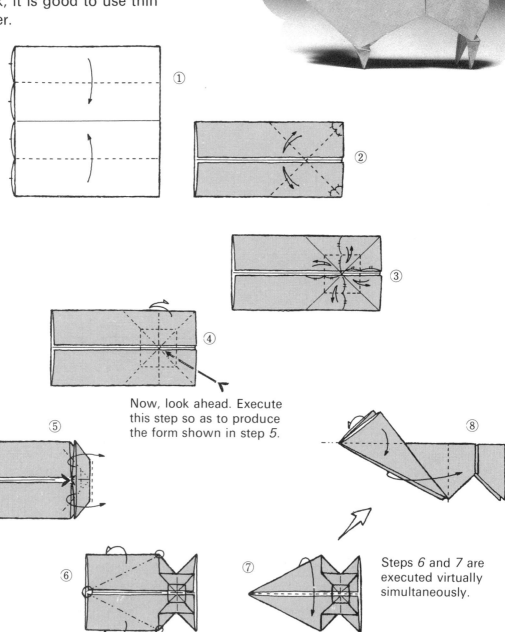

Now, look ahead. Execute this step so as to produce the form shown in step 5.

Steps 6 and 7 are executed virtually simultaneously.

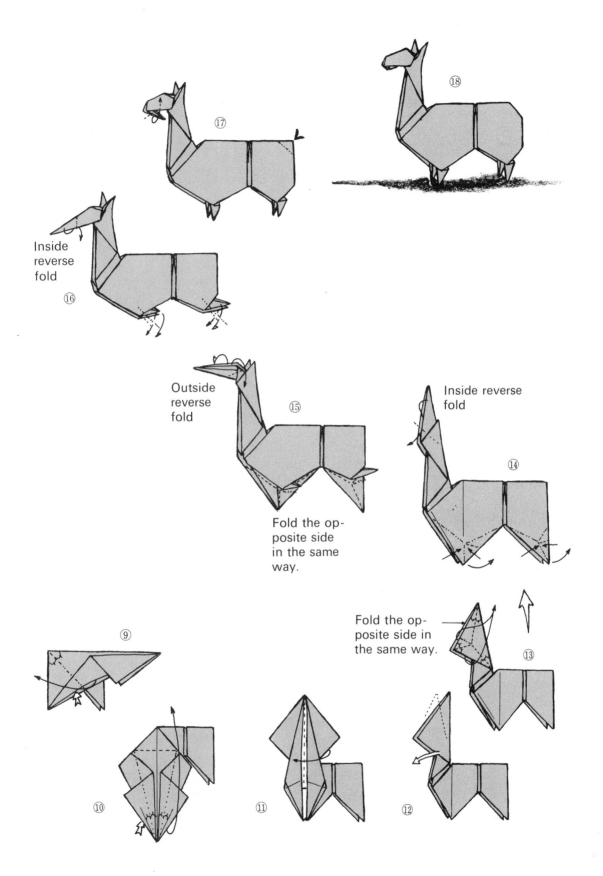

⑰

⑱

Inside
reverse
fold

⑯

Outside
reverse
fold

⑮

Fold the op-
posite side
in the same
way.

Inside reverse
fold

⑭

Fold the op-
posite side in
the same way.

⑬

⑨

⑩

⑪

⑫

145

Fox

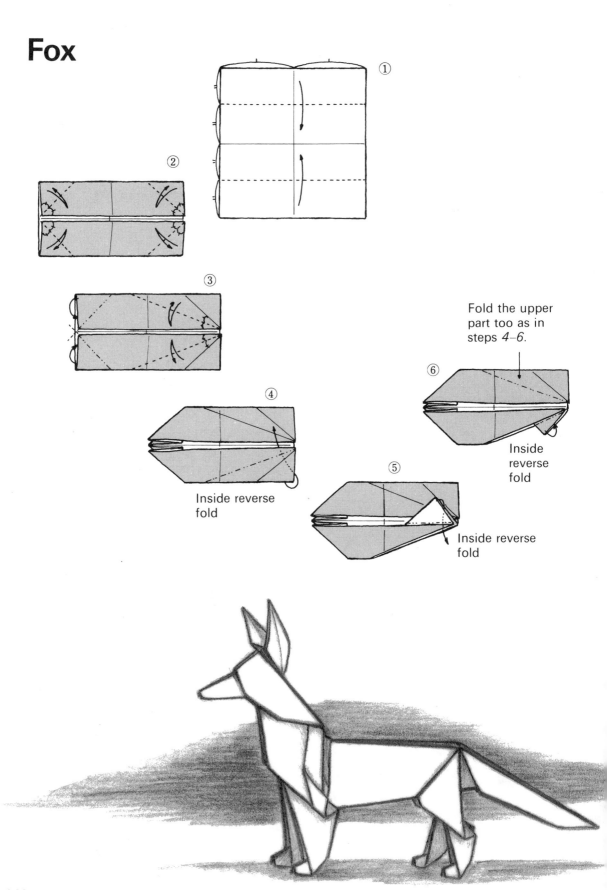

①

②

③

④

Inside reverse fold

⑤

Inside reverse fold

⑥

Fold the upper part too as in steps *4–6*.

Inside reverse fold

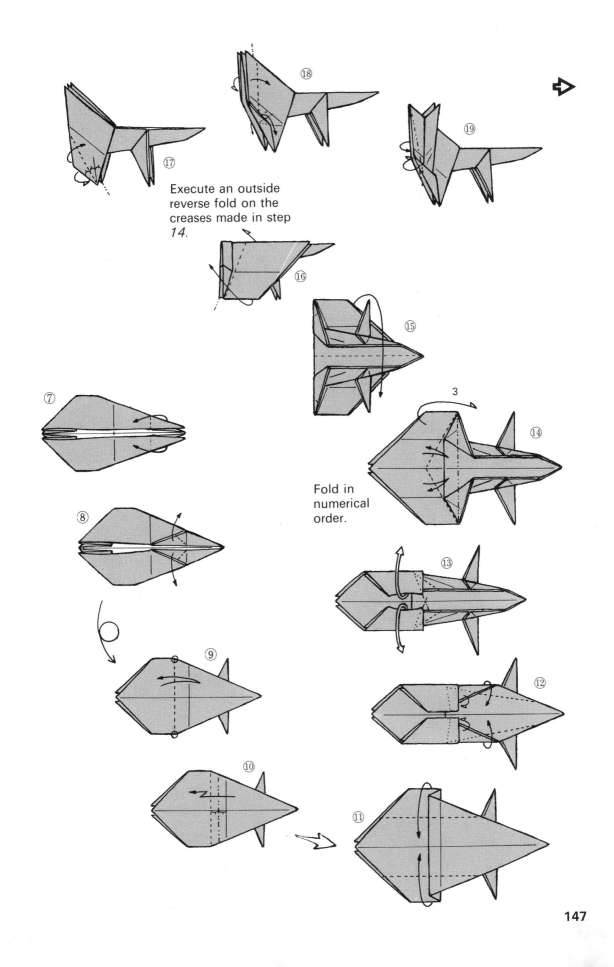

⑱

⑲

⑰

Execute an outside
reverse fold on the
creases made in step
14.

⑯

⑮

3

⑦

⑭

Fold in
numerical
order.

⑧

⑬

⑨

⑫

⑩

⑪

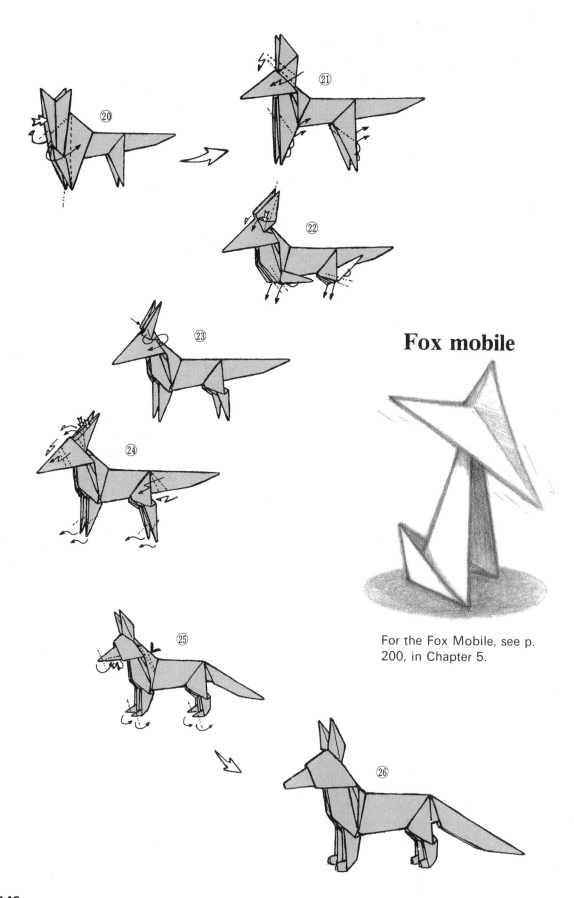

Fox mobile

For the Fox Mobile, see p. 200, in Chapter 5.

Fox on the chase

(Compound figure made from 2 sheets of paper)
The head is made exactly as is the figure in the photograph.

Origami ideals

This book presents a large number of origami works made, without cutting, from single sheets of paper because undeniably being able to produce everything needed for the four legs, ears, and tails of animals in this way generates a pure kind of happiness. But, as I have said in the introduction, ingenuity applied in this method is not necessarily supreme. The charm of unit origami or of deliberate form simplification can be as great or greater. Without adhering to the traditional restriction of no cutting and only one sheet of paper work, I have devised the three foxes shown in the photographs and drawing and am proud of them all. It is important to remember that origami ideals are richly diverse.

Symbolization of the fox

(For the folding method, see Chapter 6, p. 254.)

Beagle

Producing the beagle—a
breed made famous by
Snoopy in the celebrated
comic strip *Peanuts*—from
square paper is difficult
because folding results in
clumsy thickness. Cut a
square sheet in half on
the diagonal to make an
isosceles triangle. This
origami fold will teach
you the logic of
inventiveness.

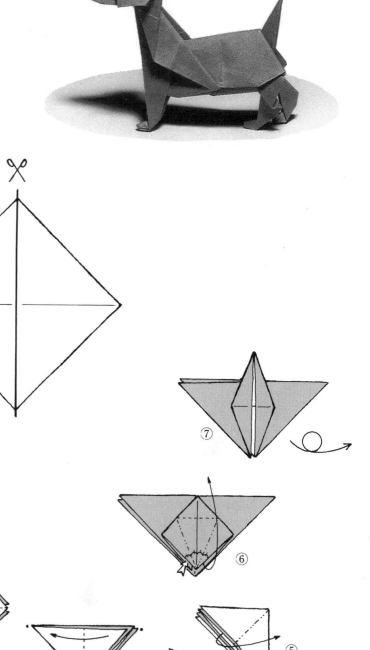

① ② ③ ④ ⑤ ⑥ ⑦

Open and crush the
second pocket from
the top.

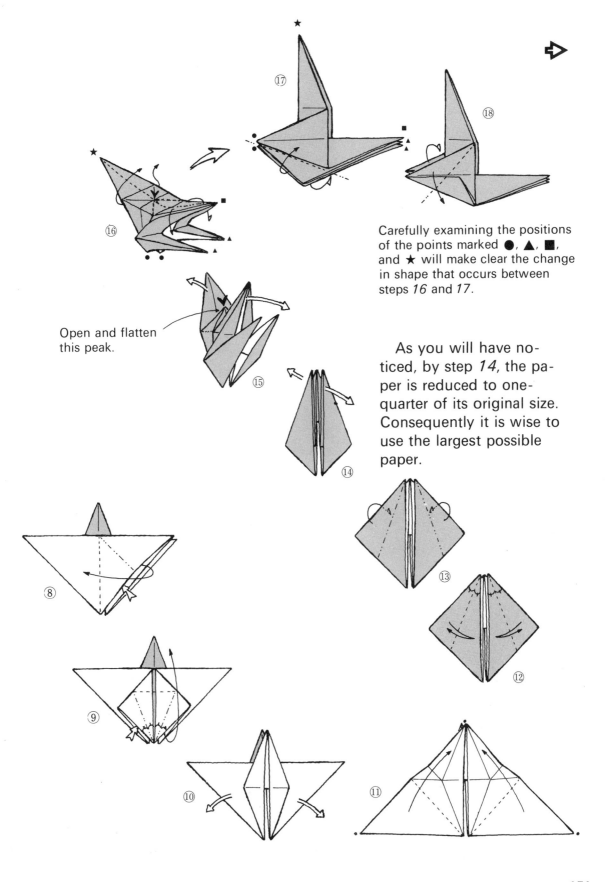

Carefully examining the positions of the points marked ●, ▲, ■, and ★ will make clear the change in shape that occurs between steps *16* and *17*.

Open and flatten this peak.

As you will have noticed, by step *14*, the paper is reduced to one-quarter of its original size. Consequently it is wise to use the largest possible paper.

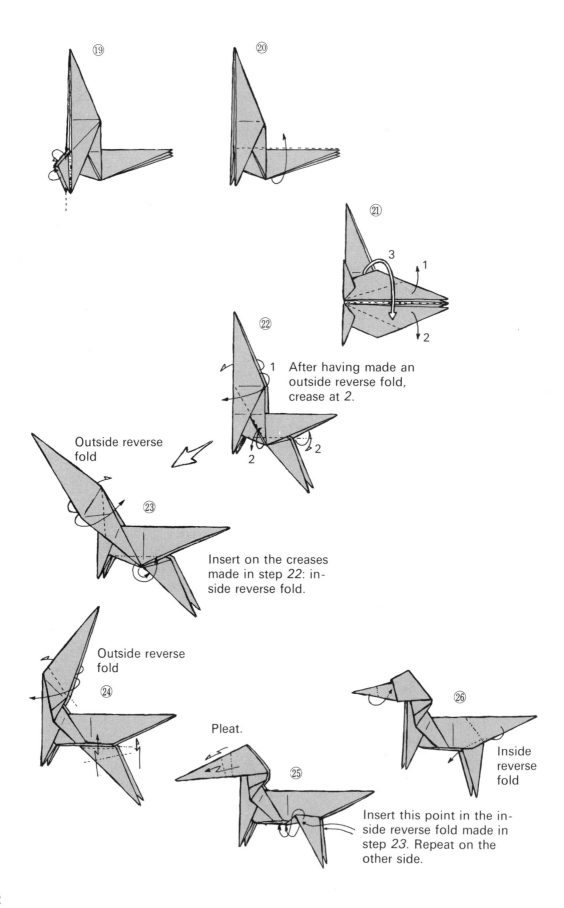

⑲

⑳

㉑

3   1

2

㉒   1   After having made an
outside reverse fold,
crease at *2*.

Outside reverse
fold

2   2

㉓

Insert on the creases
made in step *22*: in-
side reverse fold.

Outside reverse
fold

㉔

Pleat.

㉕

㉖

Inside
reverse
fold

Insert this point in the inside reverse fold made in
step *23*. Repeat on the
other side.

152

Japanese monkey

Try your hand at these 2 easy figures, which represent the kind of folding ingenuity employed in the beagle.

Giraffe

These figures, which I said at first would help make clear the nature of ingenuity in origami, explain how the two points needed for the rear legs are produced even though only four points are available from the crane base in its original square form.

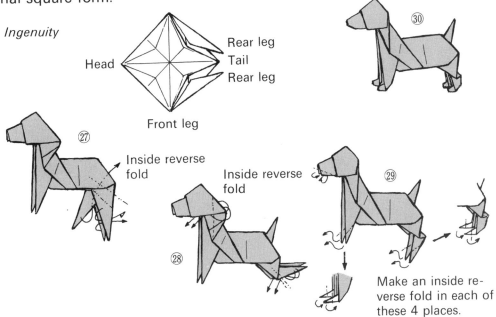

Ingenuity

Head

Rear leg
Tail
Rear leg

Front leg

Inside reverse fold

Inside reverse fold

Make an inside reverse fold in each of these 4 places.

Mother-and-child Monkeys

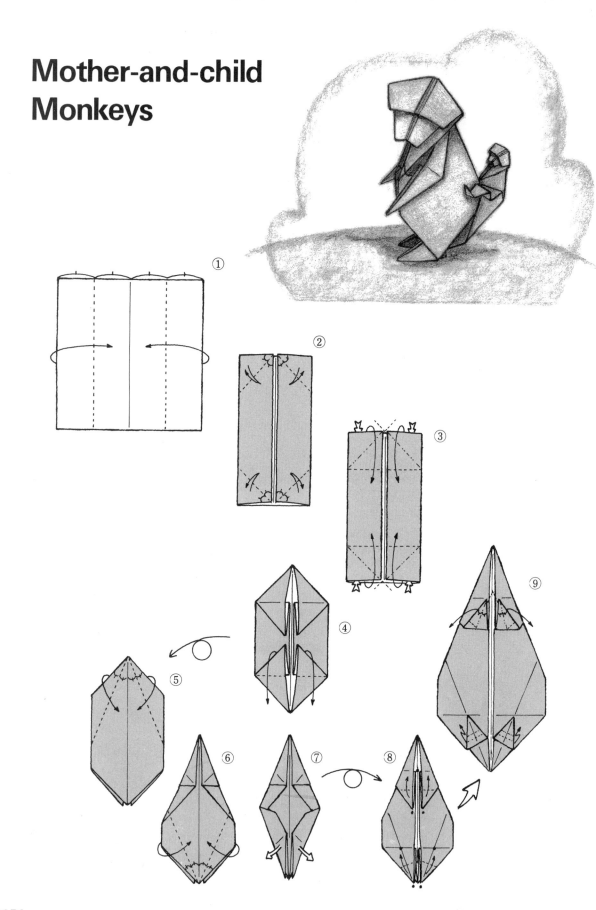

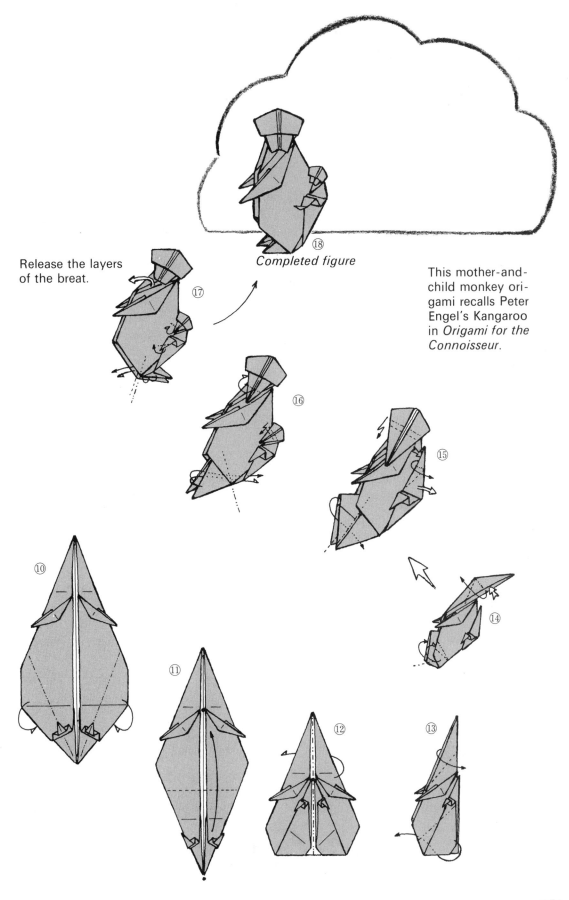

Release the layers of the breat.

⑰

⑱ *Completed figure*

This mother-and-child monkey origami recalls Peter Engel's Kangaroo in *Origami for the Connoisseur*.

⑯

⑮

⑭

⑩

⑪

⑫

⑬

Mouse

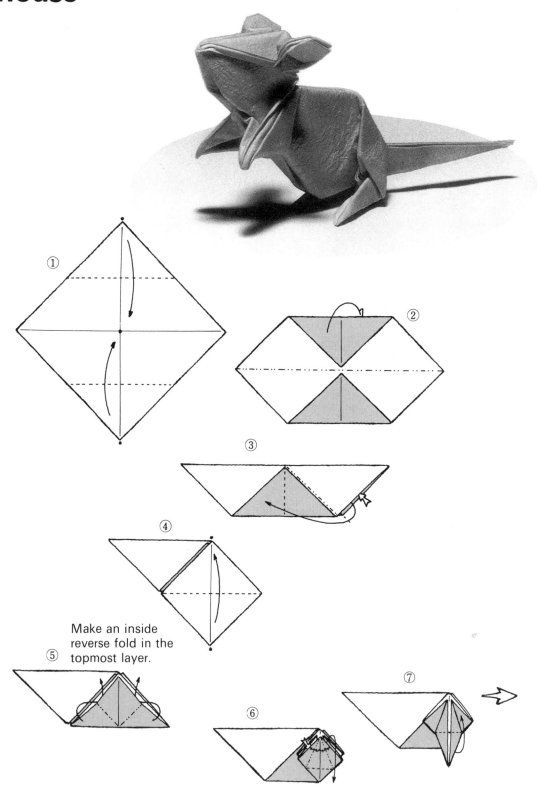

Make an inside reverse fold in the topmost layer.

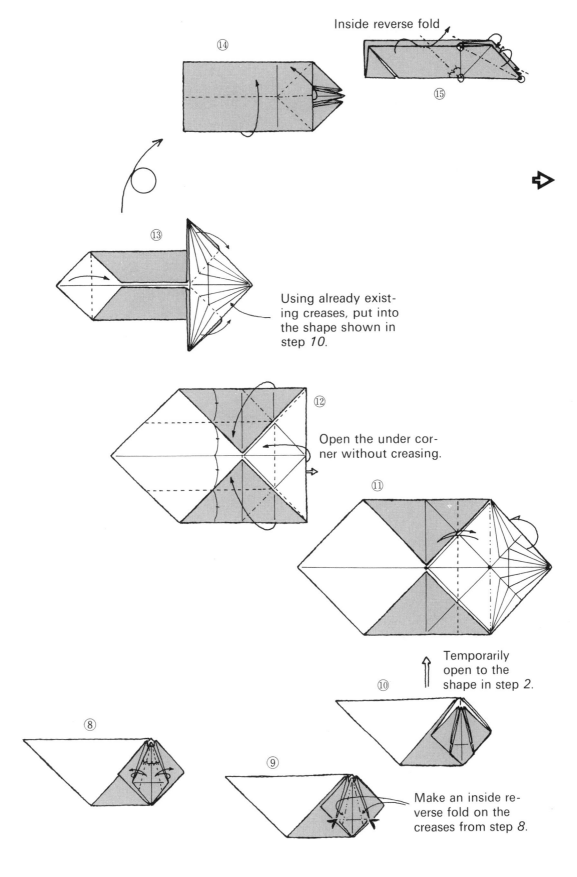

Inside reverse fold

⑭

⑮

⑬

Using already exist-
ing creases, put into
the shape shown in
step 10.

⑫

Open the under cor-
ner without creasing.

⑪

Temporarily
open to the
shape in step 2.

⑩

⑧

⑨

Make an inside re-
verse fold on the
creases from step 8.

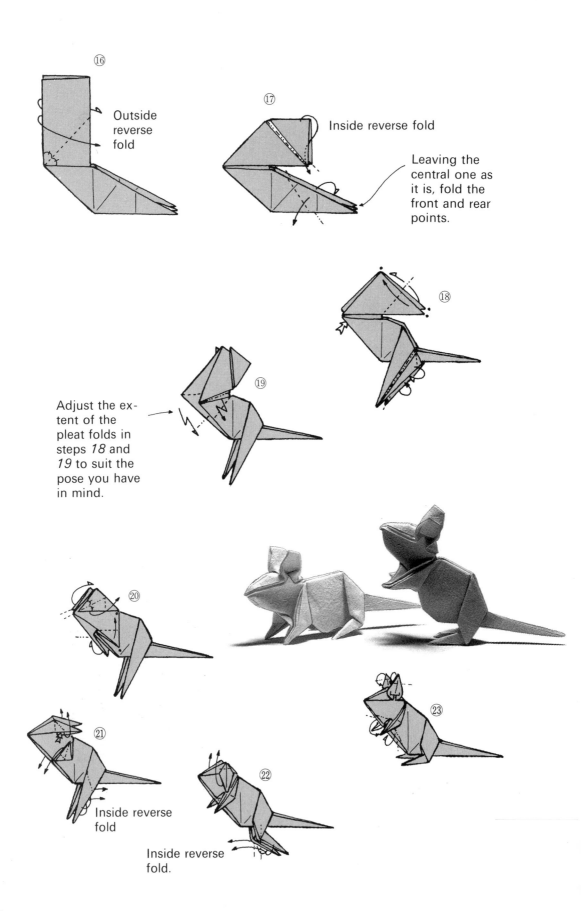

⑯

Outside reverse fold

⑰

Inside reverse fold

Leaving the central one as it is, fold the front and rear points.

⑱

⑲

Adjust the extent of the pleat folds in steps *18* and *19* to suit the pose you have in mind.

⑳

㉑

Inside reverse fold

㉒

Inside reverse fold.

㉓

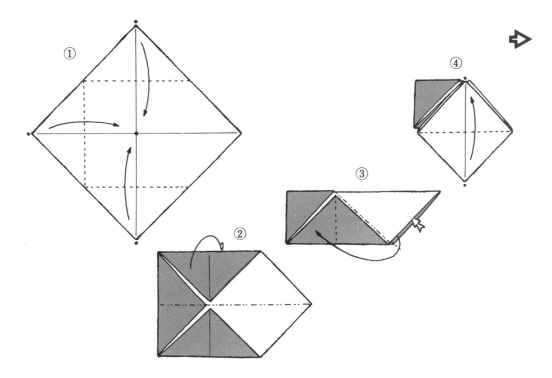

Squirrel

They are relatives in nature,
and in origami too it is possible
to fold a squirrel using the
same method used to fold a
mouse.

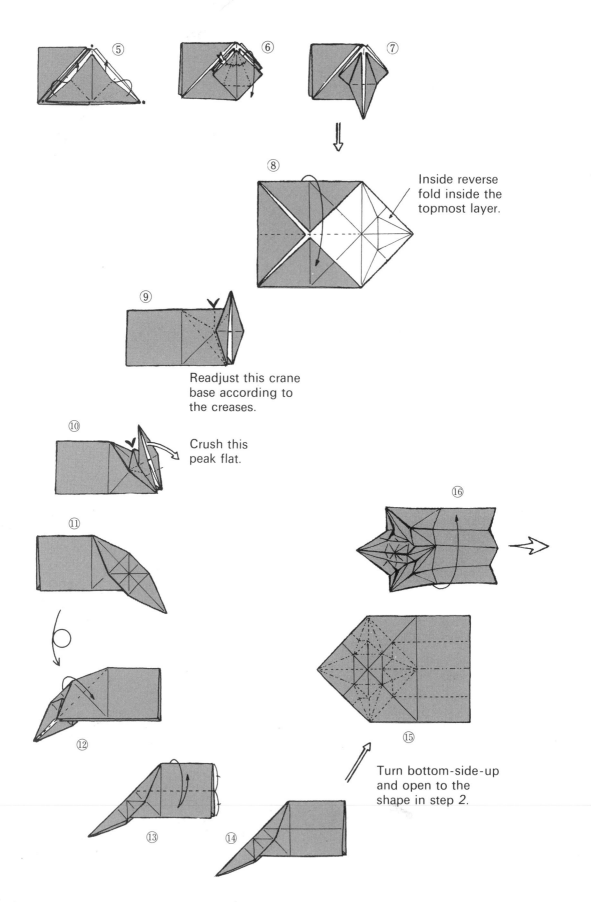

⑤ ⑥ ⑦

⑧ Inside reverse fold inside the topmost layer.

⑨ Readjust this crane base according to the creases.

⑩ Crush this peak flat.

⑪

⑫

⑬ ⑭

⑯

⑮ Turn bottom-side-up and open to the shape in step 2.

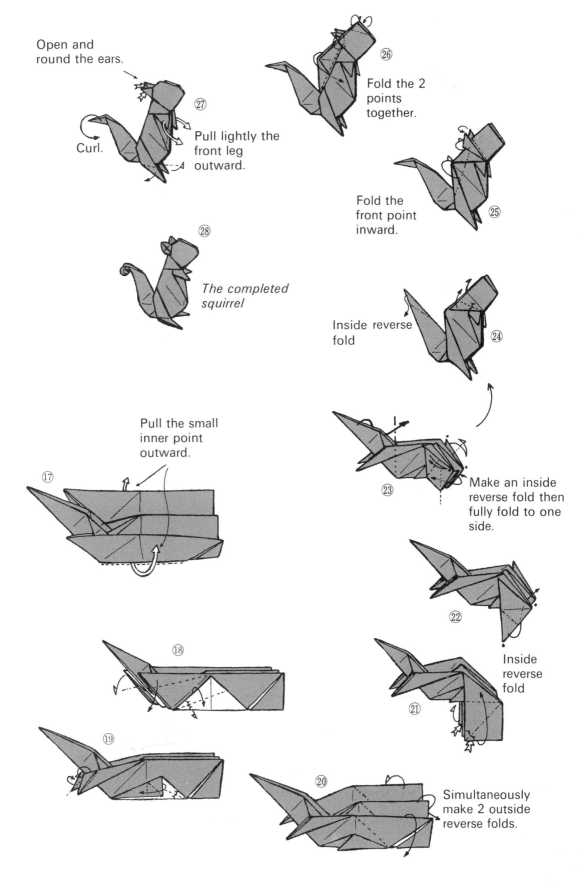

Open and round the ears.

㉗

Curl.

Pull lightly the front leg outward.

㉖ Fold the 2 points together.

Fold the front point inward. ㉕

Inside reverse fold ㉔

㉘ The completed squirrel

㉓ Make an inside reverse fold then fully fold to one side.

Pull the small inner point outward.

⑰

㉒

Inside reverse fold

㉑

⑱

⑲

⑳ Simultaneously make 2 outside reverse folds.

Elephant

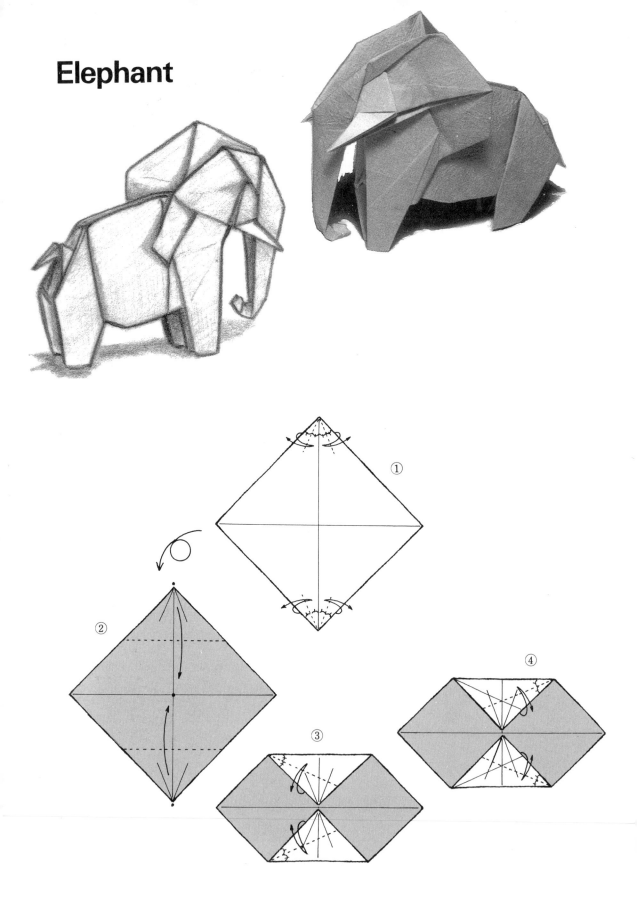

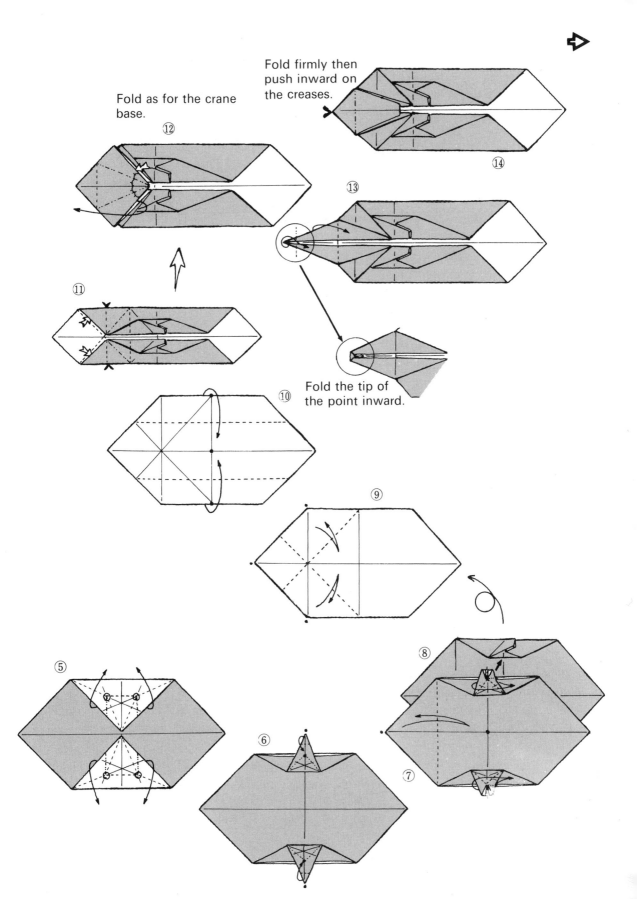

Fold as for the crane base.

⑫

Fold firmly then push inward on the creases.

⑭

⑬

Fold the tip of the point inward.

⑪

⑩

⑨

⑧

⑤

⑥

⑦

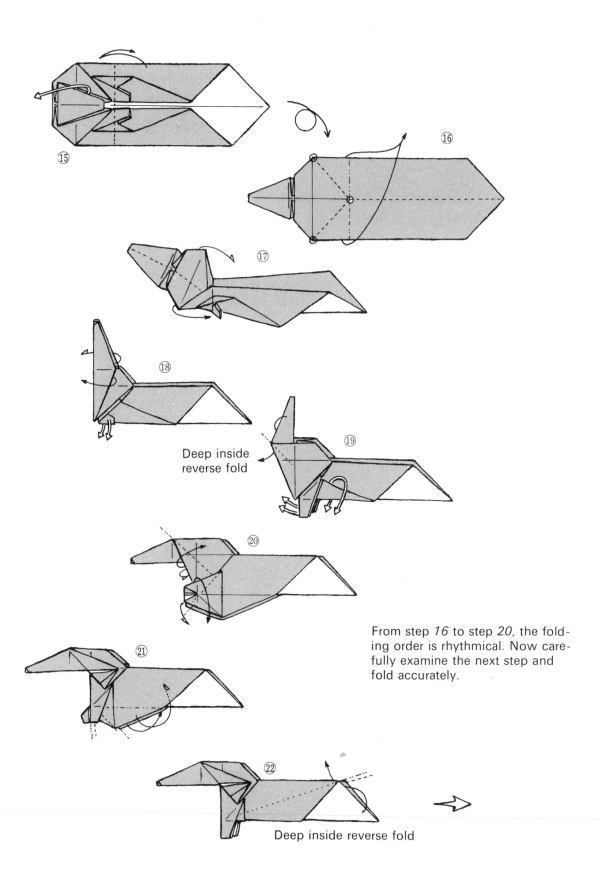

⑮

⑯

⑰

⑱

Deep inside
reverse fold

⑲

⑳

From step *16* to step *20*, the folding order is rhythmical. Now carefully examine the next step and fold accurately.

㉑

㉒

Deep inside reverse fold

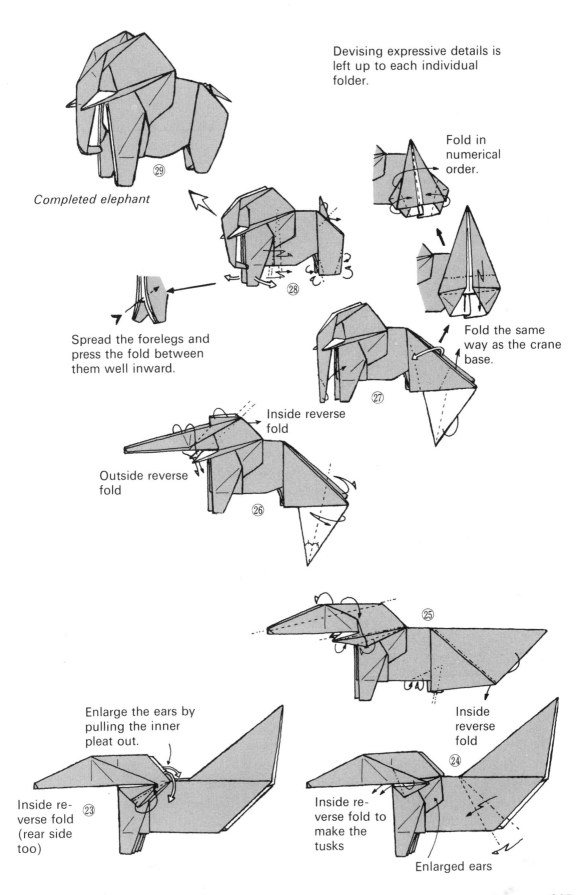

Devising expressive details is left up to each individual folder.

Fold in numerical order.

㉙

Completed elephant

Fold the same way as the crane base.

Spread the forelegs and press the fold between them well inward.

㉘

㉗

Inside reverse fold

Outside reverse fold

㉖

㉕

Inside reverse fold

Enlarge the ears by pulling the inner pleat out.

Inside reverse fold (rear side too) ㉓

Inside reverse fold to make the tusks

㉔

Enlarged ears

Lion

This difficult fold is hard to open entire once it has been made. Use a large sheet of paper.

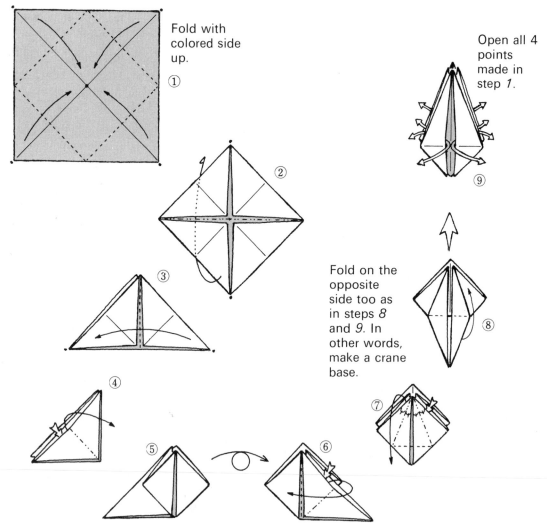

Fold with colored side up.

①

Open all 4 points made in step *1*.

⑨

②

③

Fold on the opposite side too as in steps *8* and *9*. In other words, make a crane base.

⑧

④

⑦

⑤

⑥

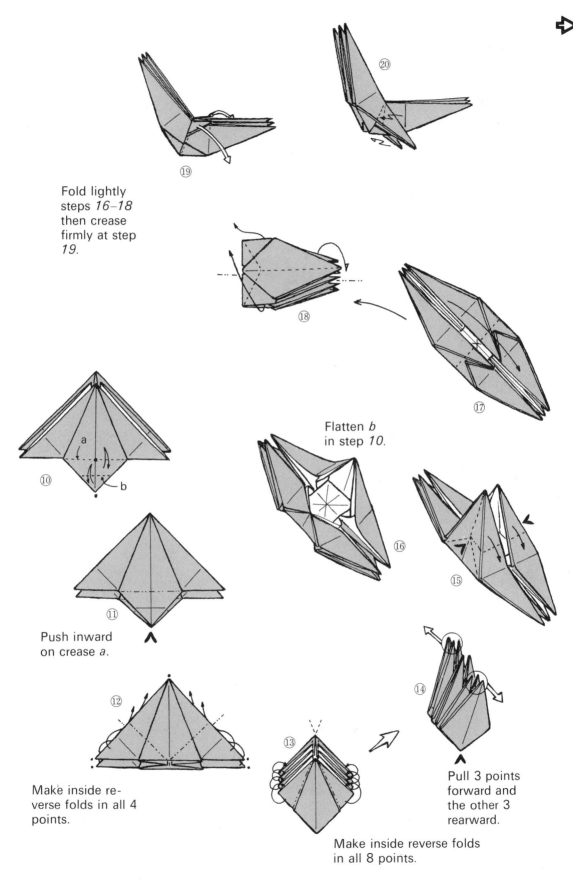

Fold lightly steps *16–18* then crease firmly at step *19*.

Flatten *b* in step *10*.

Push inward on crease *a*.

Make inside reverse folds in all 4 points.

Make inside reverse folds in all 8 points.

Pull 3 points forward and the other 3 rearward.

167

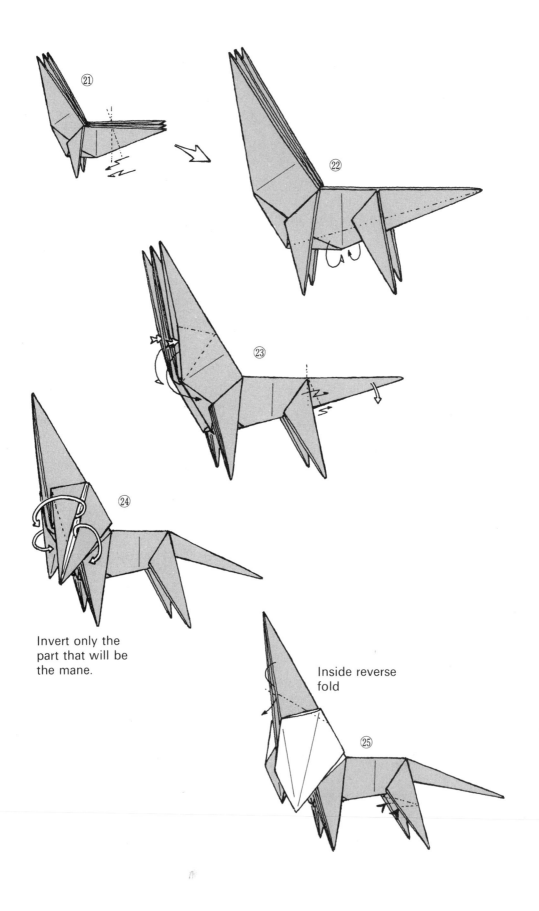

Invert only the
part that will be
the mane.

Inside reverse
fold

Because, like that of the human female body, their lithe elegance depends on predominantly curving lines and planes, most of the cats—including the lioness, the leopard, the tiger, and the cheetah—are among the most demanding creatures to express with predominantely rectilinear origami techniques. Among my own and those of other origamians, I have yet to encounter one that I find completely satisfactory. His stern cragginess makes the male lion easier to deal with. We still have a long way to go before we can treat sensuous themes in origami terms.

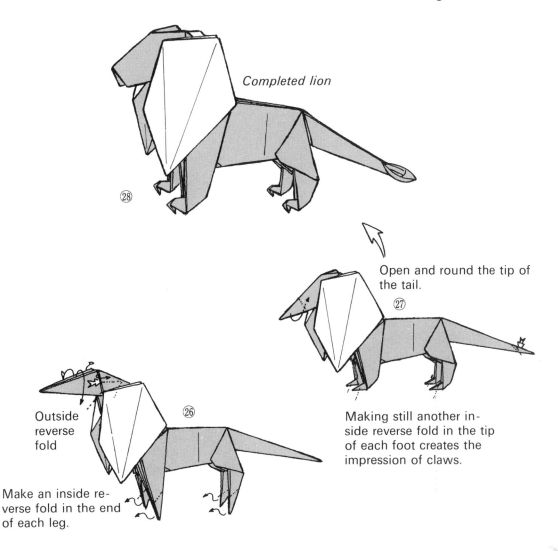

Completed lion

㉘

Open and round the tip of the tail.

㉗

Outside reverse fold

㉖

Make an inside reverse fold in the end of each leg.

Making still another inside reverse fold in the tip of each foot creates the impression of claws.

Giant Panda

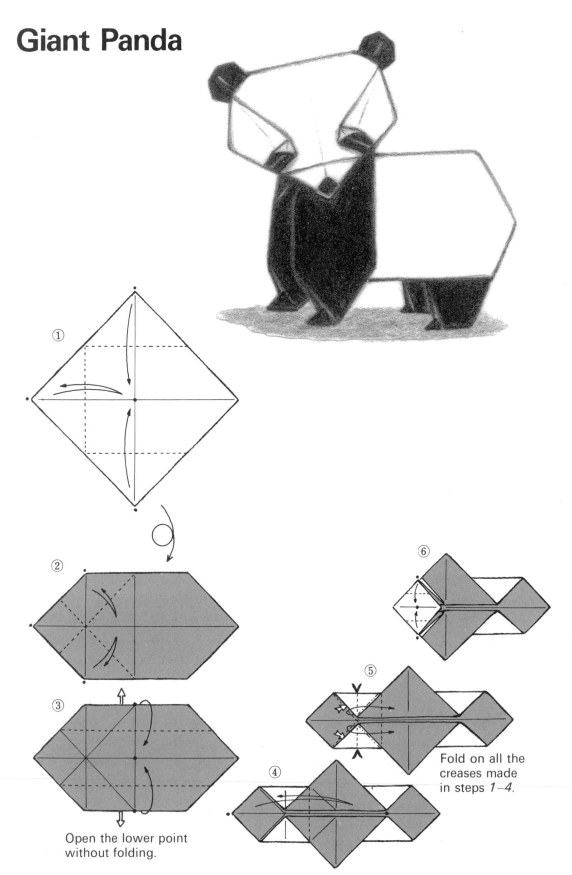

①

②

③

Open the lower point
without folding.

④

⑤

Fold on all the
creases made
in steps *1–4*.

⑥

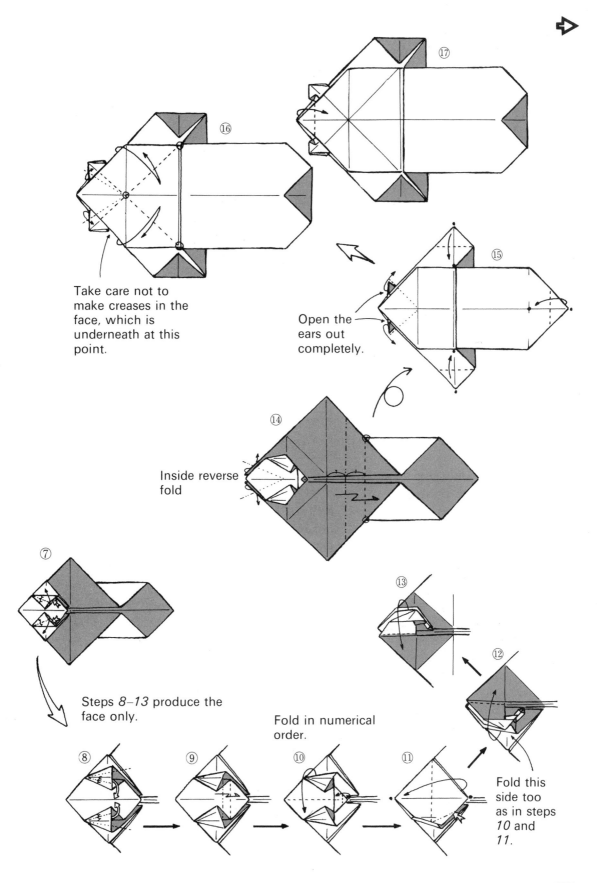

⑰

⑯

Take care not to
make creases in the
face, which is
underneath at this
point.

⑮

Open the
ears out
completely.

⑭

Inside reverse
fold

⑦

Steps *8–13* produce the
face only.

Fold in numerical
order.

⑬

⑫

Fold this
side too
as in steps
10 and
11.

⑧ ⑨ ⑩ ⑪

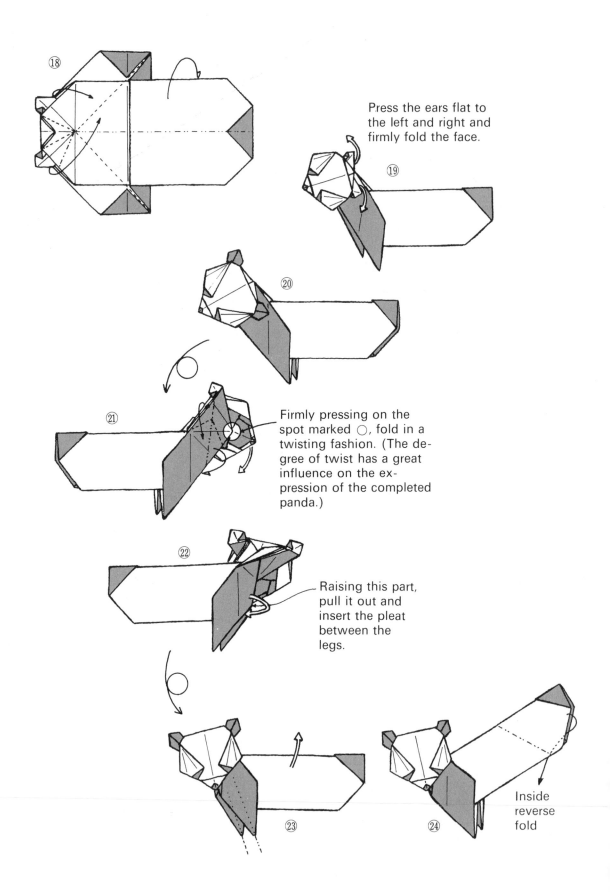

⑱

Press the ears flat to
the left and right and
firmly fold the face.

⑲

⑳

㉑

Firmly pressing on the
spot marked ○, fold in a
twisting fashion. (The degree of twist has a great
influence on the ex-
pression of the completed
panda.)

㉒

Raising this part,
pull it out and
insert the pleat
between the
legs.

㉓

㉔

Inside
reverse
fold

Vary the pose to suit yourself. The one on the left represents step 23 set on end after the legs have been folded.

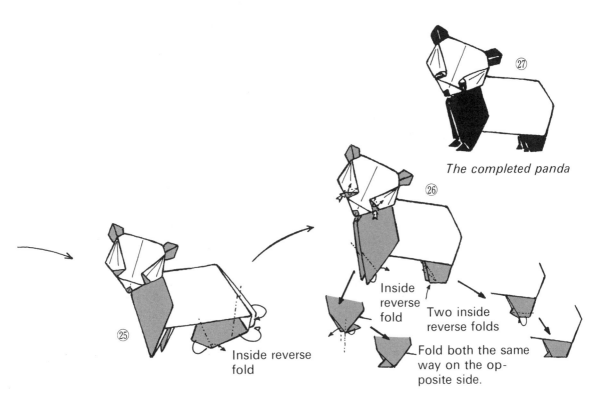

The completed panda

Inside reverse fold

Inside reverse fold

Two inside reverse folds

Fold both the same way on the opposite side.

Inside reverse fold

Donkey

Use a large sheet of paper to make the donkey, which is difficult to fold.

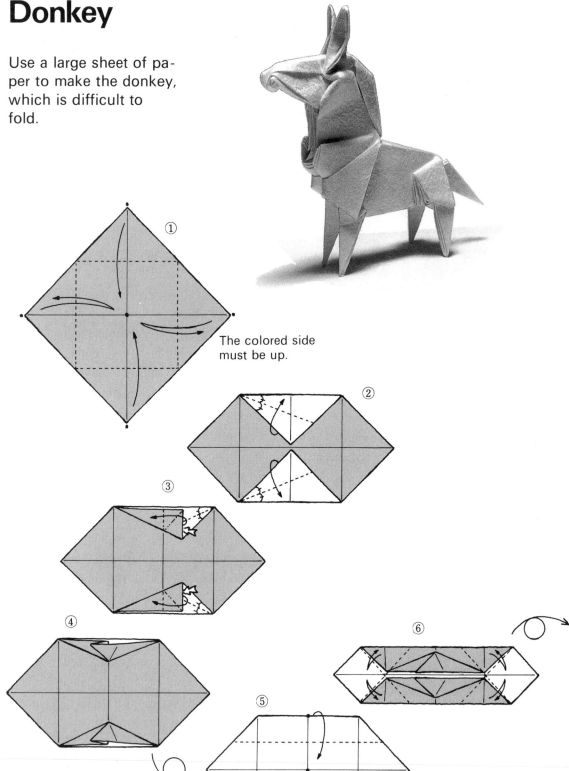

The colored side must be up.

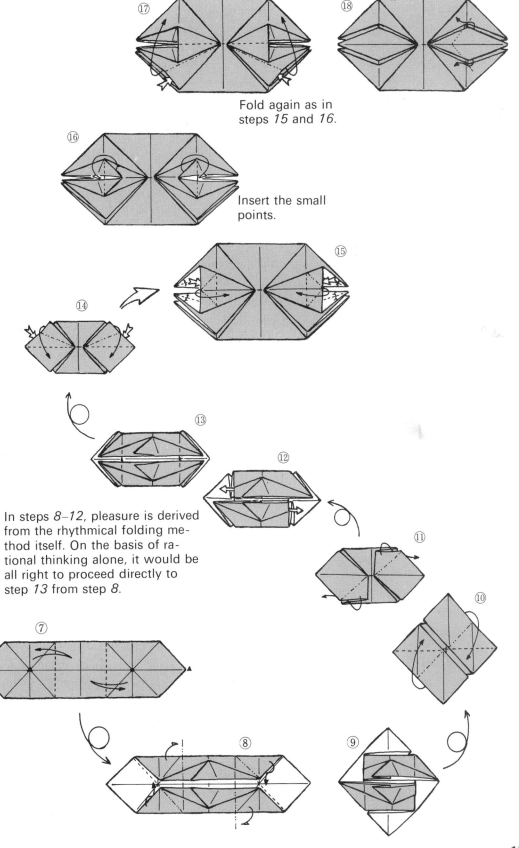

Fold again as in
steps *15* and *16*.

Insert the small
points.

In steps *8–12*, pleasure is derived
from the rhythmical folding method itself. On the basis of rational thinking alone, it would be
all right to proceed directly to
step *13* from step *8*.

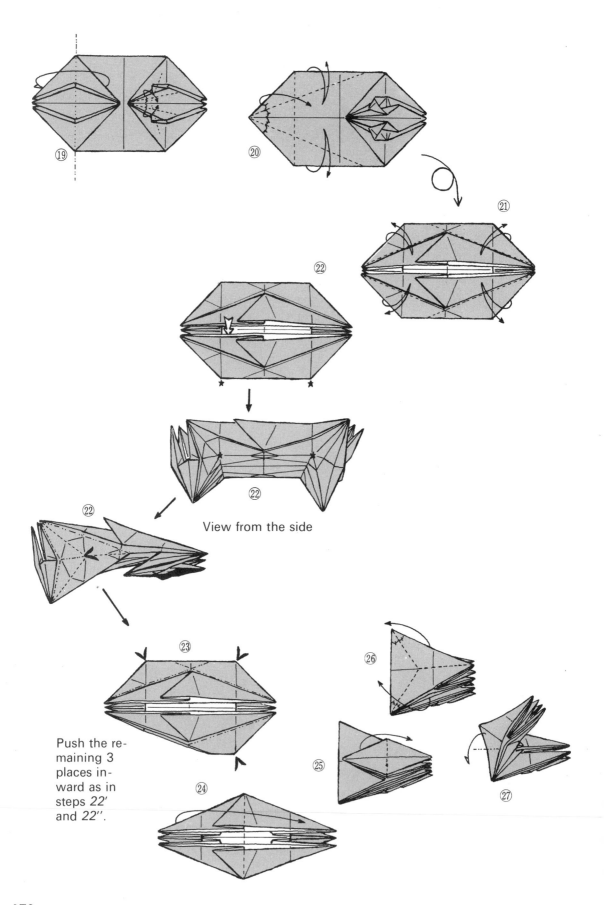

View from the side

Push the remaining 3 places inward as in steps 22' and 22".

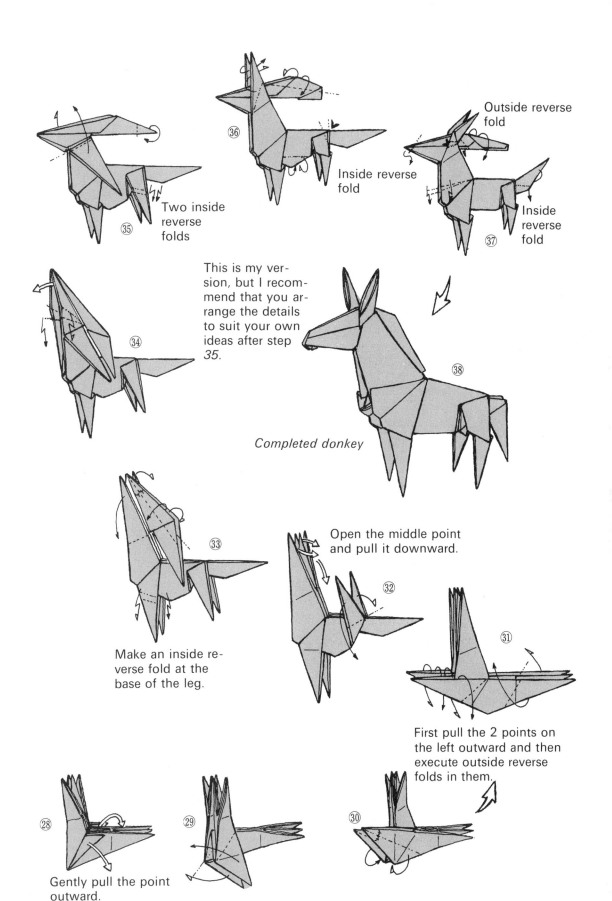

Two inside reverse folds

㉟

Inside reverse fold

㊱

Outside reverse fold

Inside reverse fold

㊲

This is my version, but I recommend that you arrange the details to suit your own ideas after step 35.

㉞

Completed donkey

㊳

㉝

Make an inside reverse fold at the base of the leg.

Open the middle point and pull it downward.

㉜

㉛

First pull the 2 points on the left outward and then execute outside reverse folds in them.

㉘

Gently pull the point outward.

㉙

㉚

Dragon

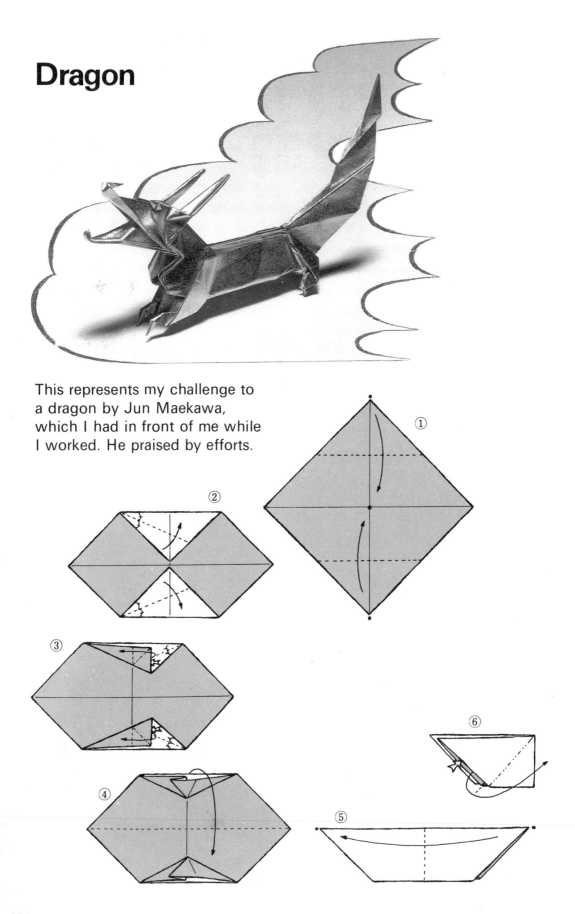

This represents my challenge to a dragon by Jun Maekawa, which I had in front of me while I worked. He praised by efforts.

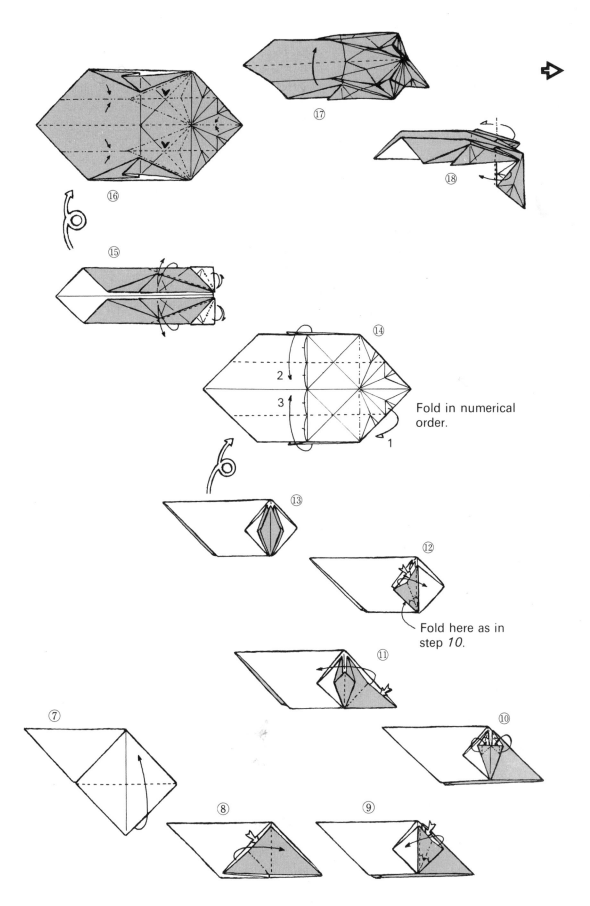

Fold in numerical order.

Fold here as in step *10*.

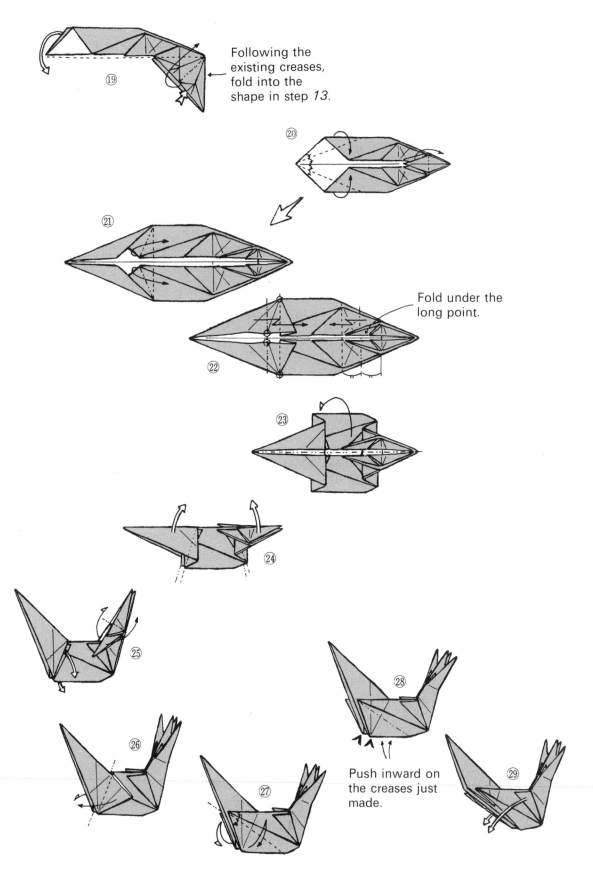

Following the existing creases, fold into the shape in step *13*.

Fold under the long point.

Push inward on the creases just made.

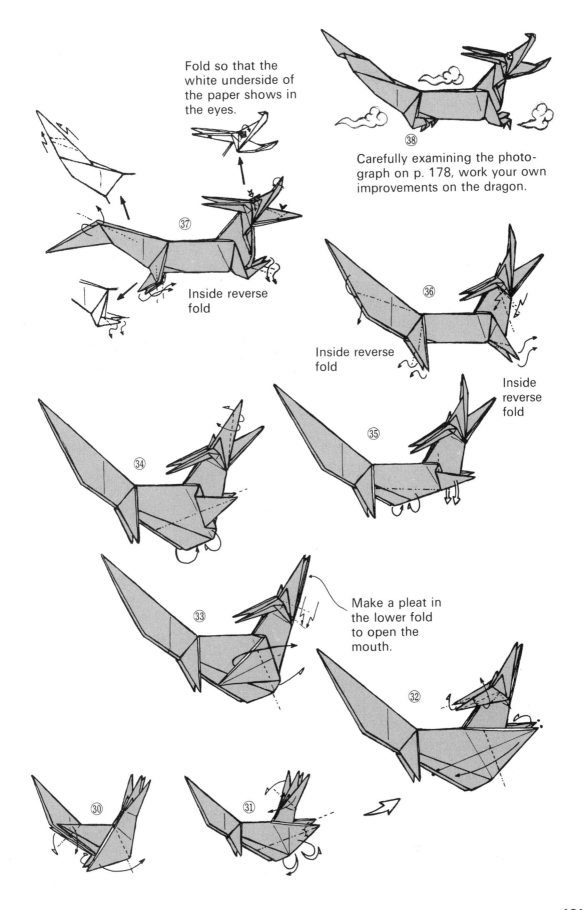

Fold so that the white underside of the paper shows in the eyes.

㊳

Carefully examining the photograph on p. 178, work your own improvements on the dragon.

㊲

Inside reverse fold

㊱

Inside reverse fold

Inside reverse fold

㉞

㉟

㉝

Make a pleat in the lower fold to open the mouth.

㉜

㉚

㉛

The Lost World of the Dinosaurs

The immense reptiles that once ruled the Earth and then suddenly and mysteriously vanished fascinate many people. As an origami theme, they are especially popular with young people. In the last pages of this chapter, I introduce a number of these representatives of a world now largely confined to fossils and hope they will please.

Dimetrodon

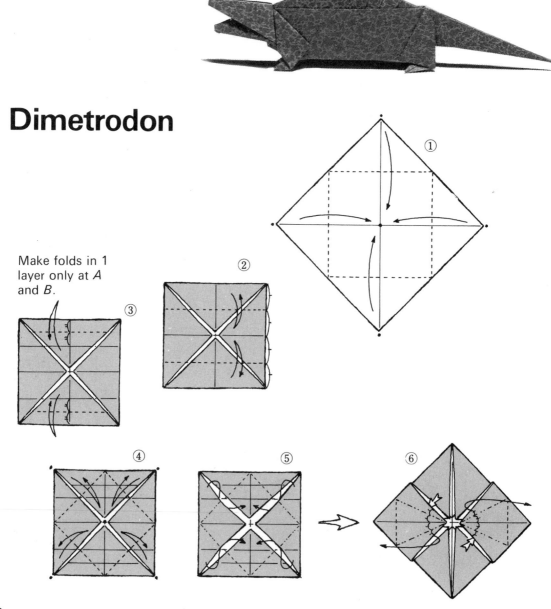

Make folds in 1 layer only at *A* and *B*.

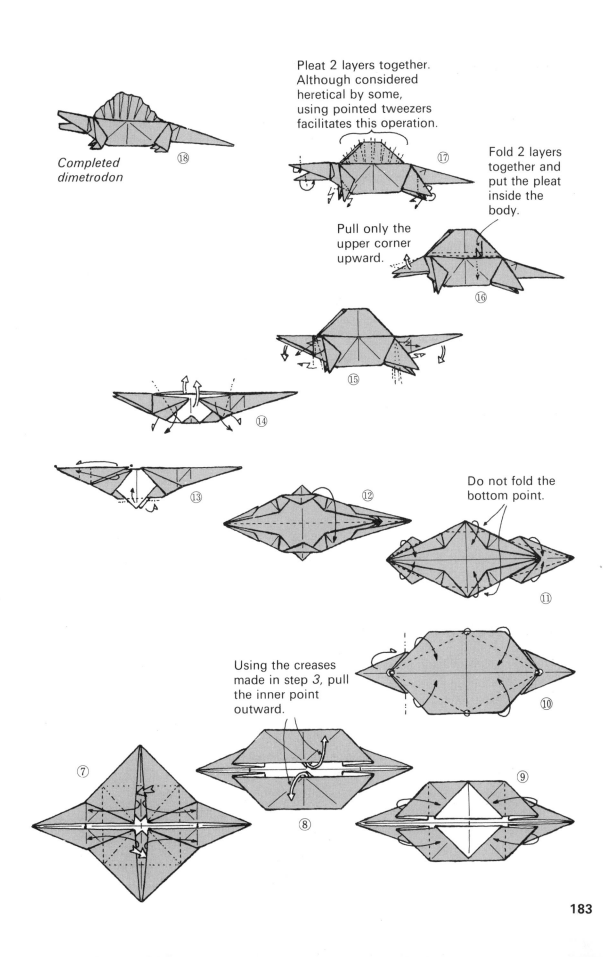

Pleat 2 layers together.
Although considered
heretical by some,
using pointed tweezers
facilitates this operation.

⑰

Fold 2 layers
together and
put the pleat
inside the
body.

Pull only the
upper corner
upward.

⑯

⑮

⑭

Completed
dimetrodon

⑱

⑬

⑫

Do not fold the
bottom point.

⑪

Using the creases
made in step *3*, pull
the inner point
outward.

⑩

⑦

⑧

⑨

Pteranodon

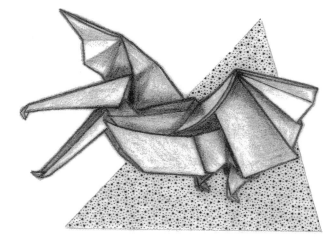

Fold in
numerical
order.

①

1 2

a   b

3

② Inside reverse
fold

③ Grip firmly and pull
outward points *a*
and *b*, visible in step *1*.

a   b

④

⑤

⑥

⑦

⑧

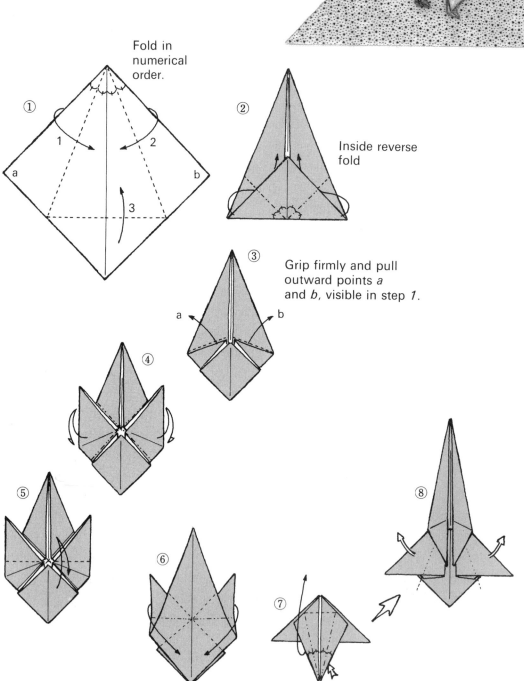

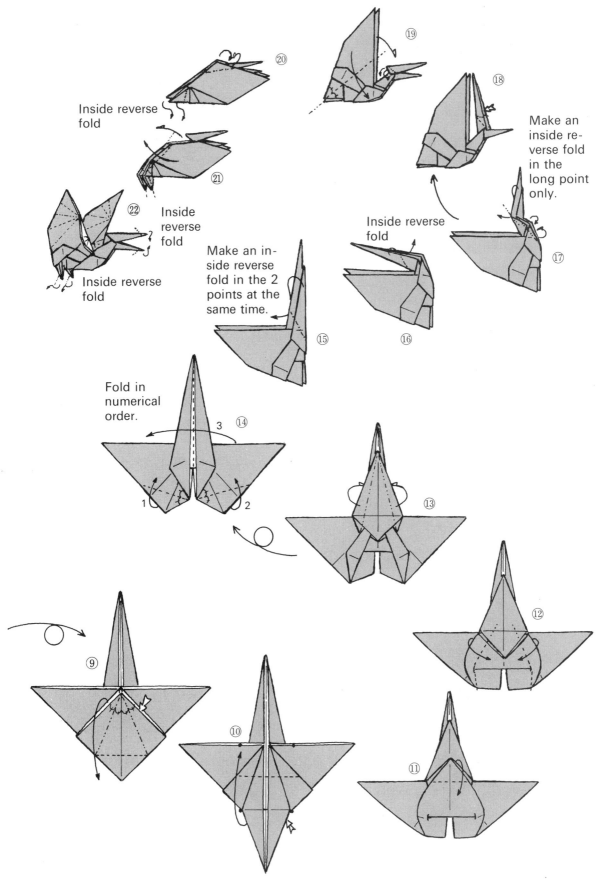

Inside reverse fold

Inside reverse fold

Inside reverse fold

Inside reverse fold

Make an inside reverse fold in the long point only.

Inside reverse fold

Make an inside reverse fold in the 2 points at the same time.

Fold in numerical order.

185

Archaeopteryx

Forerunner of the Birds
Recently much discussion
has been made of the fossils
of a now extinct, primitive bird
said to have lived seventy-five
million years ago, named
proto-avis. It closely resem-
bled this reptilelike forerunner
of the birds.

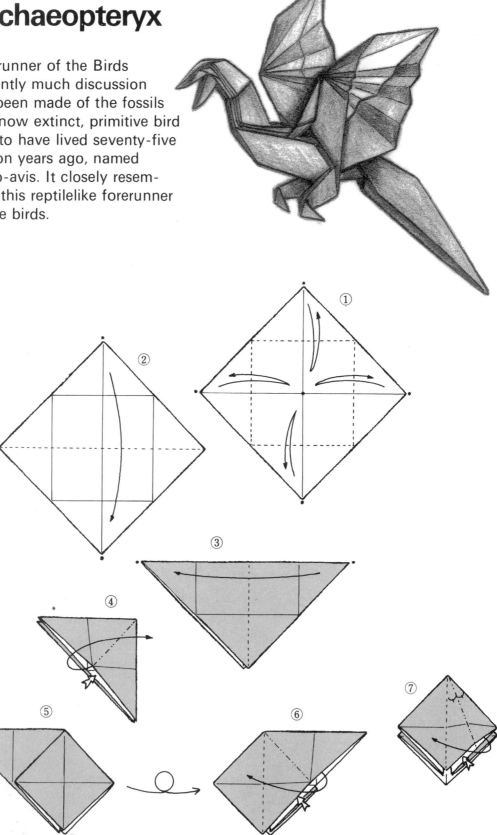

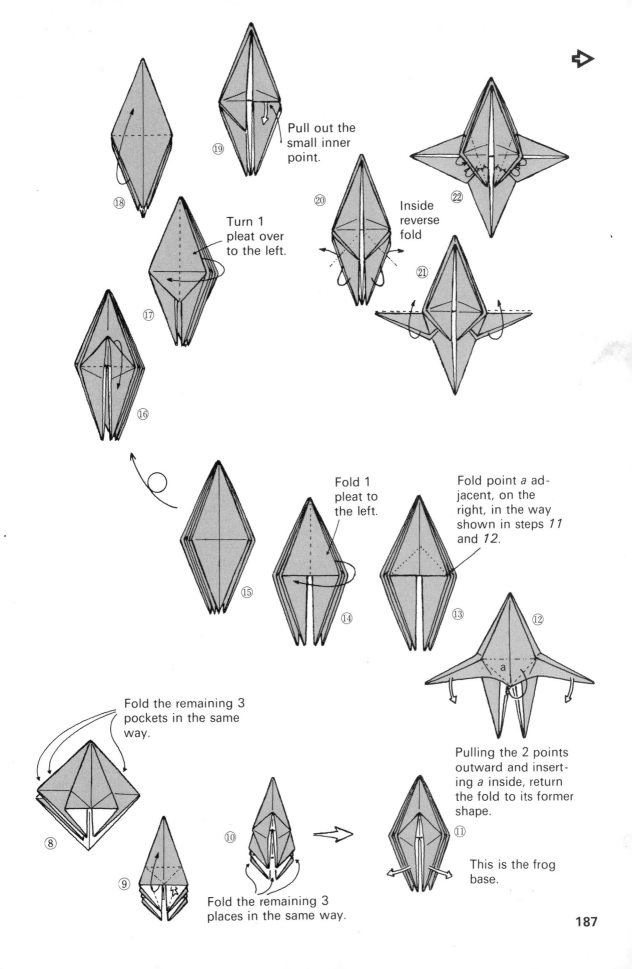

Pull out the small inner point.

Inside reverse fold

Turn 1 pleat over to the left.

Fold 1 pleat to the left.

Fold point *a* adjacent, on the right, in the way shown in steps *11* and *12*.

Fold the remaining 3 pockets in the same way.

Pulling the 2 points outward and inserting *a* inside, return the fold to its former shape.

This is the frog base.

Fold the remaining 3 places in the same way.

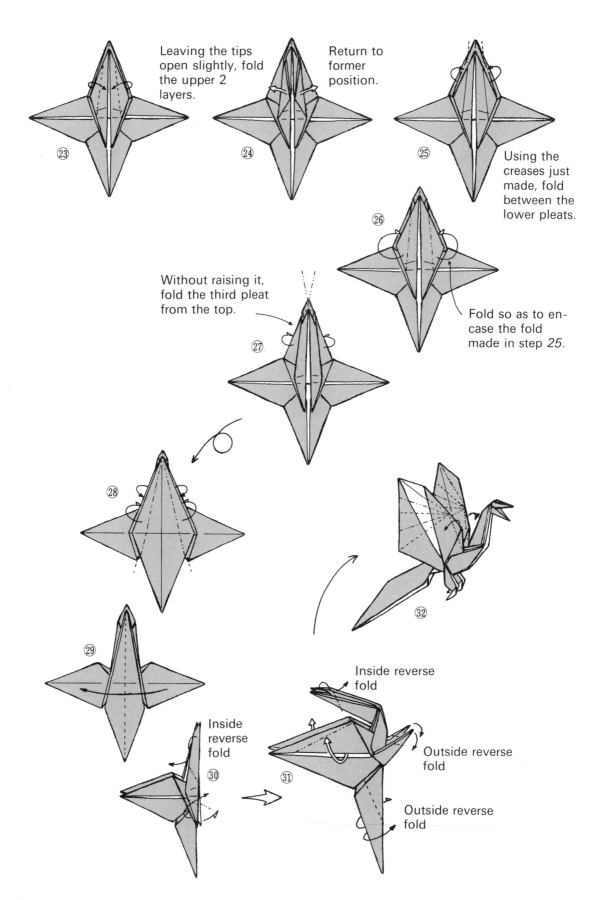

Leaving the tips open slightly, fold the upper 2 layers.

㉓

Return to former position.

㉔

㉕

Using the creases just made, fold between the lower pleats.

㉖

Without raising it, fold the third pleat from the top.

㉗

Fold so as to encase the fold made in step *25*.

㉘

㉙

Inside reverse fold

㉚

Inside reverse fold

㉛

Outside reverse fold

㉜

Outside reverse fold

Stergosaurus

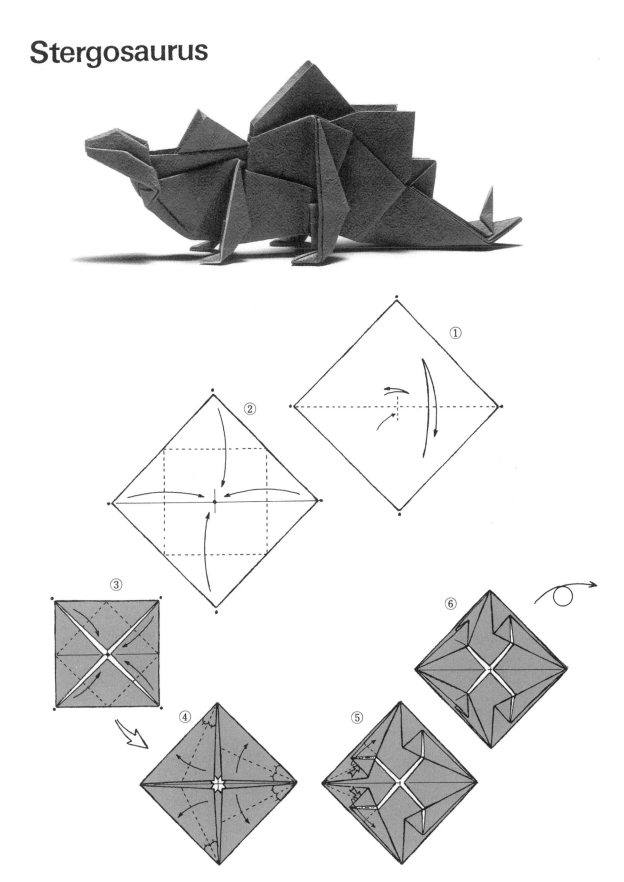

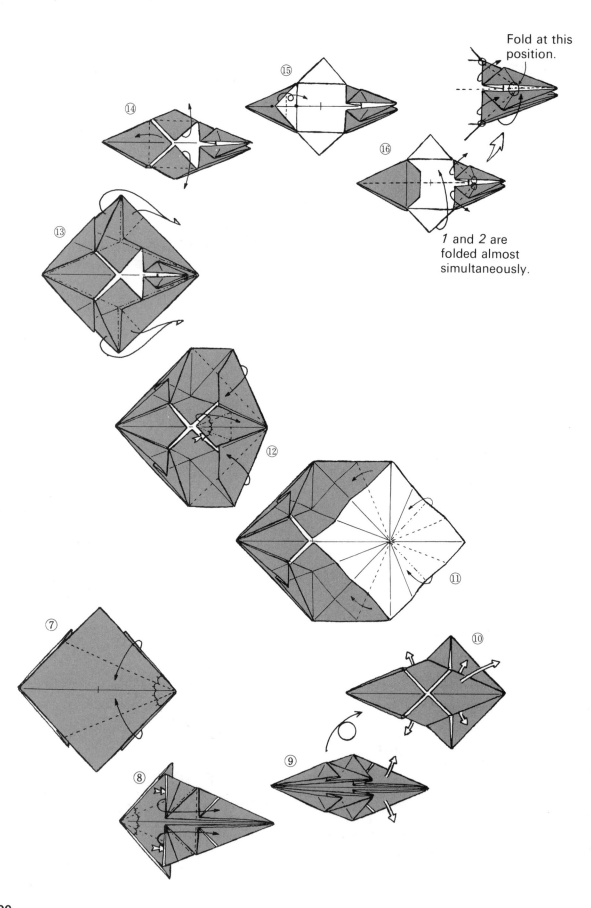

Fold at this position.

1 and 2 are folded almost simultaneously.

190

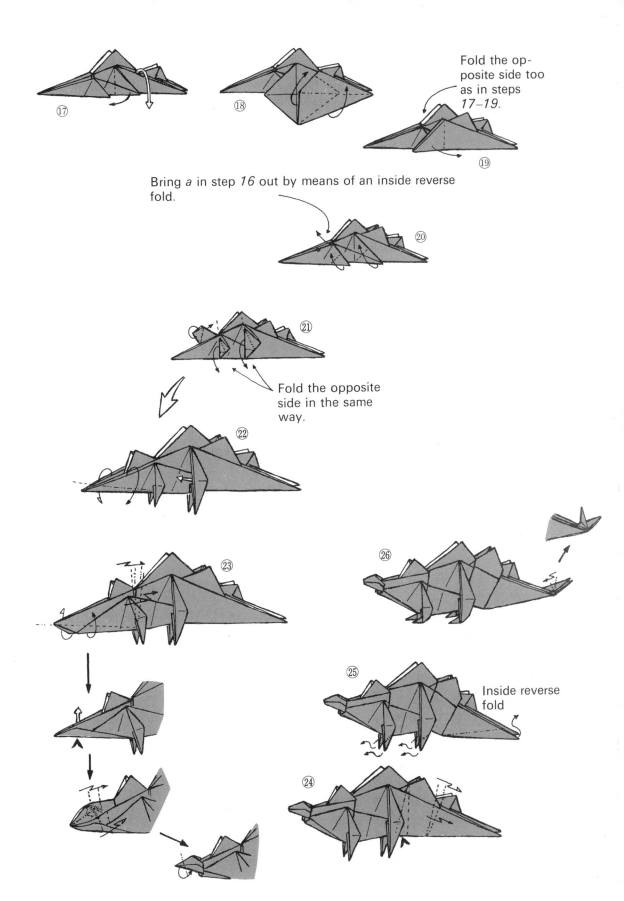

Fold the opposite side too as in steps *17–19*.

Bring *a* in step *16* out by means of an inside reverse fold.

Fold the opposite side in the same way.

Inside reverse fold

Tyrannosaurus Head

This origami is intended to be a diversion. Although the Dragon on p. 90 too is a tyrannosaurus, this one is a toylike version in which the mouth opens and closes. I am proud of it for the reason given below.

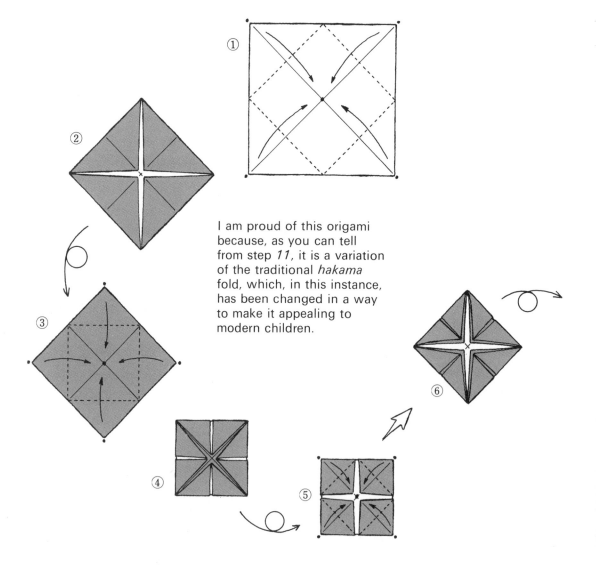

I am proud of this origami because, as you can tell from step *11*, it is a variation of the traditional *hakama* fold, which, in this instance, has been changed in a way to make it appealing to modern children.

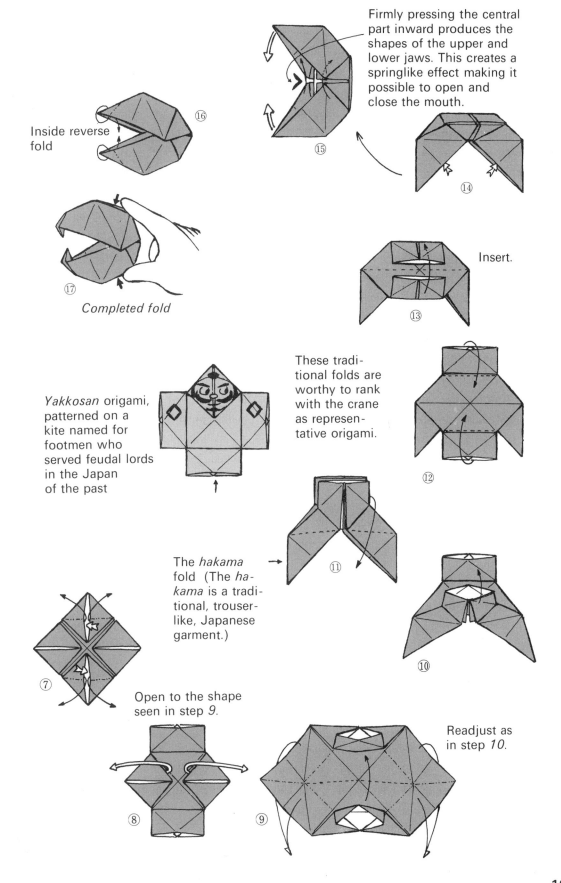

Inside reverse fold

⑯

Firmly pressing the central part inward produces the shapes of the upper and lower jaws. This creates a springlike effect making it possible to open and close the mouth.

⑮

⑭

⑰

Completed fold

Insert.

⑬

Yakkosan origami, patterned on a kite named for footmen who served feudal lords in the Japan of the past

These traditional folds are worthy to rank with the crane as representative origami.

⑫

The *hakama* fold (The *hakama* is a traditional, trouser-like, Japanese garment.)

⑪

⑩

⑦

Open to the shape seen in step *9*.

Readjust as in step *10*.

⑧

⑨

193

Brontosaurus

In actuality, one of the largest reptiles of its kind, in origami form, the brontosaurus takes a much larger piece of paper than any of the other dinosaurs. For instance, if pieces about eighteen centimeters to a side were used for the stegosaurus and tyrannosaurus, the brontosaurus will need a piece twenty-four centimeters to a side.

①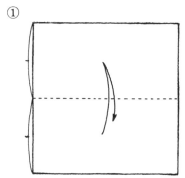

② ③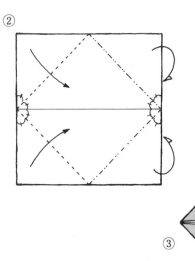

④ ⑤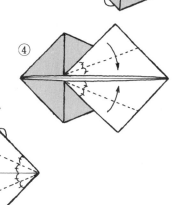

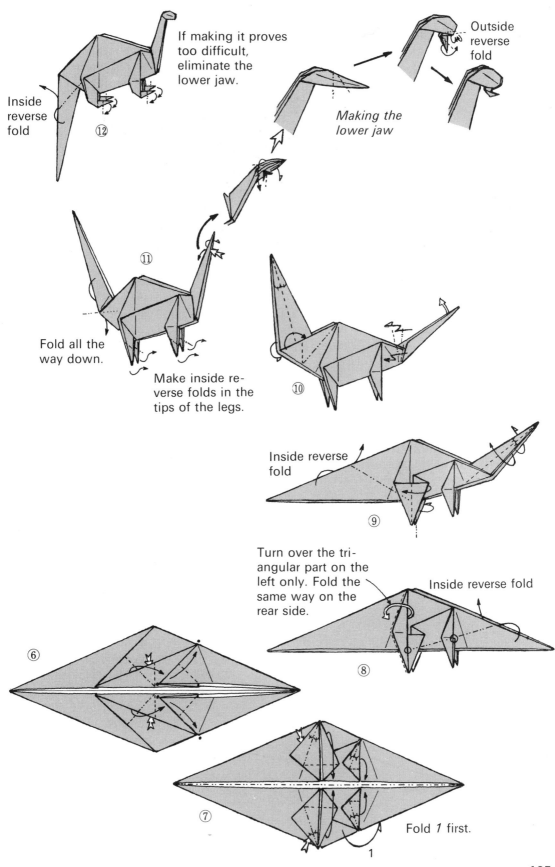

If making it proves
too difficult,
eliminate the
lower jaw.

Outside
reverse
fold

*Making the
lower jaw*

Inside
reverse
fold

⑫

Inside
reverse
fold

⑪

Fold all the
way down.

Make inside re-
verse folds in the
tips of the legs.

⑩

Inside reverse
fold

⑨

Turn over the tri-
angular part on the
left only. Fold the
same way on the
rear side.

Inside reverse fold

⑥

⑧

⑦

Fold *1* first.

1

195

Mammoth

Use a large sheet of
paper for the mammoth,
which is difficult
to fold.

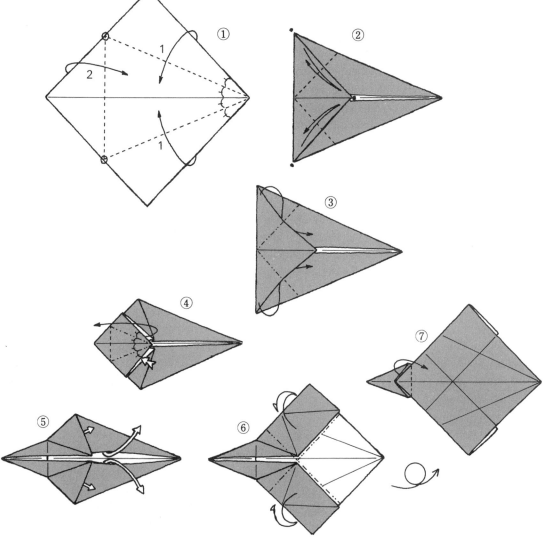

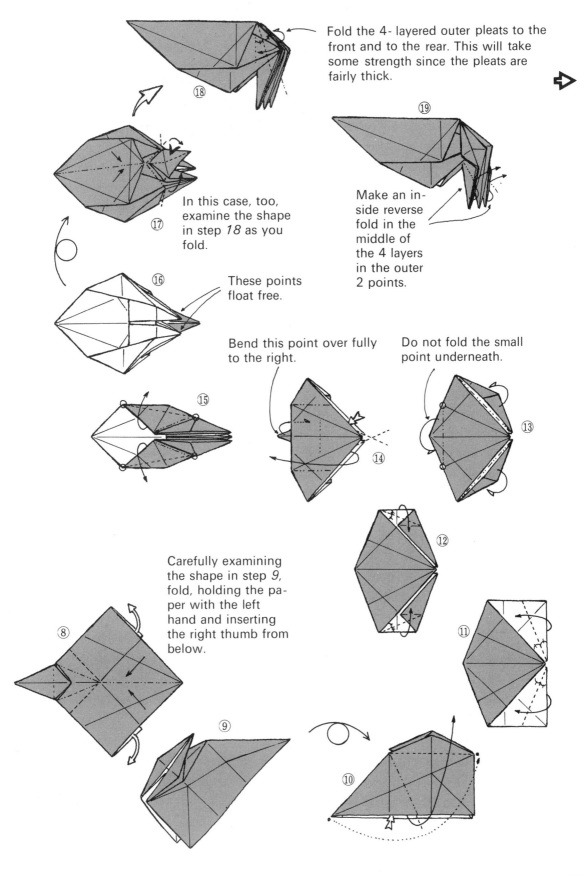

Fold the 4- layered outer pleats to the front and to the rear. This will take some strength since the pleats are fairly thick.

In this case, too, examine the shape in step *18* as you fold.

⑰

⑱

⑲

Make an in-side reverse fold in the middle of the 4 layers in the outer 2 points.

These points float free.

⑯

Bend this point over fully to the right.

Do not fold the small point underneath.

⑭

⑬

⑮

⑫

⑪

Carefully examining the shape in step *9*, fold, holding the pa-per with the left hand and inserting the right thumb from below.

⑧

⑨

⑩

197

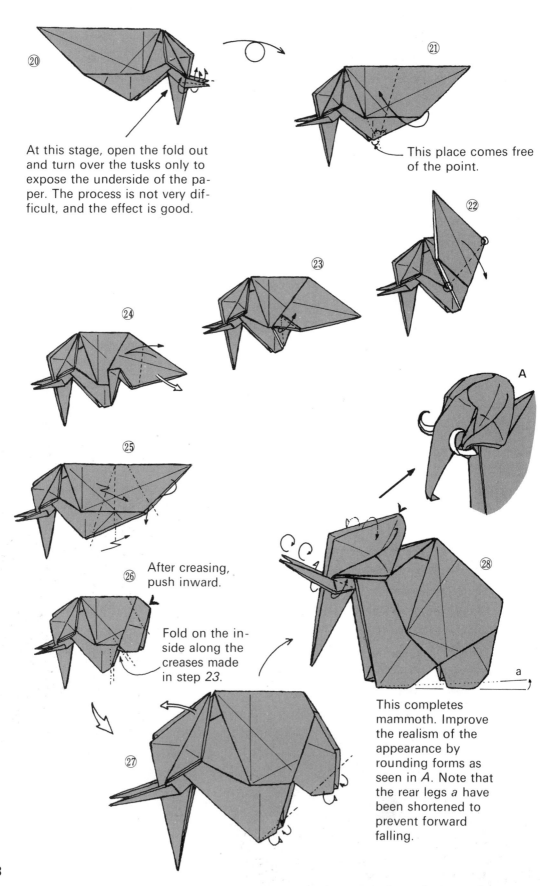

㉒

At this stage, open the fold out and turn over the tusks only to expose the underside of the paper. The process is not very difficult, and the effect is good.

㉑

This place comes free of the point.

㉓

A

㉔

㉕

After creasing, push inward.

㉖

Fold on the inside along the creases made in step 23.

㉘

a

This completes mammoth. Improve the realism of the appearance by rounding forms as seen in A. Note that the rear legs a have been shortened to prevent forward falling.

㉗

Chapter 5

Beautiful Polyhedrons

Introduction to a New World

Getting to know a number of people, including Norishige Terada, Hisashi Abè, Professor and Mrs. Kōji Fushimi, and Jun Maekawa awakened me to the mistaken nature of my previous rejection of the idea of using origami as a way of becoming more familiar with geometry. These wonderful people have helped me find the fascinating new world of origami-geometry, which I should like to introduce to all my readers. But, instead of running the risk of failing in this endeavor as a result of inept verbal explanation, I prefer to have you come to understand this appeal through your own fingertips as you practice making a number of folds. After you have done this, read the text, which concentrates on eighteen basic solid-geometric figures (regular and semiregular polyhedrons). I have included a number of frivolous folds to break the tedium.

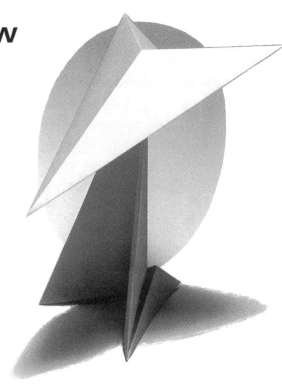

Display this together with the Fox on p. 146.

I recall Mrs. Mitsuè Fushimi's once remarking that an amusing mobile can be made by using the center of gravity produced at the point of

Fox Mobile

You will need 4 sheets of paper.

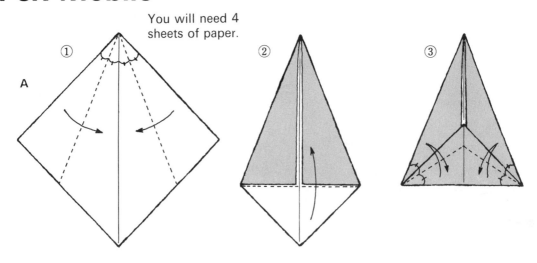

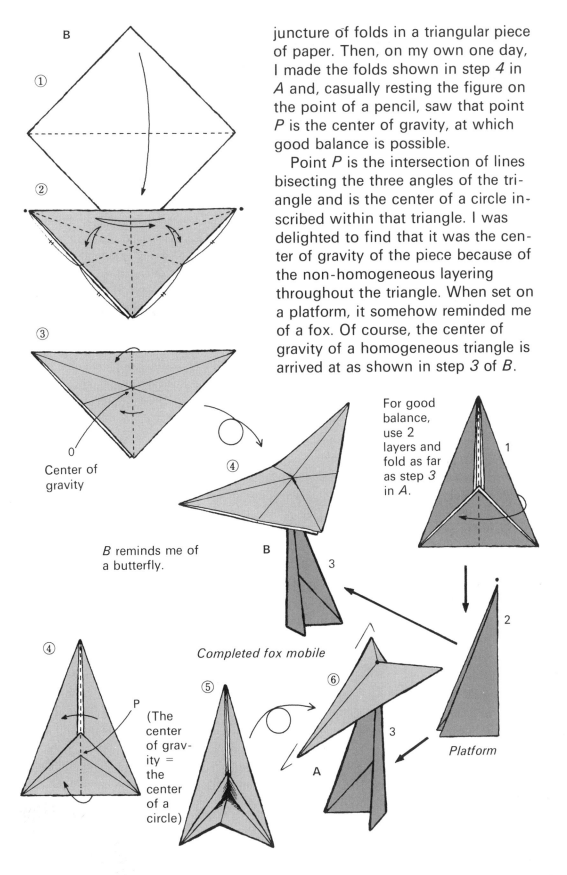

juncture of folds in a triangular piece of paper. Then, on my own one day, I made the folds shown in step *4* in *A* and, casually resting the figure on the point of a pencil, saw that point *P* is the center of gravity, at which good balance is possible.

Point *P* is the intersection of lines bisecting the three angles of the triangle and is the center of a circle inscribed within that triangle. I was delighted to find that it was the center of gravity of the piece because of the non-homogeneous layering throughout the triangle. When set on a platform, it somehow reminded me of a fox. Of course, the center of gravity of a homogeneous triangle is arrived at as shown in step *3* of *B*.

B

①

②

③

0

Center of gravity

④

B reminds me of a butterfly.

B

For good balance, use 2 layers and fold as far as step *3* in *A*.

1

3

2

Platform

3

Completed fox mobile

④

P

(The center of gravity = the center of a circle)

⑤

⑥

A

Bottomless Tetrahedron and an Equilateral-triangular Flat Unit I

Now we move into polyhedrons with the regular tetrahedron, which consists of four equilateral-triangular faces. Milk and soft drinks are often sold in paper cartons made in this shape. There are many examples of this simple form in complete condition, but I have decided to use an incomplete one.

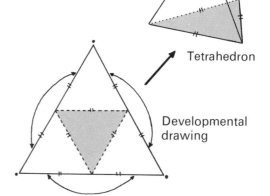

Tetrahedron

Developmental drawing

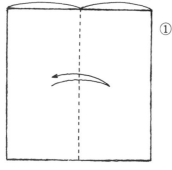

①

②

Equilateral-triangular pyramid (or a bottomless tetrahedron)

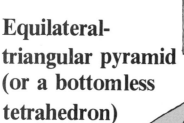

③

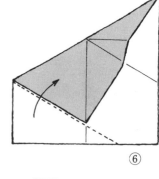

⑥

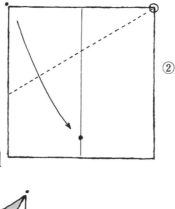

④

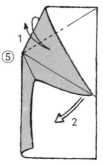

⑤

1

2

After folding at *1*, return to the former form at *2*.

202

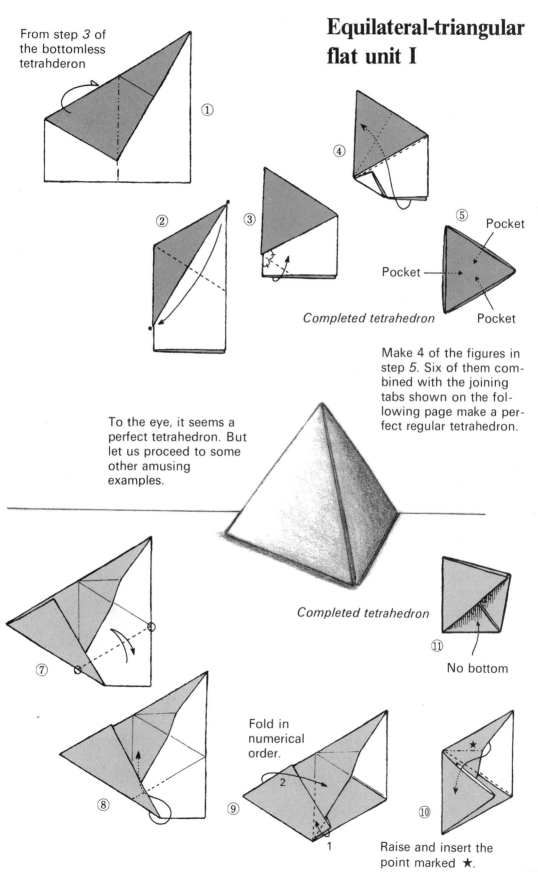

From step *3* of the bottomless tetrahderon

①

Equilateral-triangular flat unit I

④

⑤ Pocket

②

③

Pocket ←

Pocket

Completed tetrahedron

Make 4 of the figures in step *5*. Six of them combined with the joining tabs shown on the following page make a perfect regular tetrahedron.

To the eye, it seems a perfect tetrahedron. But let us proceed to some other amusing examples.

⑦

Completed tetrahedron

⑪

No bottom

⑧

Fold in numerical order.

⑨

2

1

⑩

Raise and insert the point marked ★.

203

Equilateral-triangular Flat Unit II

Unit I on the preceding page is so similar to this Unit II that there might seem to be little use in introducing both. But I have my reasons.

Before explaining them, I must say that I myself did not discover the folding method used in making Unit I. Hisashi Abè and Tomoko Fusè, at the same time, examined Unit II, which had already been made public at the time, and revised it to produce Unit I.

Folding both from pieces of paper of the same size will reveal that Unit I is larger and involves fewer folds than Unit II. The extra size means that, as is clear from the drawings on p. 205, joining tabs for Unit I are more troublesome than those for Unit II. And this problem exerts an influence on adjusting the lengths of sides of other polygonal units.

The relations between these two units suggest how hard it is to judge the superiority of one origami fold over another. Selecting either Unit I or Unit II, you should now try your hand at making the three regular polyhedrons shown on the right.

Use 2 colors in folding the regular octahedron and 3 colors in making the regular icosahedron and make sure that no units of the same color appear adjacent to each other. Each of the 4 faces of the regular tetrahedron must be of a different color.

Regular tetrahe (6 joining tabs)

Regular octahedron (12 joining tabs)

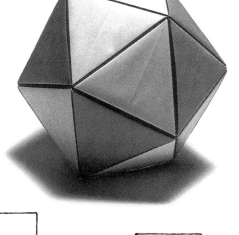

Regular icosahedron (30 joining tabs)

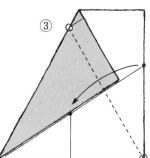

Equilateral-triangular Unit

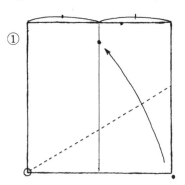

① ②

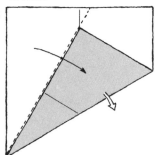

③

Regular tetrahedron, composed of 4 equilateral-triangular faces

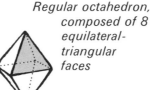 *Regular octahedron, composed of 8 equilateral-triangular faces*

 *Regular icosahedron, composed of 20 equilateral-triangular faces*

 Regular dodecahedron, composed of 12 regular-pentagonal faces

Cube (hexahedron) composed of 6 square faces

Five regular polyhedrons

In regular polyhedrons, of which there are only the five kinds listed above, all the faces are of the same shape and are all joined in such a way as to produce identical pinnacles throughout the figure. Semi-regular polyhedrons, which do not meet these same conditions, are usually the result of combining more than two regular polygons.

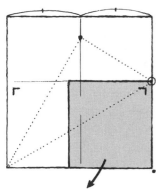

Unit I joining tab

If you attempt to make tabs like those in Unit II, only 1 can be produced from a piece of paper the same size as the one used in making Unit 1.

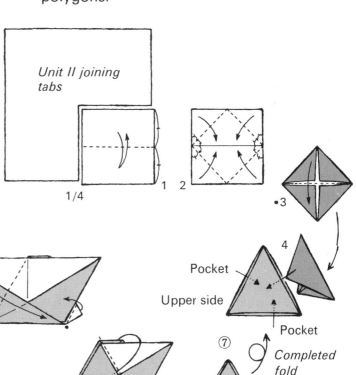

Unit II joining tabs

1/4

1   2

•3

4

Pocket

Upper side

Pocket

⑦

Completed fold

Underside

④   ⑤   ⑥

Square Flat Unit

Now, turning to the Square Flat Unit, we shall immediately see what I meant when, in comparing Equilateral-triangular Units I and II, I spoke of influences on adjusting side lengths. As is seen in the drawing in *A*, paper for the Equilateral-triangular Unit is half the size of the paper used in making the Square Flat Unit. When you have learned to combine these two kinds of units, try producing the semiregular cuboctahedron shown on p. 207. By the way, what size should the paper be if an Equilateral-triangular Flat Unit I is to be used?

Two Square Flat Units

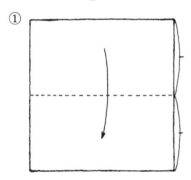

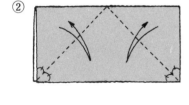

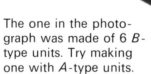

Make inside reverse folds on the creases made in step *2*.

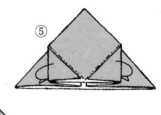

Square Flat Unit *A* type

1/2

A

Equilateral-triangular Unit 2

Thoroughly master the method for folding from half a sheet of paper. From this point on, I shall make no more use of Equilateral-triangular Flat Unit I.

The one in the photograph was made of 6 *B*-type units. Try making one with *A*-type units.

▲ *Cube (hexahedron)*

▲ *Cuboctahedron*

This figure requires 6 *A*-type units, 8 Equilateral-triangular Units (type 2), and 24 joining tabs 1/16 the size of a sheet of paper.

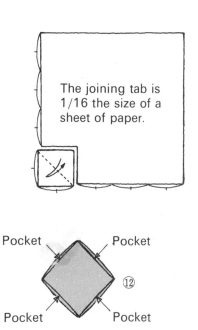

The joining tab is 1/16 the size of a sheet of paper.

Pocket   Pocket

⑫

Pocket   Pocket

Completed A-type unit

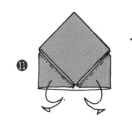

Slot   Slot

Completed B-type unit

⑫

Joining tab   Joining tab

Insert remaining corners inside the pocket.

⑪

Insert the left and right corners underneath the pocket in the *A*-type unit (as shown in step *6*) and inside the pocket in the *B*-type unit.

A-type unit

⑩

B-type unit

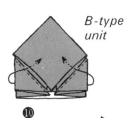
⑩

⑪

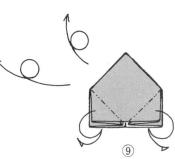
⑨

⑥

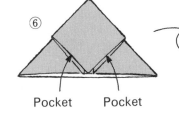

Pocket   Pocket

⑦

⑧

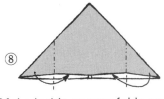

Make inside reverse folds on the creases made in step 7.

Module Cube

Modular origami, a new field that is, however, already familiar to many origami fans, entails preparing and combining numbers of units like the *B*-type Flat Square Unit, which have joining tabs and receiving slots, or pockets. Of course, even though they lack their own pockets and tabs, things like the *A*-type Square Flat Unit and the Equilateral-triangular Flat Unit fall into the same category. They are not, however, as convenient to use. Furthermore, because it has only three sides, it is impossible to work out equal numbers of tabs and pockets for the Equilateral-triangular Unit. Because of the ease with which it can be applied, the Square Flat Unit can be considered the source of modular origami. On these papers, I introduce two more cubes, but with different surface patterns.

Dice units

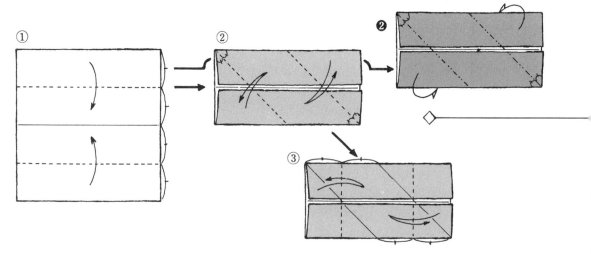

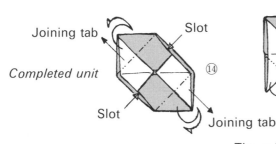

Joining tab Slot ⑭

Completed unit

Slot Joining tab

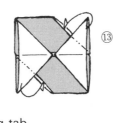
⑬

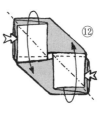
⑫

Checkerboard pattern

To produce this effect, the paper must have differently colored upper and under sides. The pinwheel pattern is attractively produced with six sheets of paper, two each of three different colors. Combining twelve units results in the checkerboard pattern.

The cubes on p. 233 were made from 12 units in the stage shown in step *14* and of 6 units in the stage shown in step *12.*

⑪

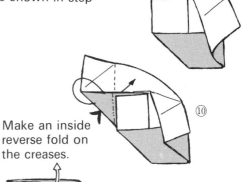

Make an inside reverse fold on the creases.
⑩

⑨

Pinwheel pattern

Joining tab

❹

Slot

Slot

❸

⑧

Make an inside reverse fold on the creases.

⑦

Joining tab
Completed unit

(Simplified Sonobè system)

Make an inside reversed fold on the creases.

Make an inside reverse fold on the creases.

④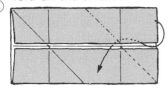

⑤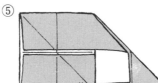

⑥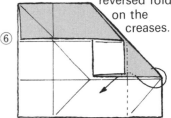

Cherry-blossom Unit

Though widely used because of convenience and versatility in production, origami units are by no means limited to the creation of polyhedrons. These Cherry-blossom Units, introduced here by way of a breather, are examples of plane applications of the system. I feel confident that both are good origami and hope you will enjoy making them.

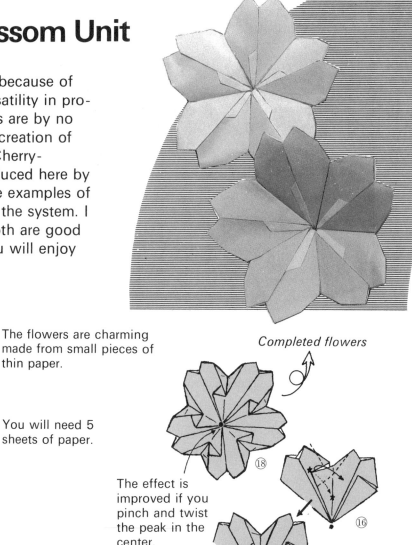

The flowers are charming made from small pieces of thin paper.

You will need 5 sheets of paper.

Completed flowers

The effect is improved if you pinch and twist the peak in the center.

Fold the remaining 4 places as the place marked ★ was folded.

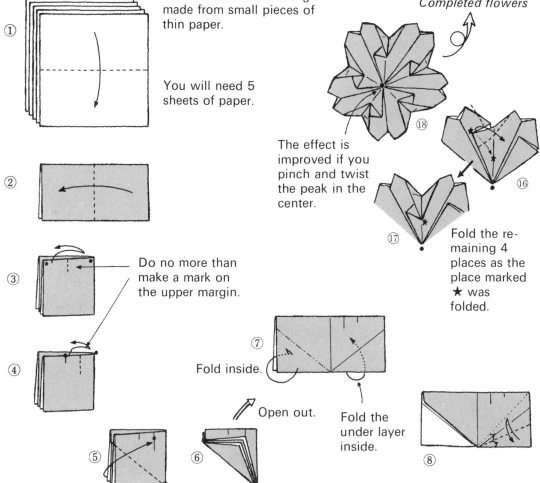

Do no more than make a mark on the upper margin.

Fold inside.

Open out.

Fold the under layer inside.

Star-within-a-star Unit

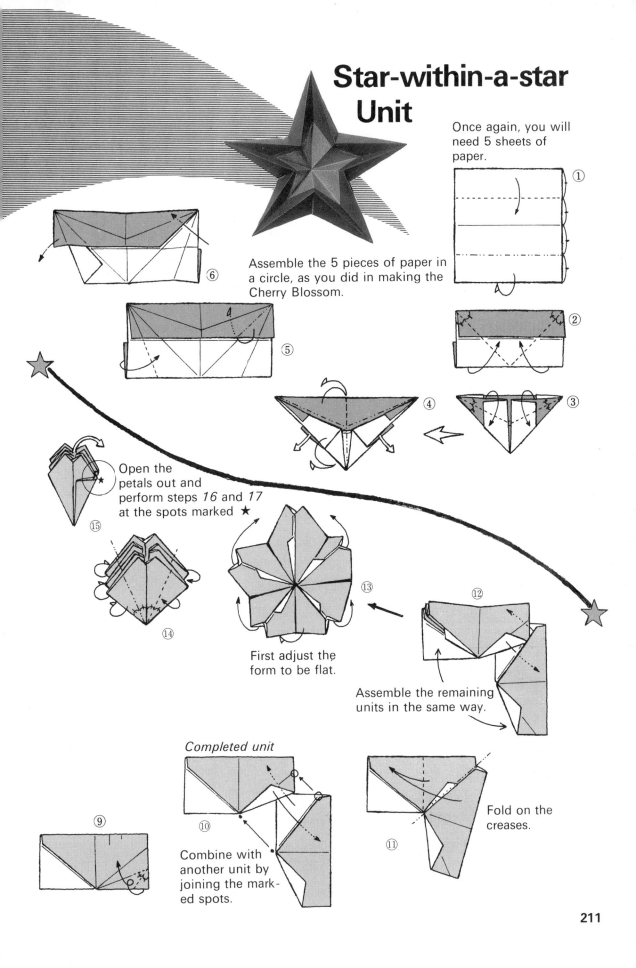

Once again, you will need 5 sheets of paper.

①

Assemble the 5 pieces of paper in a circle, as you did in making the Cherry Blossom.

②

⑥

③

⑤

④

Open the petals out and perform steps *16* and *17* at the spots marked ★

⑮

⑭

⑬

First adjust the form to be flat.

⑫

Assemble the remaining units in the same way.

Completed unit

⑨

⑩

Combine with another unit by joining the marked spots.

⑪

Fold on the creases.

Combining the Cube and the Regular Octahedron

As an examination of the figures makes obvious, this interesting variation is a combination of the cube and the regular octahedron. It can be reconverted into a simple cube.

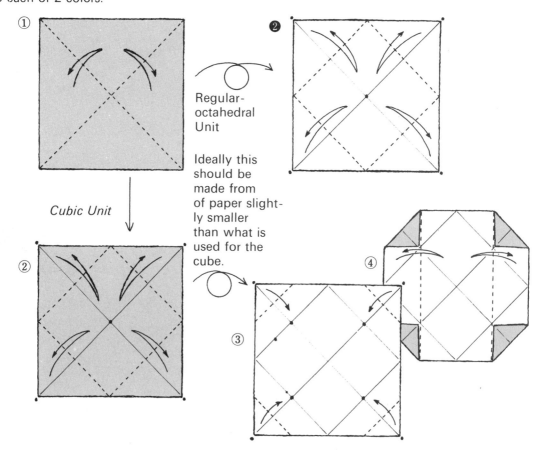

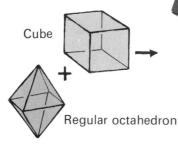

Cube

+

Regular octahedron

You will need 12 sheets of paper, 6 each of 2 colors.

①

Cubic Unit

②

②

❷ Regular-octahedral Unit

Ideally this should be made from of paper slightly smaller than what is used for the cube.

③

④

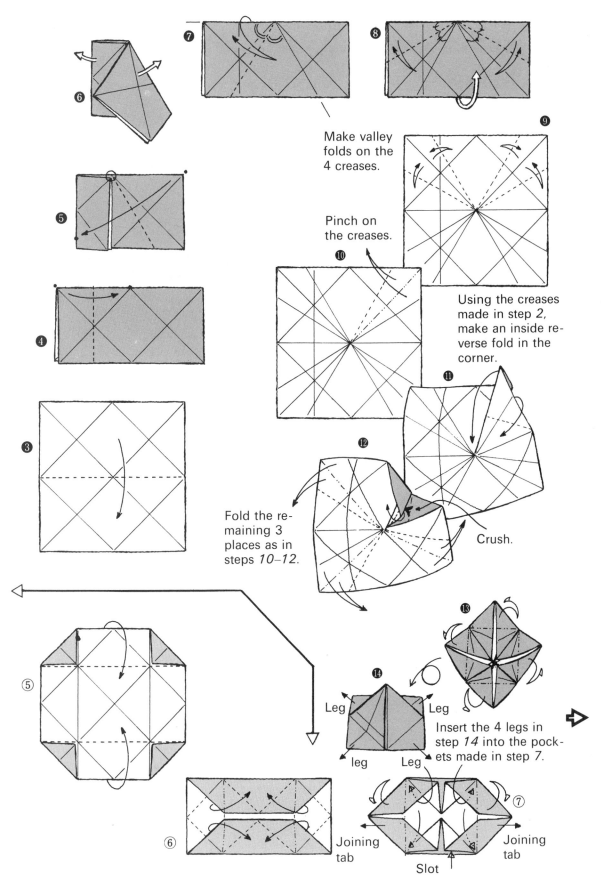

7

8

Make valley folds on the 4 creases.

6

9

5

Pinch on the creases.

Using the creases made in step 2, make an inside reverse fold in the corner.

4

10

11

3

12

Fold the remaining 3 places as in steps 10–12.

Crush.

13

14

Leg   Leg

leg   Leg

Insert the 4 legs in step 14 into the pockets made in step 7.

⑤

⑥

⑦

Joining tab

Joining tab

Slot

213

Union of Two Regular Tetra-hedrons: Kepler's Star

Give some thought to the relation between this figure and the regular octa-hedron and the cube.

This attractive combination of two regular tetrahedrons is named Kepler's Star because it is a form first-explained by the German astronomer and mathe-matician Johannes Kepler (1571–1630).

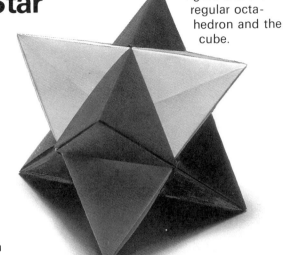

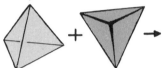

Regular tetrahedron   Regular tetrahedron

Joining unit

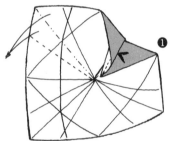

❶ **❷** **❸**

Begin with step *12* of the regular octahedron on p. 213.

Fold this multilayered point too as in step *1*.

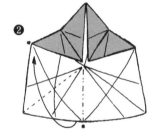

Completing the Figure Started on the Preceding Pages

Make six of the combined units seen in the photo-graph below and arrange them as shown in the figure on the right.

An example of the developmental form.

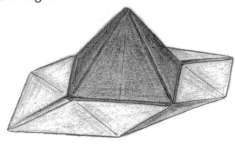

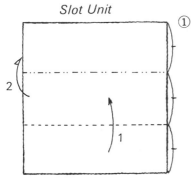

Slot Unit

①

2

1

Fold in numerical order to divide the paper horizontally into 3 equal parts.

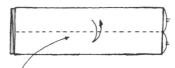

②

Crease the upper layer.

Make 4 each, in different colors, of steps *5* and *9* and insert the tabs into the slots. Assembly is easy because 9 is slightly larger. A dab of glue on each tab will ensure firm assembly.

② It is important that there be space left over at the place marked ★ in step *4*.

③

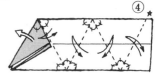
④ ★

Inside reverse fold on the creases

⑤

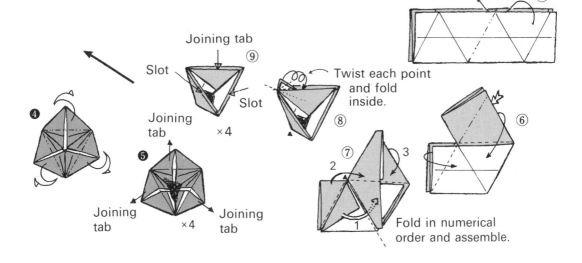

Joining tab

Slot

⑨

Slot

Joining tab ×4

Twist each point and fold inside.

⑧

⑥

Joining tab

❹

❺

Joining tab ×4

Joining tab

⑦

2

1

3

Fold in numerical order and assemble.

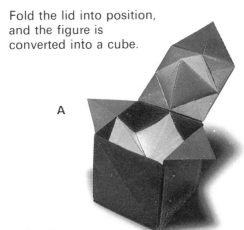

Fold the lid into position, and the figure is converted into a cube.

A

If glue has been used up to the stage shown in the drawing on the left, the assembly will be strong enough to permit you to convert the cube into a combination cube and octahedron and reconvert into a cube many times.

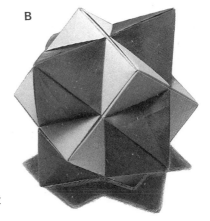

As is apparent from the view in *A*, the apexes of the regular octahedron correspond with the centers of the faces of the cube.

B

Spirals

Folding paper is necessarily a rectilinear process. And the straight lines and forms produced in this way are one of origami's aesthetic characteristics. At the same time, however, inability to produce curved lines and planes appears to be one of origami's weaknesses. Nonetheless, using origami methods to produce something suggestive of curves is a challenging topic. I shall have succeeded if the two forms introduced here remind you of spirals.

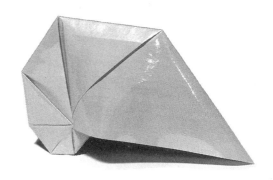

People of more than middle-school age should try to work out the length proportions of *a–f* in step *14*.

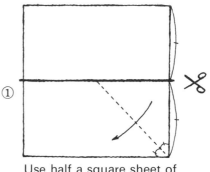

Use half a square sheet of paper.

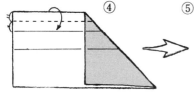

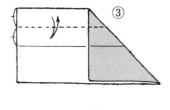

Univalve Shell

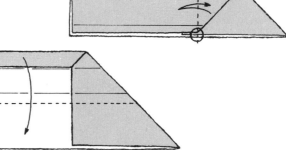

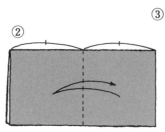

Object d'Art

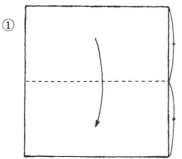

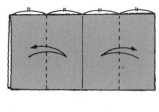

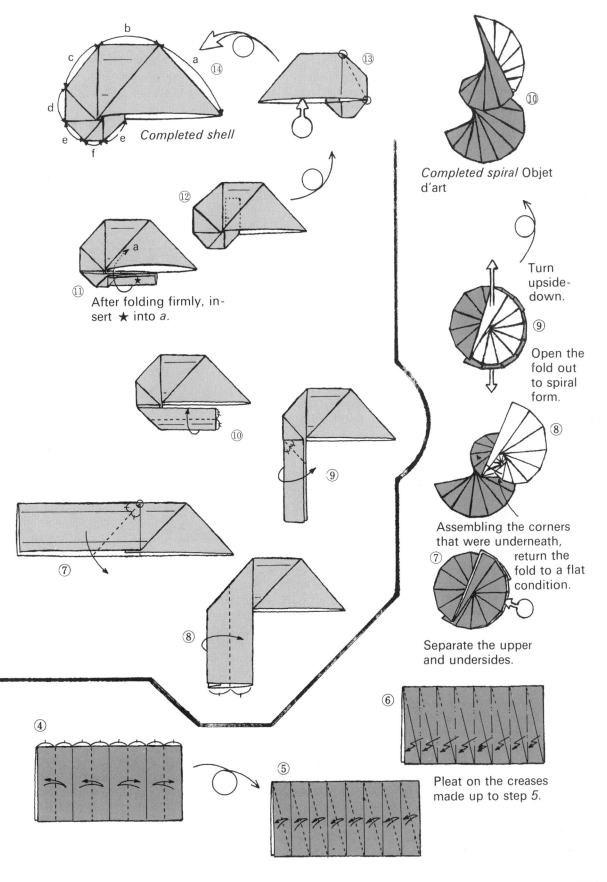

b

c

a

⑭

d

e   e

f

Completed shell

⑬

Completed spiral Objet
d'art

⑩

Turn
upside-
down.

⑫

⑨

Open the
fold out
to spiral
form.

a

⑪ After folding firmly, insert ★ into *a*.

⑧

Assembling the corners
that were underneath,
return the
fold to a flat
condition.

⑩

⑦

⑨

⑦

Separate the upper
and undersides.

⑧

⑥

④

⑤

Pleat on the creases
made up to step *5*.

217

Regular-pentagonal Flat Unit

Dodecahedron

After a considerable digression, I return to the regular dodecahedron, the sole remaining regular polyhedron to be covered. To produce it, we require a Regular-pentagonal Flat Unit. But this unit is much more difficult to make than the Equilateral-triangular or the Square versions. Once you have made it, you may want to do some extra research in written matter on the subject.

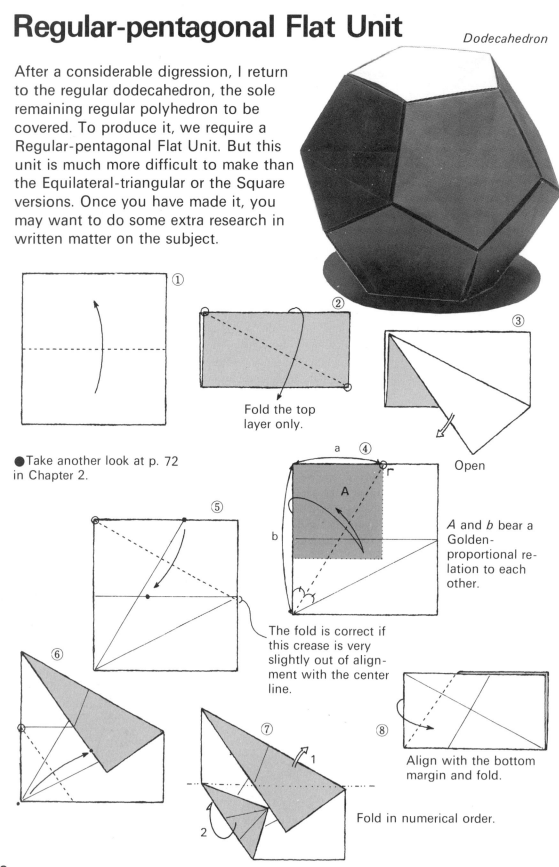

● Take another look at p. 72 in Chapter 2.

①

② Fold the top layer only.

③ Open

④ *A* and *b* bear a Golden-proportional relation to each other.

The fold is correct if this crease is very slightly out of alignment with the center line.

⑤

⑥

⑦ Fold in numerical order.

⑧ Align with the bottom margin and fold.

218

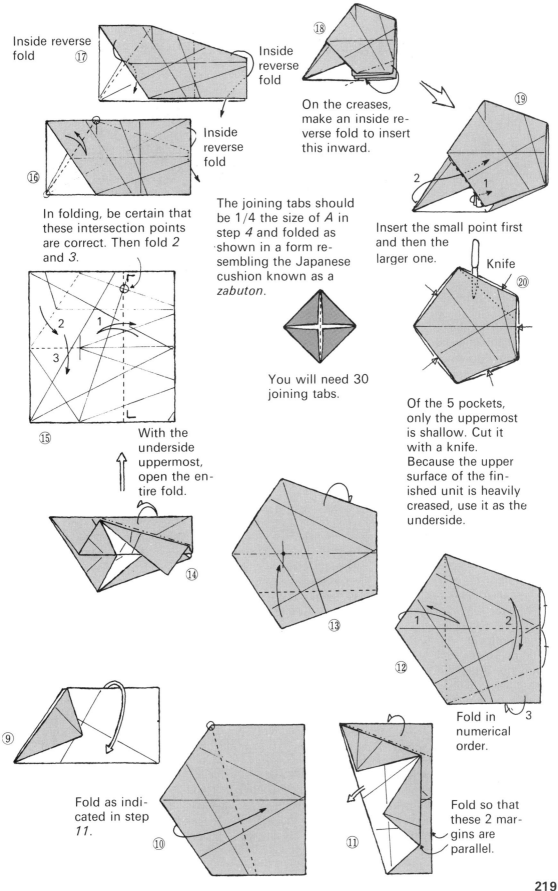

Inside reverse fold ⑰

Inside reverse fold

Inside reverse fold

⑯ In folding, be certain that these intersection points are correct. Then fold *2* and *3*.

⑱

On the creases, make an inside reverse fold to insert this inward.

⑲

Insert the small point first and then the larger one.

The joining tabs should be 1/4 the size of *A* in step *4* and folded as shown in a form resembling the Japanese cushion known as a *zabuton*.

You will need 30 joining tabs.

Knife

⑳

Of the 5 pockets, only the uppermost is shallow. Cut it with a knife. Because the upper surface of the finished unit is heavily creased, use it as the underside.

⑮

With the underside uppermost, open the entire fold.

⑭

⑬

⑫

Fold in numerical order.

⑨

Fold as indicated in step *11*.

⑩

⑪

Fold so that these 2 margins are parallel.

From Regular to Semiregular Polyhedrons

Now that we have made Equilateral-triangular, Square, and Regular-pentagonal Flat Units, we are able to produce all five of the regular polyhderons. Furthermore, combining these three basic flat units enables us to produce the six semiregular polyhderons shown in the photograph on p. 221. But such combinations entail joining the sides of the flat units. And this is somewhat difficult in the case of the Regular-pentagonal Unit, the relation of the side and diagonal of which is the Golden Proportion ($\sqrt{5} - 1 : 2$). A practical solution is presented on the next page, but it would be a good idea for you to approach the matter as a sophisticated and amusing puzzle to tackle on your own. In succeeding papers, I shall introduce Regular-hexagonal, Regular-decagonal, and Regular-octagonal Flat Units that will enable us to produce all eighteen of the basic polyhedrons.

Complete team of regular polyhedrons

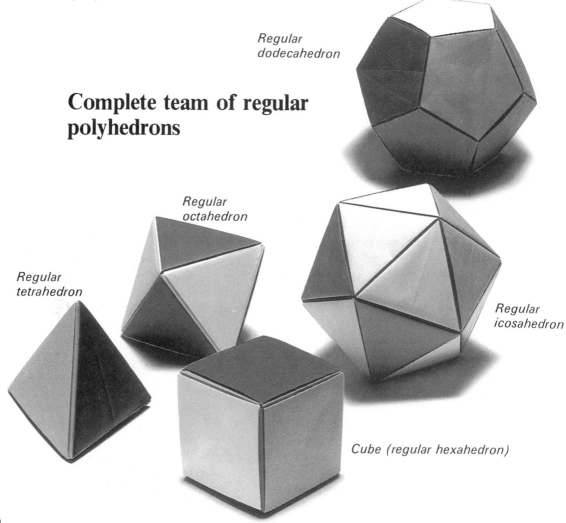

Regular dodecahedron

Regular octahedron

Regular tetrahedron

Regular icosahedron

Cube (regular hexahedron)

Six semiregular polyhedrons produced with units already introduced

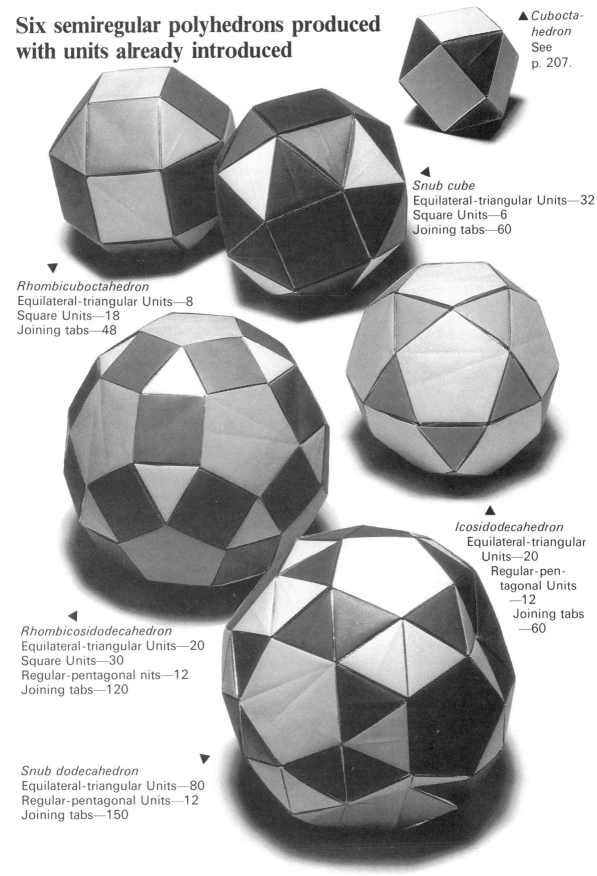

▲ *Cubocta-hedron*
See
p. 207.

◀
Snub cube
Equilateral-triangular Units—32
Square Units—6
Joining tabs—60

▼
Rhombicuboctahedron
Equilateral-triangular Units—8
Square Units—18
Joining tabs—48

▲
Icosidodecahedron
Equilateral-triangular
Units—20
Regular-pen-
tagonal Units
—12
Joining tabs
—60

◀
Rhombicosidodecahedron
Equilateral-triangular Units—20
Square Units—30
Regular-pentagonal nits—12
Joining tabs—120

▼
Snub dodecahedron
Equilateral-triangular Units—80
Regular-pentagonal Units—12
Joining tabs—150

Lengths of Sides

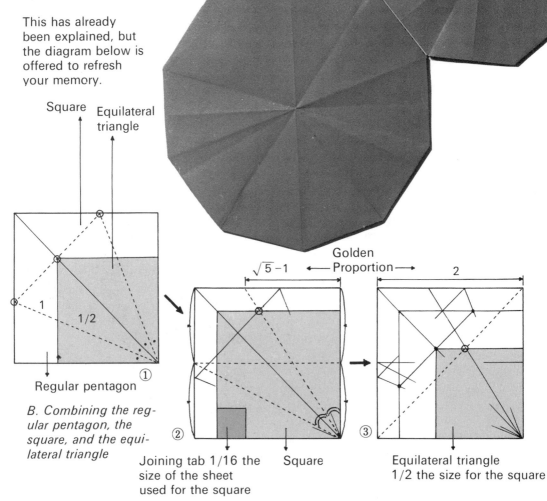

To ensure that the sizes of all the six kinds of polygons used in flat units are the same, different sizes of paper must be used. Of course, in any single semiregular polyhedron, only two or three of those flat units will be combined. Paper for the figure with the smaller number of angles should be smaller. All joining tabs are the squares without folding.

A. Combining the square and the equilateral triangle

This has already been explained, but the diagram below is offered to refresh your memory.

Square   Equilateral triangle

Regular pentagon   ①

B. Combining the regular pentagon, the square, and the equilateral triangle

Golden Proportion

$\sqrt{5}-1$ 2

② Joining tab 1/16 the size of the sheet used for the square   Square

③ Equilateral triangle 1/2 the size for the square

C. Combining the regular hexagon, the regular pentagon, the square, and the equilateral triangle

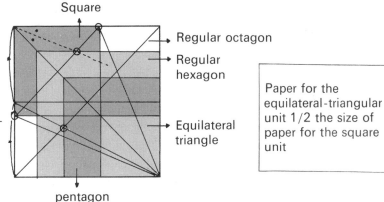

Regular hexagon ←

Square

① ②

Regular pentagon

Equilateral triangle

D. Combining the regular octagon, the regular hexagon, the square, and the equilateral triangle

The combination of regular octagon and regular pentagon occurs in none of the semiregular polyhedrons.

Square

Regular octagon

Regular hexagon

Equilateral triangle

pentagon

Paper for the equilateral-triangular unit 1/2 the size of paper for the square unit

Note: The relations for adjusting side lengths given here are solely for the units employed in this book to produce flat units for polyhedrons.

E. Combining the regular decagon, the regular hexagon, the square, and the equilateral triangle

These are given for the sake of reference; the combination of regular decagon, regular octagon, and regular pentagon does not occur.

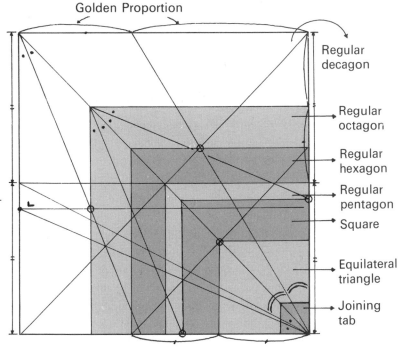

Golden Proportion

Regular decagon

Regular octagon

Regular hexagon

Regular pentagon

Square

Equilateral triangle

Joining tab

Note: Roughly half of the ratios worked out here are practically useful approximations.

Regular-hexagonal Flat Unit

Now that the problem of adjusting lengths of sides has been dealt with, we can turn to the remaining three polygonal flat units. First I present the Regular-hexagonal Unit. The Regular-octagonal and Regular-decagonal Units cannot be used by themselves to produce solid figures but must be combined with other polygons.

Joining tabs
Joining tabs are the same size, and a simple proportional relation has been selected.

1/16

Make an inside reverse fold on the creases.

224

Three more semiregular polyhedrons become possible

▲
Truncated tetrahedron
Equilateral-triangular Units—4
Regular-hexagonal Units—4
Joining tabs—18

▲
Truncated octahedron
Square units—6
Regular-hexagonal Units—8
Joining tabs—36

▼
Turncated icosahedron
Regular-pentagonal
Units—12
Regular-hexagonal
Units—20
Joining tabs
—90

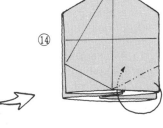

Two of the pockets are shallow and require that the joining tabs be adjusted as shown in *A* on the left.

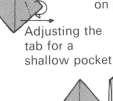

Adjusting the tab for a shallow pocket

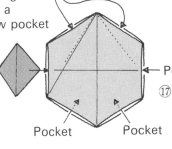

← Pocket

⑰

Pocket   Pocket

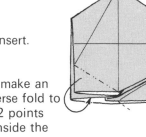

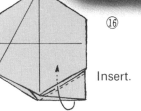

⑯

Insert.

This time, make an inside reverse fold to bring the 2 points together inside the lower part.

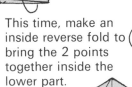

⑮

⑭

Make an inside reverse fold on the creases in the upper right layer only.

Make the inside reverse fold in this fashion. Repeat on the left side.

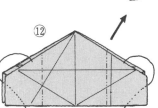

⑫

Inside reverse fold

⑬

225

Decagonal Flat Unit

The folding style used in this Regular-octagonal and in the succeeding Regular-decagonal Flat Units is different from the one used in preceding units. Since it results in beautiful forms well before the units are finished, this style is rhythmical and truly origamilike.

The colored side is upper.

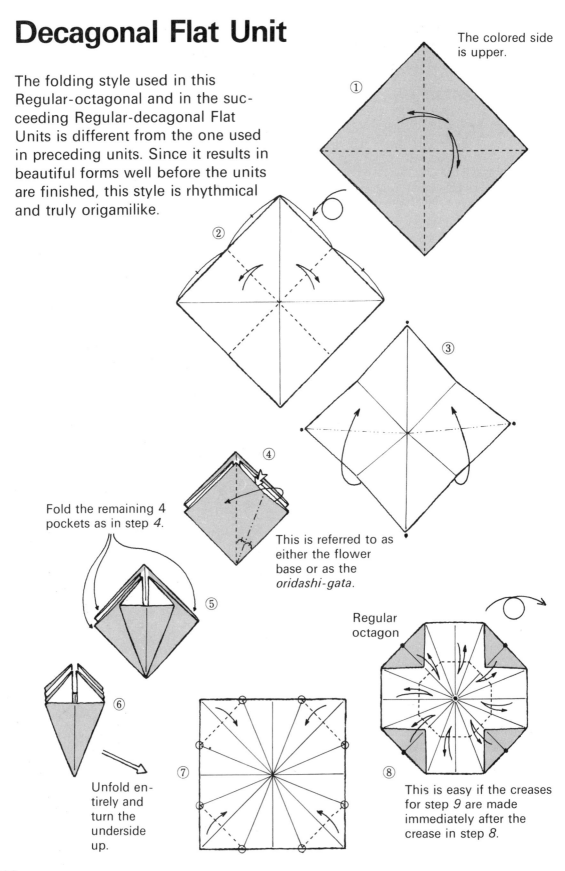

This is referred to as either the flower base or as the *oridashi-gata*.

Fold the remaining 4 pockets as in step *4*.

Unfold entirely and turn the underside up.

Regular octagon

This is easy if the creases for step *9* are made immediately after the crease in step *8*.

226

Two new semiregular polyhedrons

◀

Truncated hexahedron
Equilateral-triangular Units—8
Regular-octagonal Units—6
Joining tabs—36

▲

Rhombitruncated cuboctahedron
Square Units—12
Regular-hexagonal Units—8
Regular-octagonal Units—6
Joining tabs—72

Joining tabs

Though we do not actually use them, I present these joining tabs as samples for judging side length.

Pocket

Pocket   Pocket

Pocket

Pocket

⑬

Pocket

Pocket

Fix in place by folding the small point inward.

⑫

⑪

⑨

⑩

Using creases produced in step *9*, fold into the shape seen in step *12*.

227

Regular-octogonal Flat Unit

The final stages of the folding process of this last of the polygonal flat units has the pleasing rhythmical feel of the folding of the Regular-octagonal Unit. Though the unit is not theoretically 100 percent accurate, this degree of accuracy makes for folding ease and beauty in the completed form. People who require total accuracy should attempt to work out their own variations on the regular pentagon shown on p. 218.

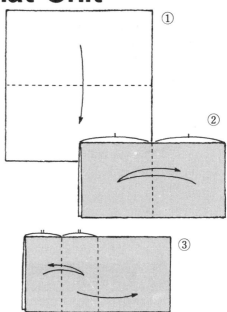

Fold in numerical order.

Fold point *a* as firmly as possible. Fold point *b* so that it is very slightly out of alignment.

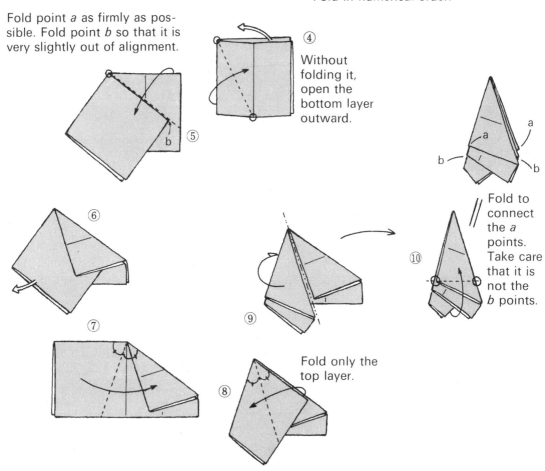

Without folding it, open the bottom layer outward.

Fold to connect the *a* points. Take care that it is not the *b* points.

Fold only the top layer.

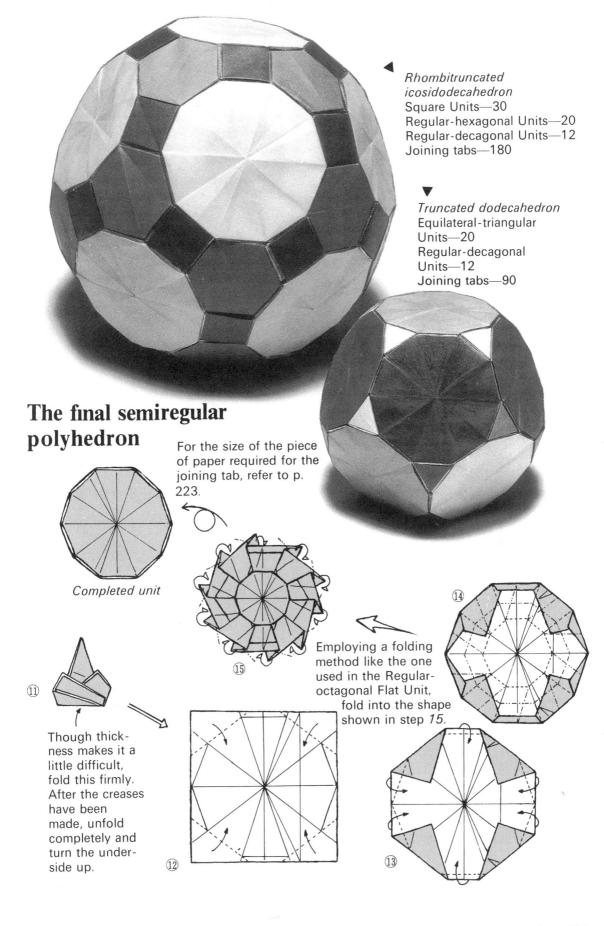

*Rhombitruncated
icosidodecahedron*
Square Units—30
Regular-hexagonal Units—20
Regular-decagonal Units—12
Joining tabs—180

Truncated dodecahedron
Equilateral-triangular
Units—20
Regular-decagonal
Units—12
Joining tabs—90

The final semiregular polyhedron

For the size of the piece of paper required for the joining tab, refer to p. 223.

Completed unit

⑪

Though thickness makes it a little difficult, fold this firmly. After the creases have been made, unfold completely and turn the underside up.

⑮

⑭

⑫

⑬

Employing a folding method like the one used in the Regular-octagonal Flat Unit, fold into the shape shown in step *15*.

229

At the Threshold

The energetic reader will already have made and arranged on his desk the eighteen basic polyhedrons, the theme of this chapter. But, since these eighteen are all produced from only six polygonal flat units—from the equilateral triangular to the regular-deoagonal —having made all of them does not mean that we have graduated from the course. As is clear from the extent to which these six units can be applied, it is possible to take many different approaches to each form and polyhedron. In other words, at this stage, we have arrived at the threshold of a whole new field of origami inquiry.

I should now like to present a few works that will stimulate awareness of the limitless possibilities for ingenuity lying ahead. You will recall that we had to cut the pocket of the Regular-pentagonal Flat Unit on p. 218. Thinking that there ought to be a better way to solve the problem of a shallow pocket, I worked out the method shown on the right. *B* and *C* on the opposite page represent folds that have developed from the slot unit on p. 215.

From step *11* on p. 219

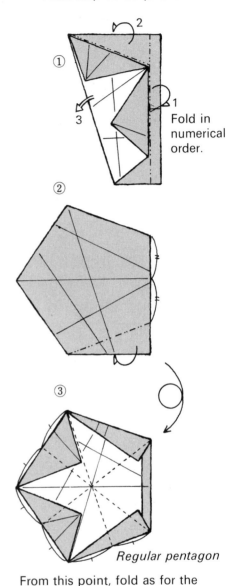

① Fold in numerical order.

②

③

Regular pentagon

From this point, fold as for the Regular-octagonal and Regular-decagonal Flat Units.

Variant version of the Regular-pentagonal Flat Unit

This variation is not an alteration of size. But, since the pocket is slightly shallow, it is necessary to fold the joining tab as shown.

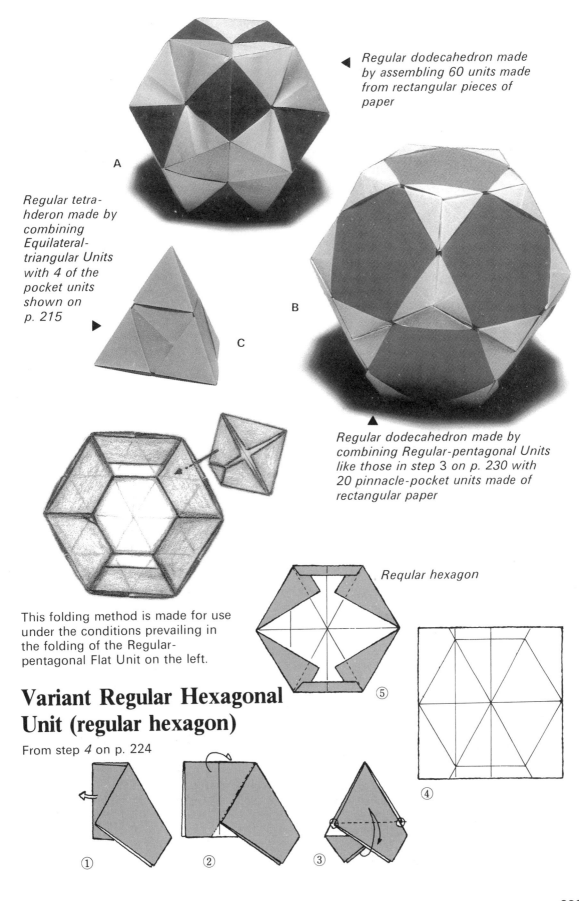

Regular dodecahedron made by assembling 60 units made from rectangular pieces of paper

A

Regular tetra-hderon made by combining Equilateral-triangular Units with 4 of the pocket units shown on p. 215

C

B

Regular dodecahedron made by combining Regular-pentagonal Units like those in step 3 on p. 230 with 20 pinnacle-pocket units made of rectangular paper

This folding method is made for use under the conditions prevailing in the folding of the Regular-pentagonal Flat Unit on the left.

Reqular hexagon

⑤

④

Variant Regular Hexagonal Unit (regular hexagon)

From step *4* on p. 224

①

②

③

231

The Inexhaustible Fascination of Polyhedrons

Now let us go a little more deeply into the virtually boundless possibilities inherent in even a single polyhedron. Up to this point, the cube, the most basic of the basic polyhedrons, has already played a part in more than eight of the figures I have presented. For doubters, I have lined them up in the photographs below.

I have said "more than eight" because, in the case of units, 6-sheet and 12-sheet assemblies too can be squares, raising the numbers of possibilities to 24, 54, 96, and so on. But without going too much into detail, I merely wish to point out the abundant possibilities of a single polyhedron. Developments become even more varied when the cube is viewed from different viewpoints as in *A*.

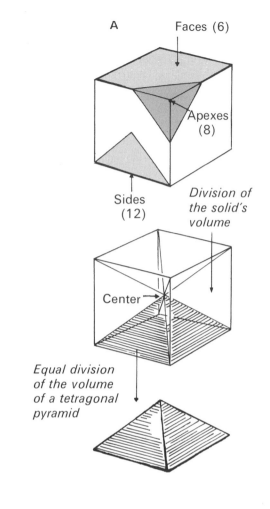

A

Faces (6)

Apexes (8)

Sides (12)

Division of the solid's volume

Center

Equal division of the volume of a tetragonal pyramid

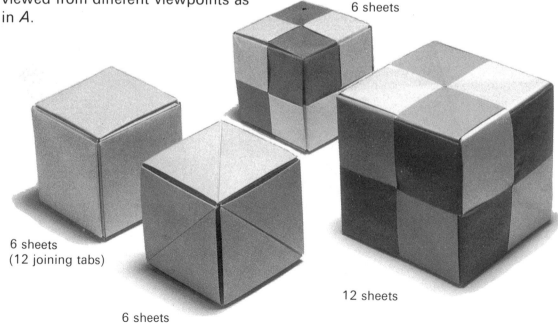

6 sheets

6 sheets (12 joining tabs)

6 sheets

12 sheets

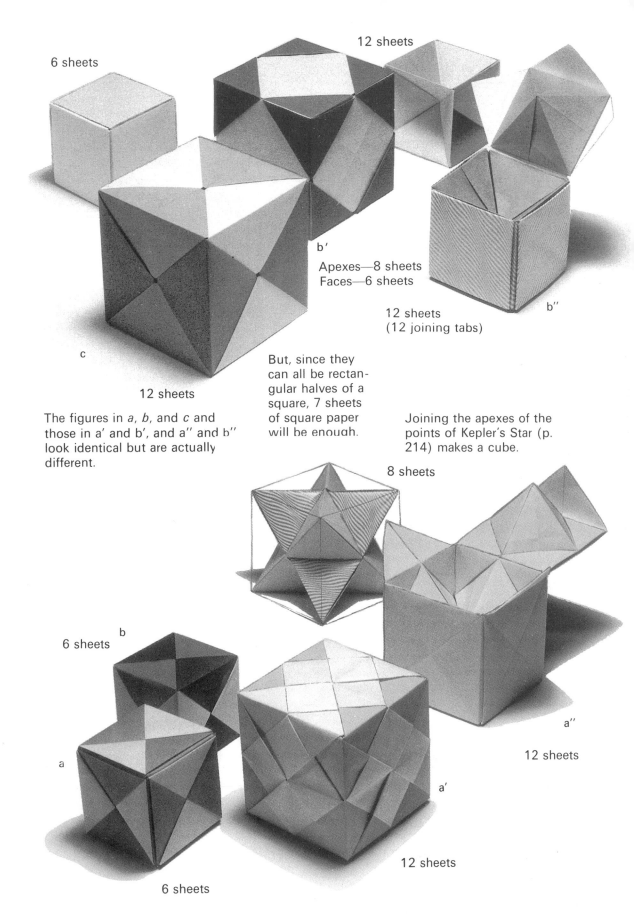

6 sheets

12 sheets

b'

Apexes—8 sheets
Faces—6 sheets

12 sheets
(12 joining tabs)

c

12 sheets

The figures in *a*, *b*, and *c* and those in a' and b', and a'' and b'' look identical but are actually different.

But, since they can all be rectangular halves of a square, 7 sheets of square paper will be enough.

Joining the apexes of the points of Kepler's Star (p. 214) makes a cube.

8 sheets

b

6 sheets

a

a''

12 sheets

a'

6 sheets

12 sheets

The Reversible Stellate Icosahedron

Though Chapter 2 pursues a new origami field, in attempting something similar, Chapter 5 has caused a great deal more hard work and probably considerable fatigue. This work has been included to provide relief.

The peculiar name requires some explanation. As an examination of *A* shows, the regular icosahedron can be viewed as having an interior composed of three intersecting parallelograms with long and short sides illustrating the Golden Proportion. The apex of a trigonal pyramid the base of which is equal to the short side of one of those parallelograms and the edge of which is equal to one-half the diagonal of such a parallelogram becomes the center of a regular icosahedron. The volume of the icosahedron may be divided into twenty equal parts by twenty such trigonal pyramids. Consequently, as is shown on the right, this fascinating stellar form can be reassembled into a regular icosahedron by turning all the apexes of the pyramids inward to the center.

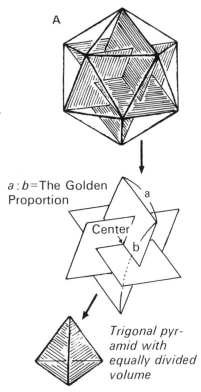

A

$a : b$ = The Golden Proportion

Center

a

b

Trigonal pyramid with equally divided volume

Trigonal pyramid for the regular icosahedron

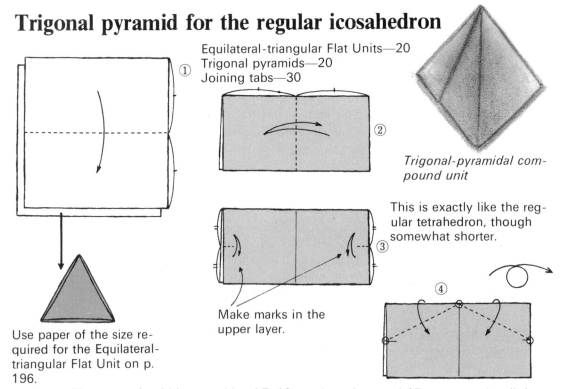

Equilateral-triangular Flat Units—20
Trigonal pyramids—20
Joining tabs—30

Trigonal-pyramidal compound unit

This is exactly like the regular tetrahedron, though somewhat shorter.

Make marks in the upper layer.

Use paper of the size required for the Equilateral-triangular Flat Unit on p. 196.

●The paper should have a side of 7–10 cm since the usual 15-cm paper is a little too large for the inversion and reassembly.

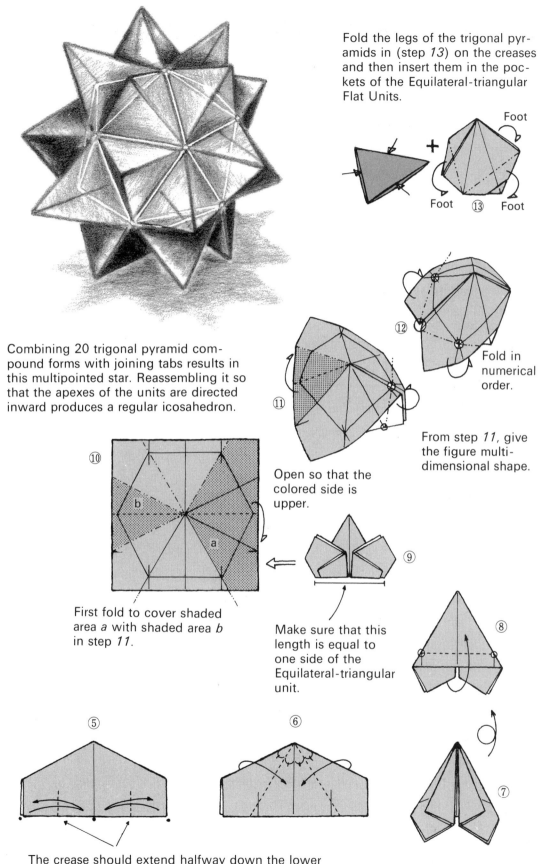

Fold the legs of the trigonal pyramids in (step *13*) on the creases and then insert them in the pockets of the Equilateral-triangular Flat Units.

Foot

Foot

Foot

⑬

⑫

Fold in numerical order.

⑪

From step *11*, give the figure multi-dimensional shape.

Combining 20 trigonal pyramid compound forms with joining tabs results in this multipointed star. Reassembling it so that the apexes of the units are directed inward produces a regular icosahedron.

⑩

b

a

Open so that the colored side is upper.

First fold to cover shaded area *a* with shaded area *b* in step *11*.

⑨

⑧

Make sure that this length is equal to one side of the Equilateral-triangular unit.

⑤

⑥

⑦

The crease should extend halfway down the lower side.

The Reversible Stellate Regular Dodecahedron

This very rewarding work is similar to the preceding one except that in this instance the pyramidal units have pentagonal bases and divide the volume of the solid figure into twelve equal parts when the apexes are turned inward.

The apex (*P*) corresponds to the center of the pentagonal base.

Pentagonal pyramid with equally divided volume

Use paper of the size required for the Regular-pentagonal Flat Unit on p. 218.

Regular-pentagonal Flat Units—12
Pentagonal pyramid units—12
Joining tabs—30

Pentagonal-pyramidal compound unit

At *a*, do no more than make a mark. At *b*, crease for about 1/4 of the way.

The process is easier if you fold *1* before folding *2*.

236

As was the case with the regular icosahedron, the regular dodecahedron can be viewed as composed of 3 intersecting parallelograms the relation of the sides of which illustrates the Golden Proportion. It is troublesome, however, that in this instance the short and long sides of the parallelograms fail to correspond directly with the base or the edge of the pentagonal pyramid.

Assemble in multi-dimensional form.

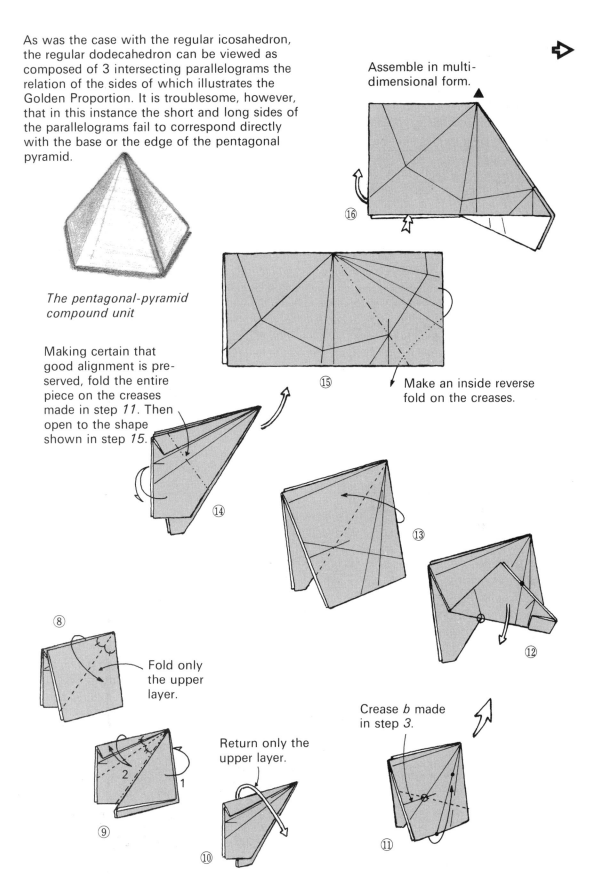

The pentagonal-pyramid compound unit

Making certain that good alignment is preserved, fold the entire piece on the creases made in step *11*. Then open to the shape shown in step *15*.

Make an inside reverse fold on the creases.

Fold only the upper layer.

Return only the upper layer.

Crease *b* made in step *3*.

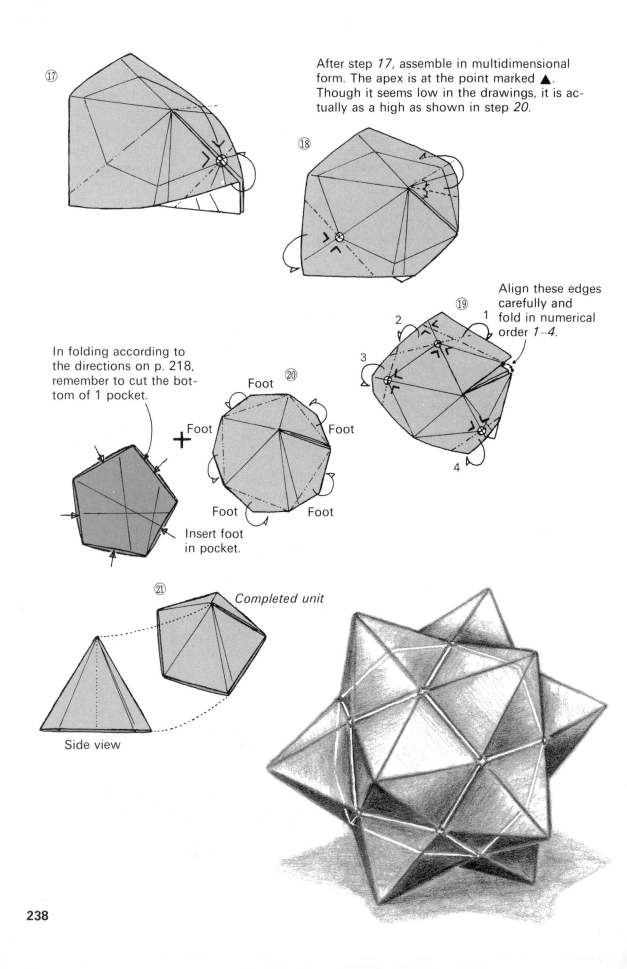

⑰

After step *17*, assemble in multidimensional form. The apex is at the point marked ▲. Though it seems low in the drawings, it is actually as a high as shown in step *20*.

⑱

Align these edges carefully and fold in numerical order *1–4*.

⑲

2

1

3

4

In folding according to the directions on p. 218, remember to cut the bottom of 1 pocket.

⑳

Foot

Foot

Foot

Foot

Foot

Foot

+

Insert foot in pocket.

㉑

Completed unit

Side view

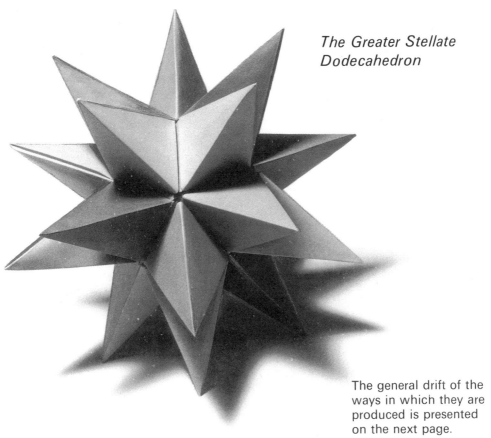

The Greater Stellate Dodecahedron

The general drift of the ways in which they are produced is presented on the next page.

Two stellate dodecahedrons

Unlike the ones on the preceding pages, these two beautiful stellar forms cannot be converted into their corresponding solid-geometric figures. Give some thought to the differences in their appearances.

The Lesser Stellate Dodecahedron

●The large one too is a dodecahedron but is composed of 12 star faces.

The extra height of the pyramidal units (*B*) used in the two figures on the preceding page makes it impossible to invert them to convert the star form into its corresponding solid-geometric figure: the apexes would all pass through the center.

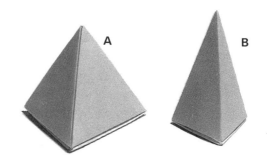

Greater and Lesser Stellate Dodecahedrons

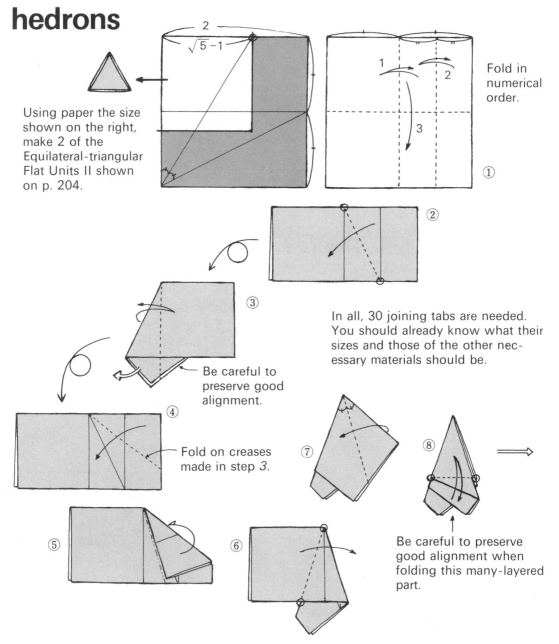

Using paper the size shown on the right, make 2 of the Equilateral-triangular Flat Units II shown on p. 204.

Fold in numerical order.

In all, 30 joining tabs are needed. You should already know what their sizes and those of the other necessary materials should be.

Be careful to preserve good alignment.

Fold on creases made in step *3*.

Be careful to preserve good alignment when folding this many-layered part.

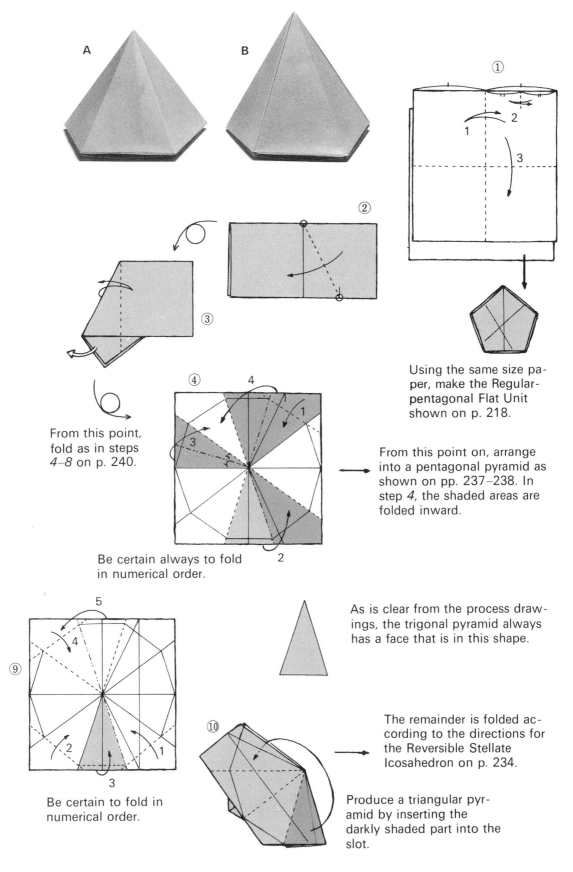

A

B

①

②

③

④

4
1
3
2

Using the same size paper, make the Regular-pentagonal Flat Unit shown on p. 218.

From this point on, arrange into a pentagonal pyramid as shown on pp. 237–238. In step *4*, the shaded areas are folded inward.

From this point, fold as in steps *4–8* on p. 240.

Be certain always to fold in numerical order.

As is clear from the process drawings, the trigonal pyramid always has a face that is in this shape.

⑨

5
4
2
1
3

Be certain to fold in numerical order.

⑩

The remainder is folded according to the directions for the Reversible Stellate Icosahedron on p. 234.

Produce a triangular pyramid by inserting the darkly shaded part into the slot.

241

Stellate Regular Octahedron

By now we have produced all five of the regular polyhedrons plus convertible stellate versions of two with the largest number of faces. Now we shall turn to the remaining three by beginning with the easiest, the regular octahedron, with which the introduction should already have made you very familiar.

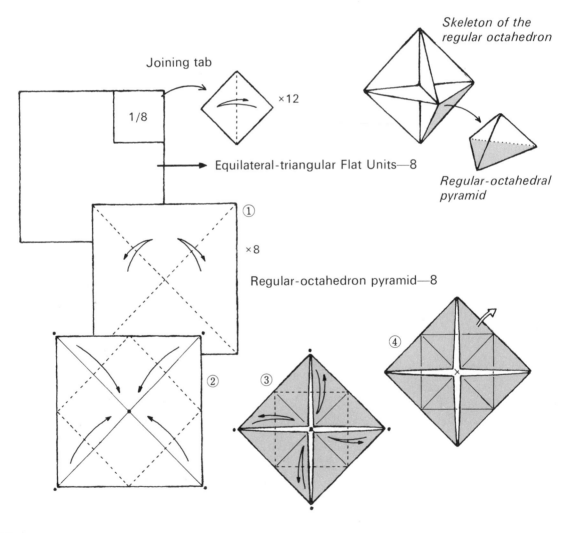

Joining tab

×12

1/8

Equilateral-triangular Flat Units—8

Skeleton of the regular octahedron

Regular-octahedral pyramid

① ×8

Regular-octahedron pyramid—8

② ③ ④

242

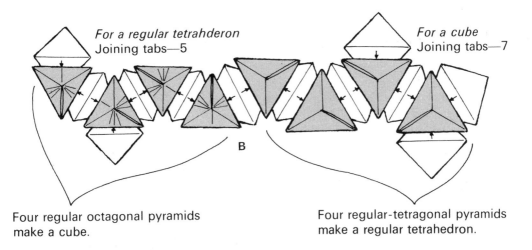

For a regular tetrahderon
Joining tabs—5

For a cube
Joining tabs—7

B

Four regular octagonal pyramids make a cube.

Four regular-tetragonal pyramids make a regular tetrahedron.

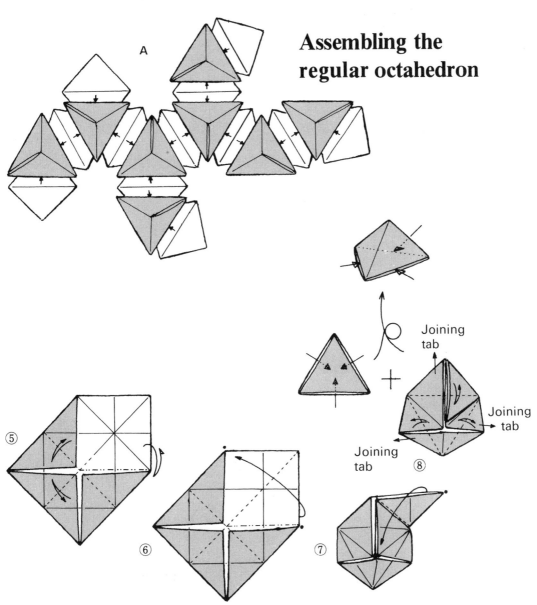

A

Assembling the regular octahedron

Joining tab

Joining tab

Joining tab

Joining tab

⑤

⑥

⑦

⑧

Stellate Tetrahedron

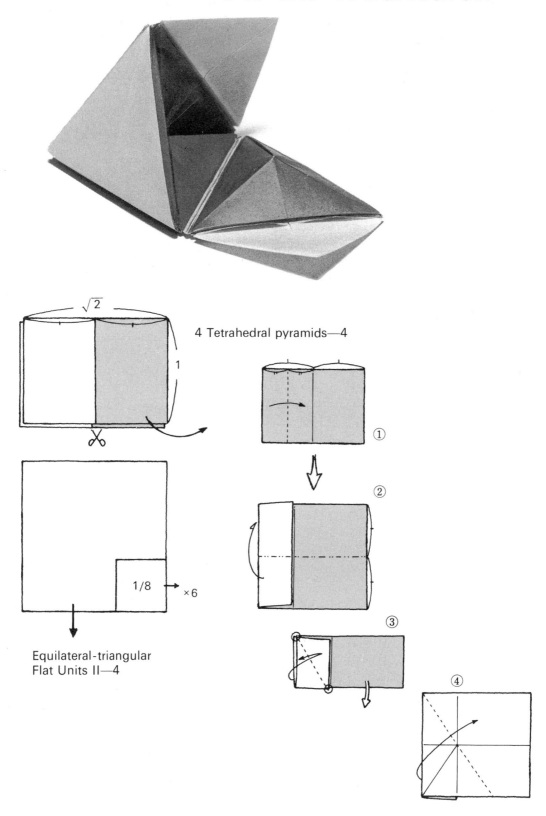

4 Tetrahedral pyramids—4

$\sqrt{2}$

1

1/8 →×6

Equilateral-triangular
Flat Units II—4

① ② ③ ④

Toy puzzle

The photograph below shows the completed appearance of the form presented in developmental drawings in *B* on p. 243. An excellent display of the relations between the cube and the regular tetrahedron, it is a delightful puzzle toy as well. You should have fun making it.

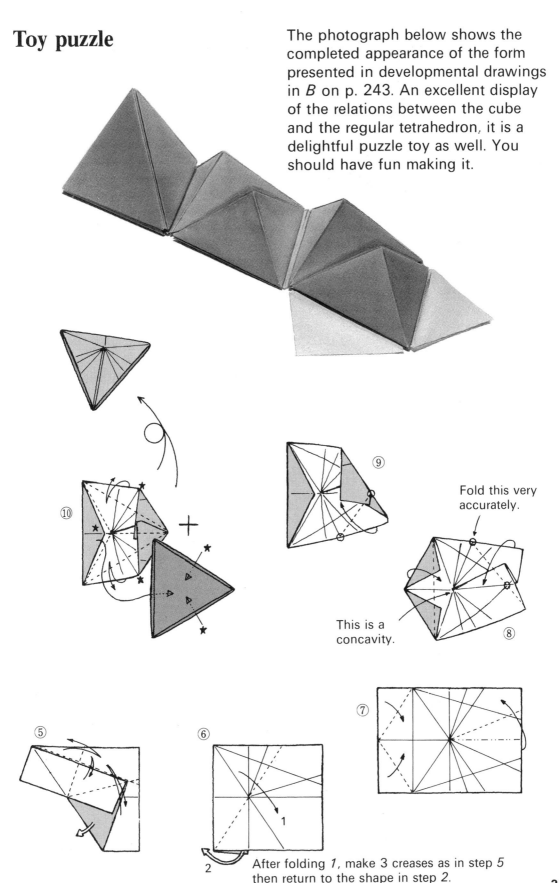

⑨

Fold this very accurately.

⑩

This is a concavity.

⑧

⑦

⑤

⑥

1

2 After folding *1*, make 3 creases as in step *5* then return to the shape in step *2*.

Stellate Square

The photograph on the right is the puzzle on p. 245 immediately before assembly into a cube. The photograph of the stellate square appears on p. 247. Actually, as was the case with the tetrahedron, there is very little stellar about its appearance. Its converted version, however, is the beautiful rhomboid dodecahedron.

Cube pyramid

Make a Square Flat Unit of the A type, as shown on p. 207.

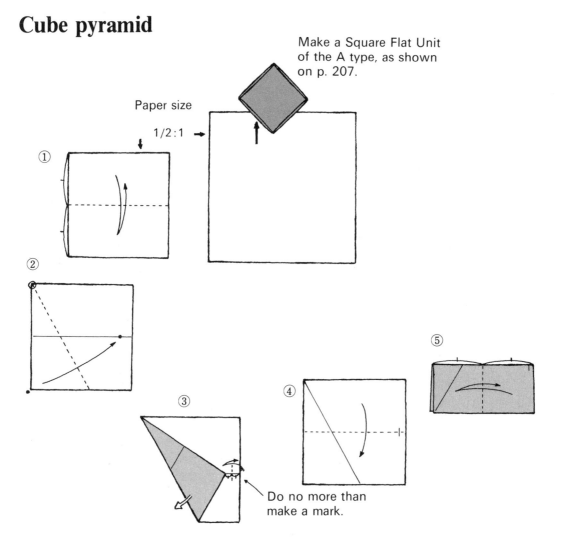

Paper size

1/2 : 1 →

①

②

③

④

⑤

Do no more than make a mark.

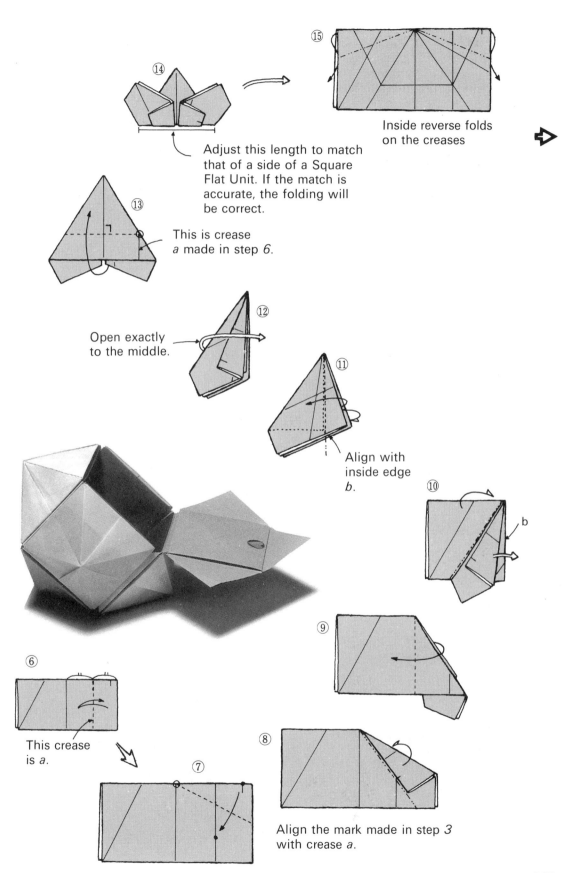

⑮ Inside reverse folds on the creases

⑭ Adjust this length to match that of a side of a Square Flat Unit. If the match is accurate, the folding will be correct.

⑬ This is crease *a* made in step *6*.

Open exactly to the middle.

⑫

⑪ Align with inside edge *b*.

⑩ b

⑨

⑥ This crease is *a*.

⑦

⑧ Align the mark made in step *3* with crease *a*.

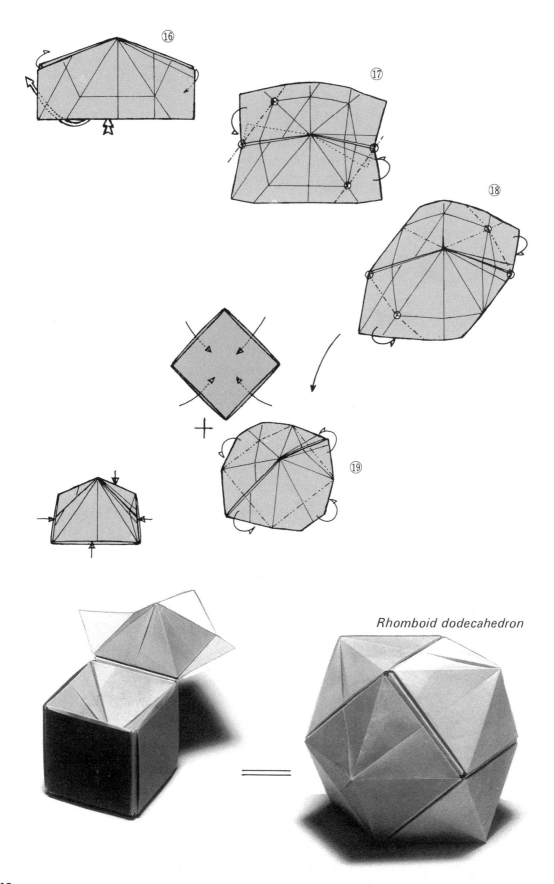

⑯

⑰

⑱

⑲

Rhomboid dodecahedron

Chapter **6**

Viva Origami

Doubling the Pleasure

I decided to think of origami in two categories—the lyrical category of representations of bird and animals and the theoretical category including the works presented in the preceding chapter—precisely because many origamians seems to dislike the second category. The attitude of such people, however, is inconsistent. As long as they are produced by accurately folding from square pieces of paper, origami animals do not differ materially from purely geometric folds.

Nonetheless, a clear difference of mood sets one category apart from the other. While realizing this, I believe that striving to unite the two as skillfully as possible doubles the pleasure to be enjoyed—as amphibians can enjoy living both on the land and in the water. Though my actions may fall short of my words, in this final chapter, I present a random selection of themes incorporating the aim of blending the two categories.

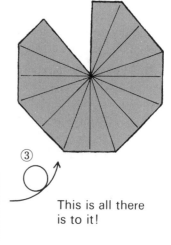

Completed water-lily pad

Water-lily Pad

①

A little ingenuity can change a purely geometric form into representational origami.

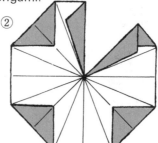

②

③

This is all there is to it!

Begin with step *8* of the Regular-octagonal Flat Unit on p. 226.

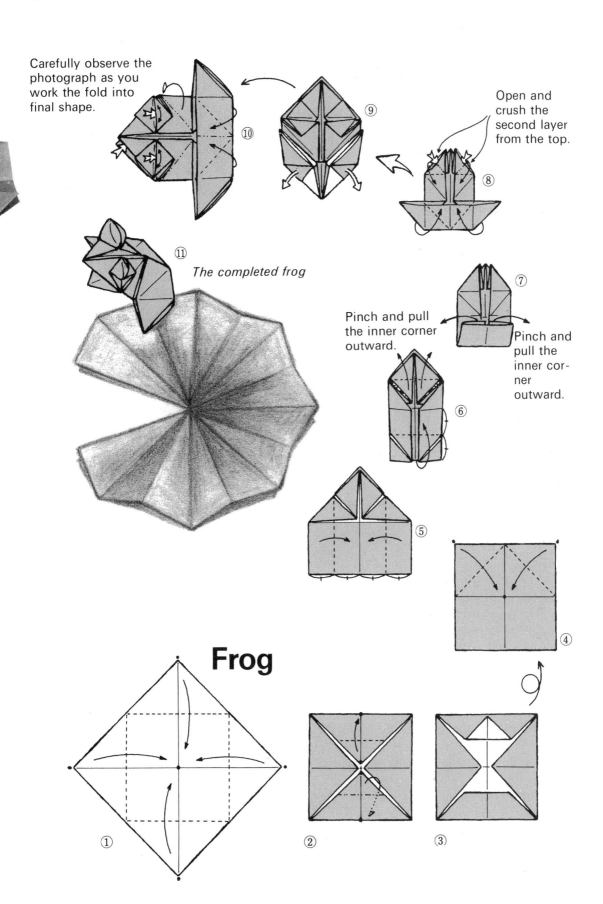

Carefully observe the photograph as you work the fold into final shape.

⑩

⑨

Open and crush the second layer from the top.

⑧

⑪

The completed frog

⑦

Pinch and pull the inner corner outward.

Pinch and pull the inner corner outward.

⑥

⑤

④

Frog

①

②

③

The Ambitious Frog

As you will see as you fold it, this frog is very different from the one presented on pp. 250–251. In this virtually unprecedented work, halfway opening something that has already been folded produces the froglike quality. This is why it is ambitious.

Use paper 15 cm to a side or smaller.

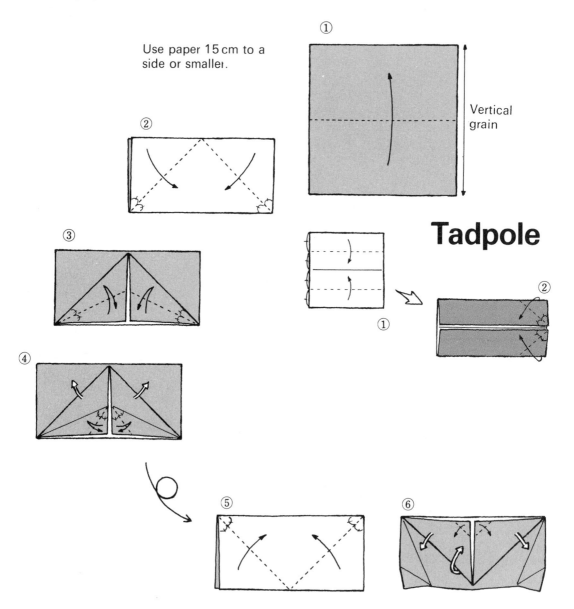

Tadpole

252

In machine-made paper, the fibers are uniformly oriented in the vertical direction to produce what is called the vertical grain. The cross grain, of course, runs at ninety degrees to it. When making paper airplanes, it is important to know about the grain. As is shown in *A* and *B*, paper curls when held so that the vertical grain is horizontally oriented.

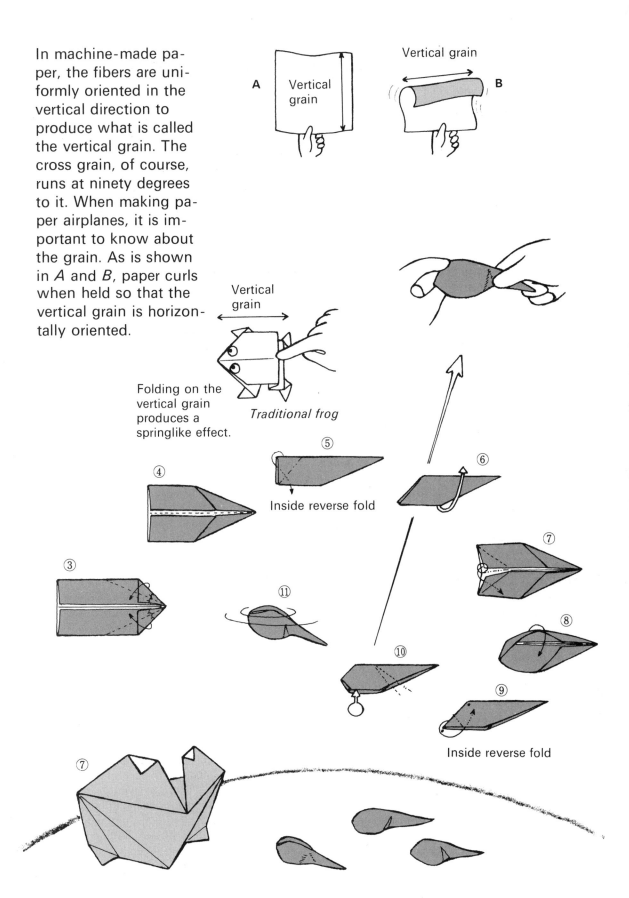

A
Vertical grain

Vertical grain

B

Vertical grain

Folding on the vertical grain produces a springlike effect.

Traditional frog

③

④

⑤
Inside reverse fold

⑥

⑦

⑧

⑨
Inside reverse fold

⑩

⑪

⑦

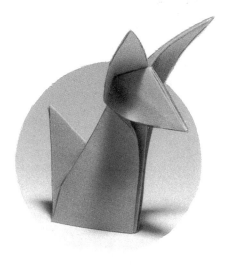

My Favorite Fox

This fold has already appeared in a photograph in Chapter 4 (p. 149). Although perhaps, having commented on the difficulty of producing them, I should not stress my feelings about a work in which curved planes play a prominent

①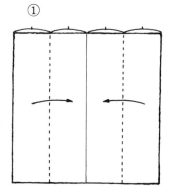

②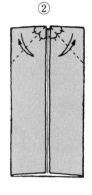

③

Fold firmly.

④

⑤

⑥

⑦

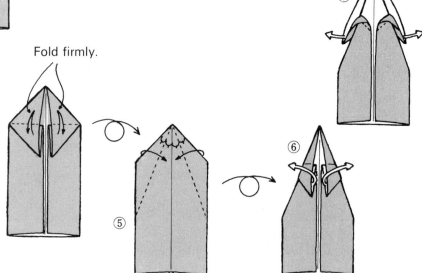

role, this fox completely delights
me. Try your hand at folding the
four legs from the kind of rectangular paper shown in A.

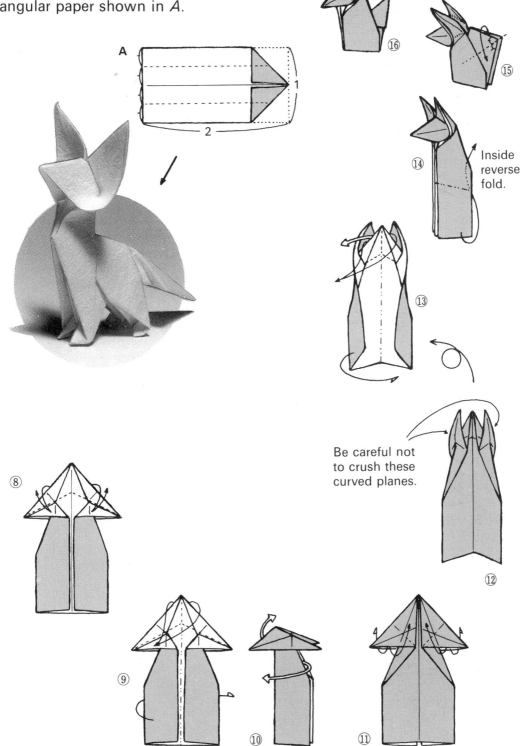

The completed fox

Inside
reverse
fold.

Be careful not
to crush these
curved planes.

Cicada

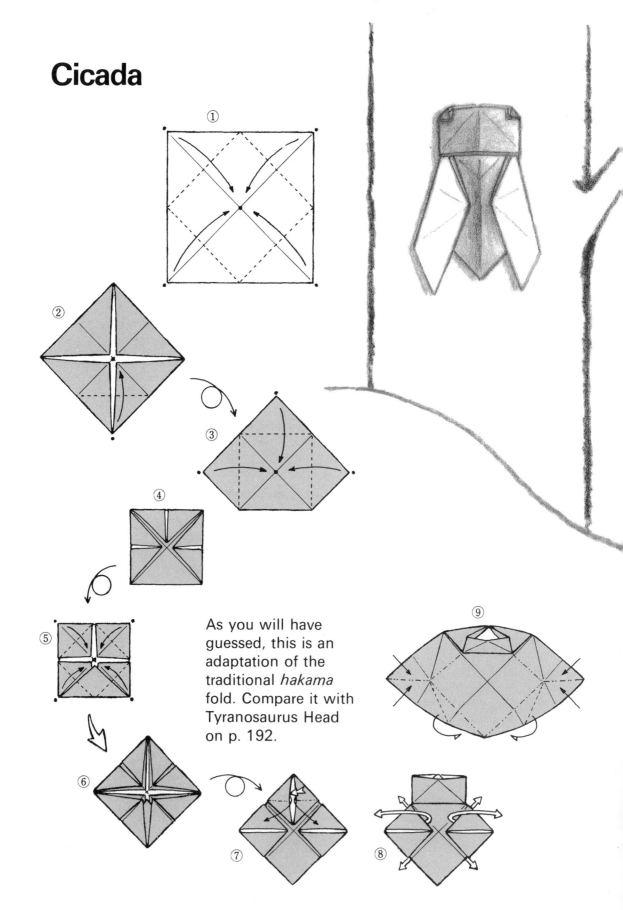

As you will have guessed, this is an adaptation of the traditional *hakama* fold. Compare it with Tyranosaurus Head on p. 192.

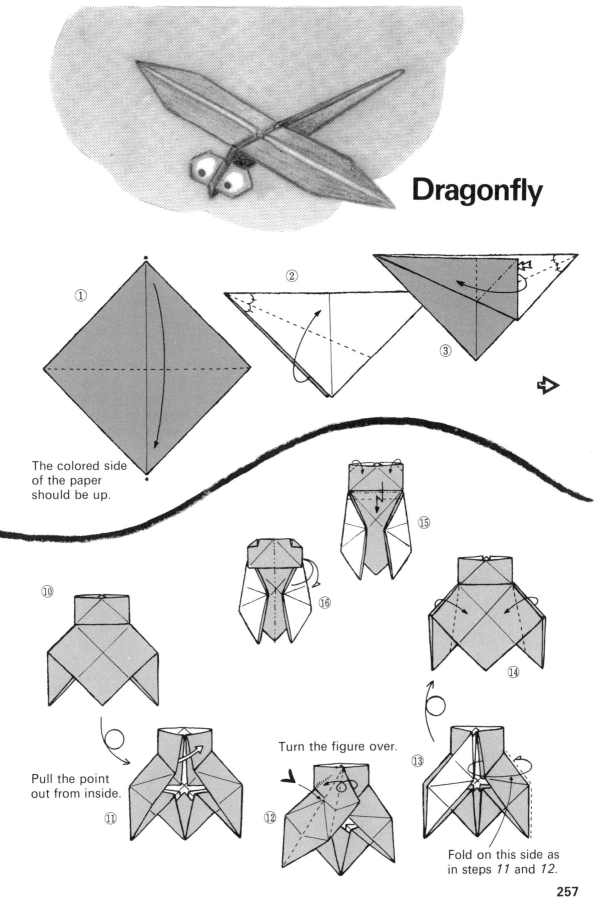

Dragonfly

① The colored side of the paper should be up.

②

③

⑩

⑪ Pull the point out from inside.

⑫ Turn the figure over.

⑬ Fold on this side as in steps *11* and *12*.

⑭

⑮

⑯

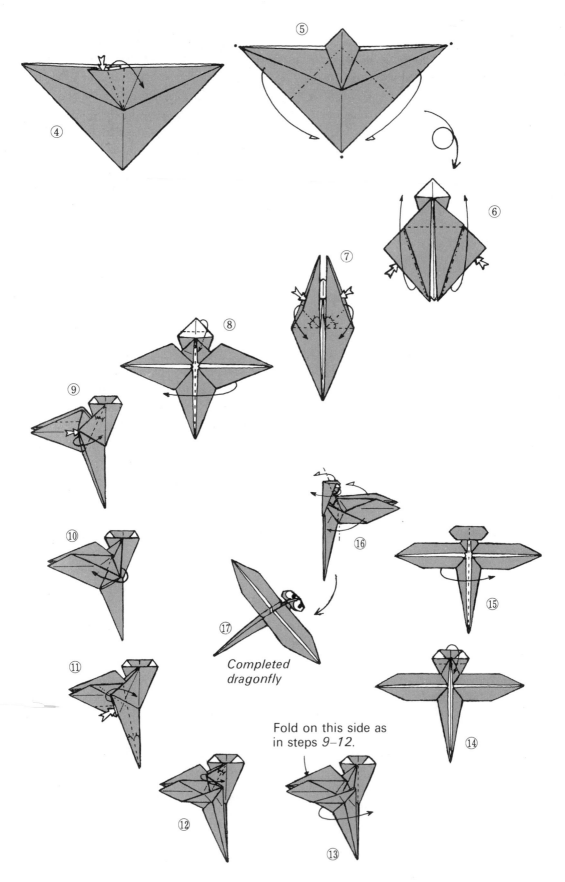

④

⑤

⑥

⑦

⑧

⑨

⑩

⑪

⑫

⑬

⑭

⑮

⑯

⑰

Completed
dragonfly

Fold on this side as
in steps *9–12.*

Hopping Grasshopper

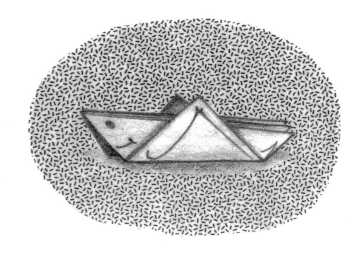

①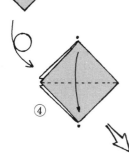

②

③

④

For fun

Because of my own interests, this book may lean a little in the direction of theory. But origami is essentially fun. And it is all the more enjoyable if its theoretical aspects are taken into consideration in a way that makes it an intellectual hobby. Nonetheless, as the outstanding origami masters of the past discovered and passed on to us, with or without theory, the important thing is to have a good time while folding.

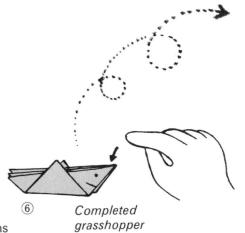

⑥ *Completed grasshopper*

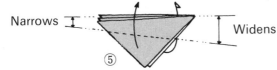

Narrows

Widens

⑤

Carp

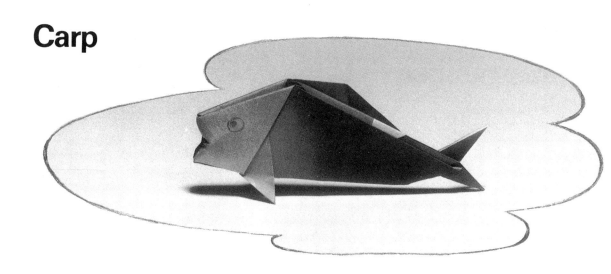

The colored side of the paper must be up.

①

②

③

④

⑤

⑥

㉑

Completed carp

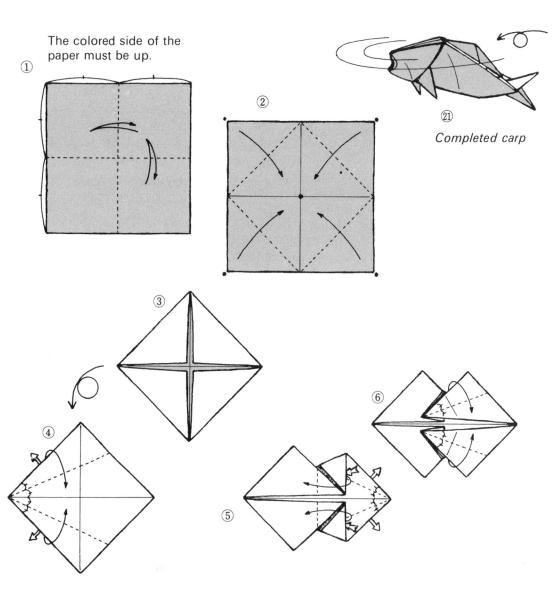

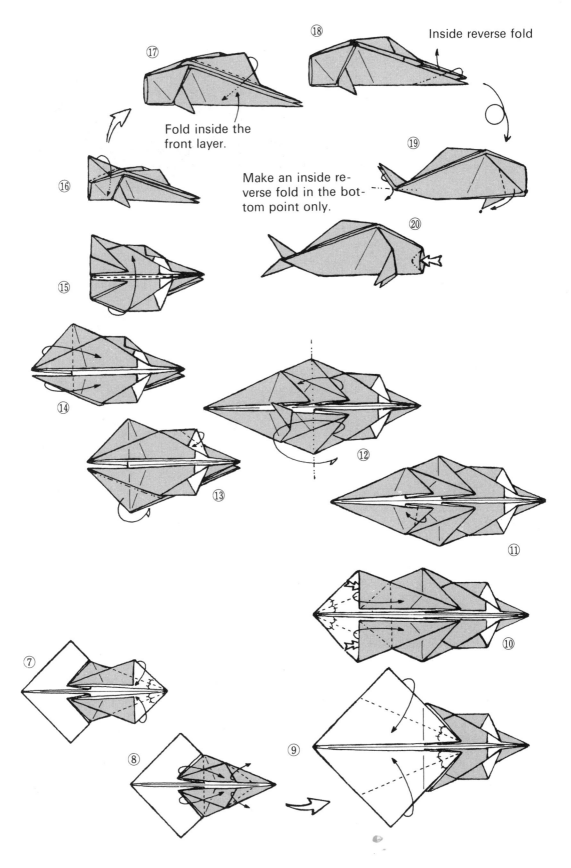

Fold inside the front layer.

Inside reverse fold

Make an inside reverse fold in the bottom point only.

Shark

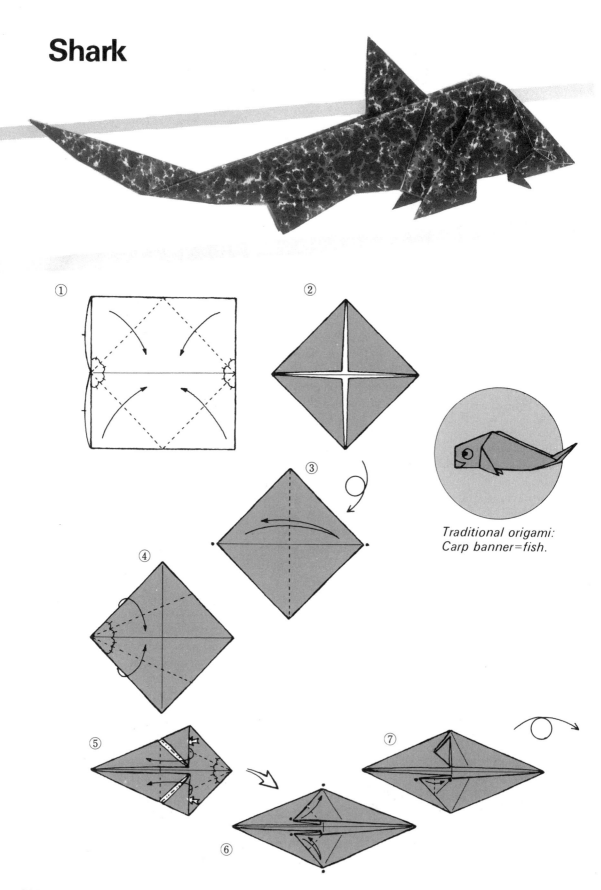

Traditional origami:
Carp banner=fish.

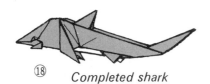

⑱ *Completed shark*

Inside reverse fold

⑰

⑯

⑮

⑭

Fold so as to leave this point to serve as the dorsal fin.

Like Carp (p. 260), this Shark is based on the traditional blintz (fish) fold. As you will see, this method is used to increase the number of points available in the blintz fold.

⑬

⑫

⑪

Insert point *a* under point *b*.

⑧

⑨

⑩

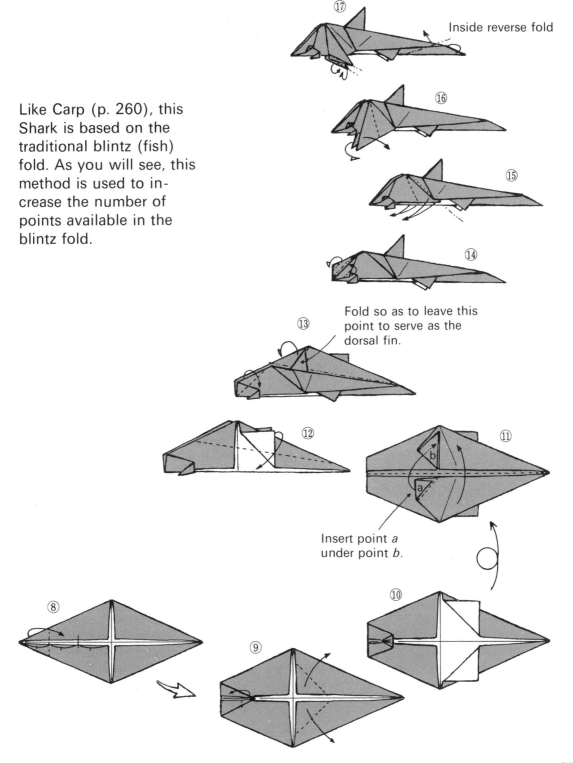

Tropical Fish

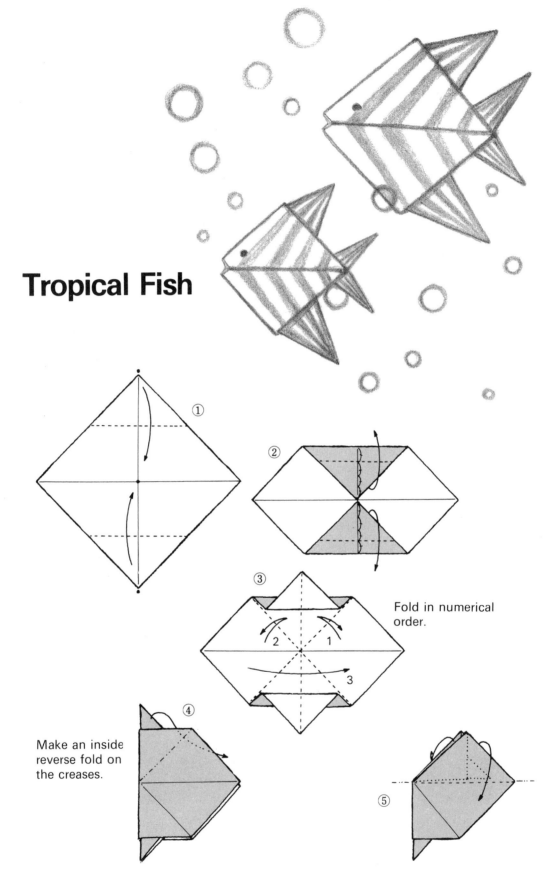

①

②

③ Fold in numerical order.

2 1

3

④ Make an inside reverse fold on the creases.

⑤

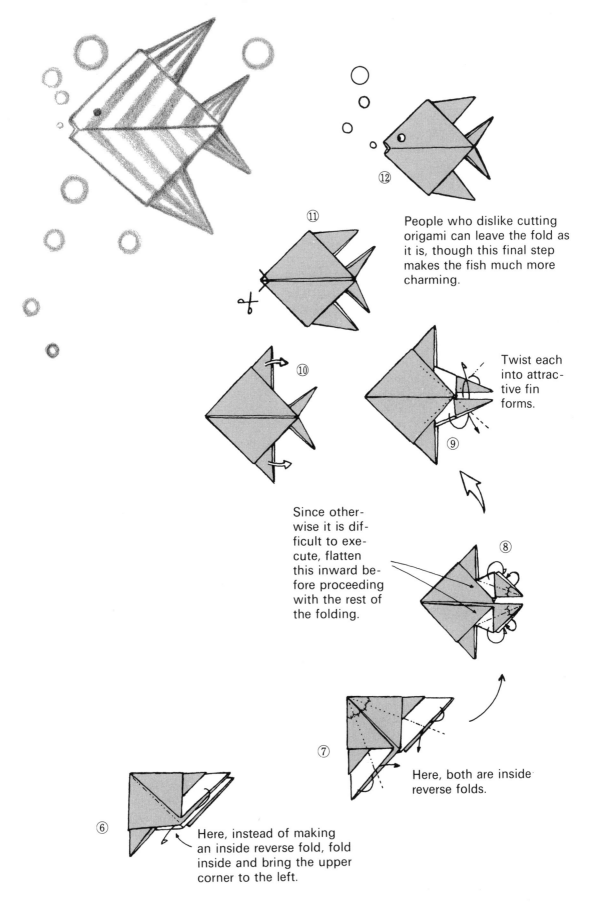

⑫

⑪

People who dislike cutting origami can leave the fold as it is, though this final step makes the fish much more charming.

⑩

Twist each into attractive fin forms.

⑨

Since otherwise it is difficult to execute, flatten this inward before proceeding with the rest of the folding.

⑧

⑦

Here, both are inside reverse folds.

⑥

Here, instead of making an inside reverse fold, fold inside and bring the upper corner to the left.

Hermit Crab

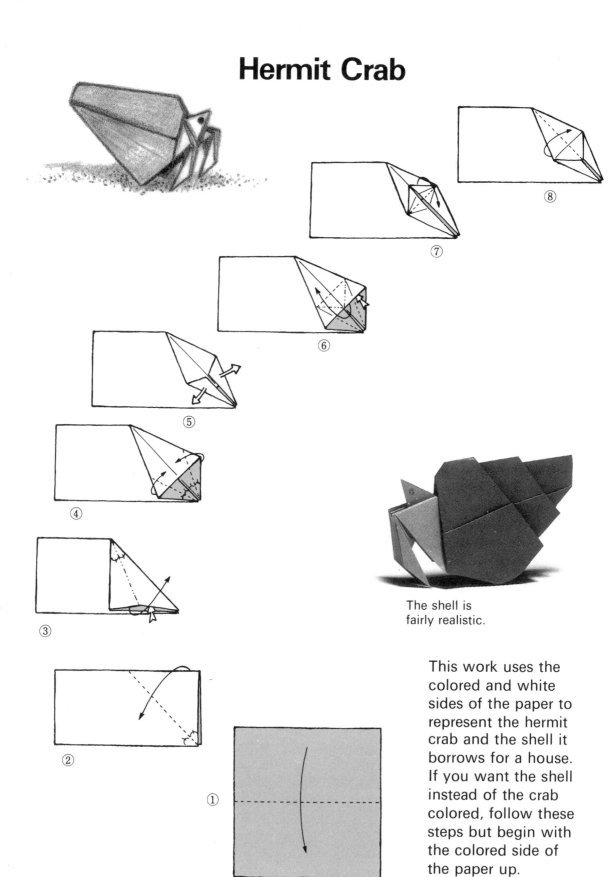

The shell is
fairly realistic.

This work uses the
colored and white
sides of the paper to
represent the hermit
crab and the shell it
borrows for a house.
If you want the shell
instead of the crab
colored, follow these
steps but begin with
the colored side of
the paper up.

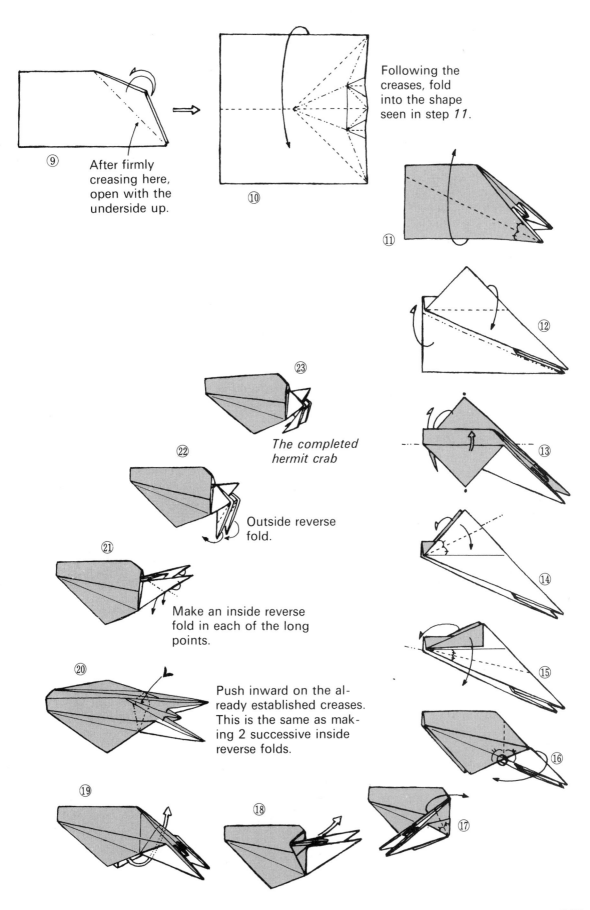

⑨ After firmly creasing here, open with the underside up.

Following the creases, fold into the shape seen in step *11*.

⑩

⑪

⑫

⑬

⑭

⑮

⑯

⑰

⑱

⑲

Push inward on the already established creases. This is the same as making 2 successive inside reverse folds.

⑳

Make an inside reverse fold in each of the long points.

㉑

Outside reverse fold.

㉒

㉓

The completed hermit crab

Univalve Shell

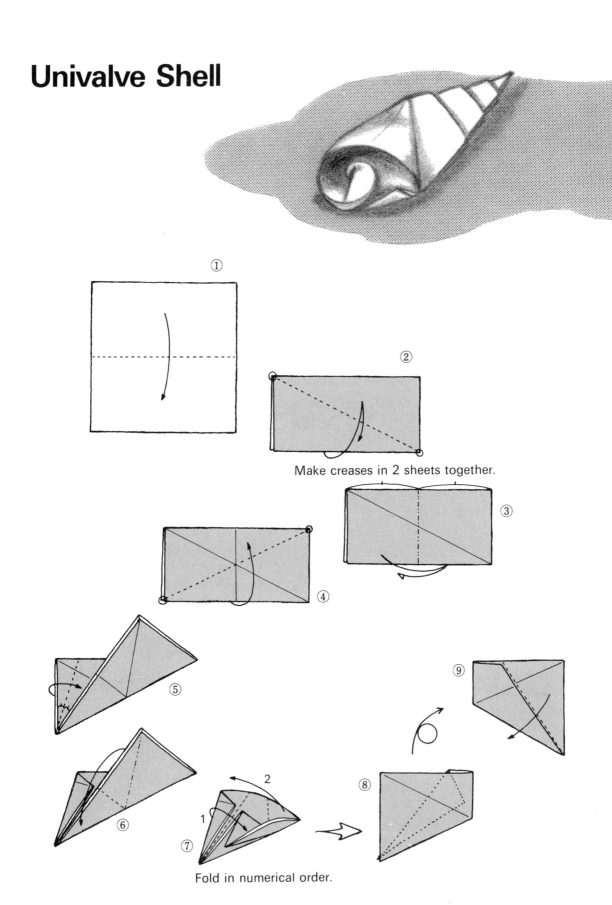

①

②

Make creases in 2 sheets together.

③

④

⑤

⑥

⑦

1 2

⑧

⑨

Fold in numerical order.

268

By the sea, by the sea, by the beautiful sea

A different univalve shell may be found on p. 216. The starfish is the star form shown on p. 100.

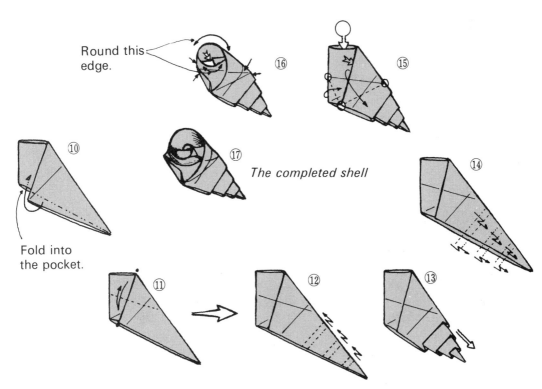

Round this edge.

⑯

⑮

⑩

⑰ *The completed shell*

Fold into the pocket.

⑭

⑪

⑫

⑬

Bivalve Shell

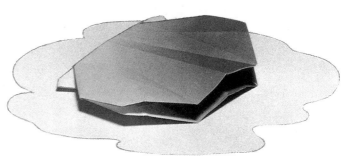

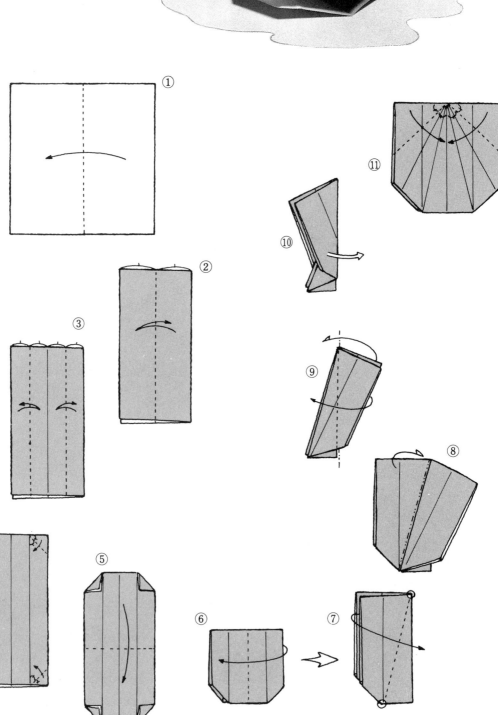

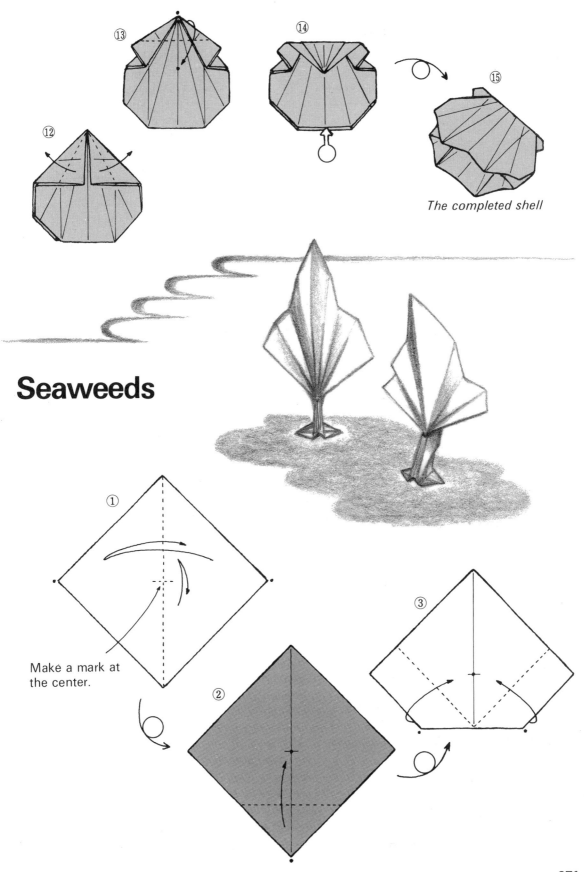

⑬

⑭

⑫

⑮

The completed shell

Seaweeds

① Make a mark at the center.

②

③

Sea Anemones

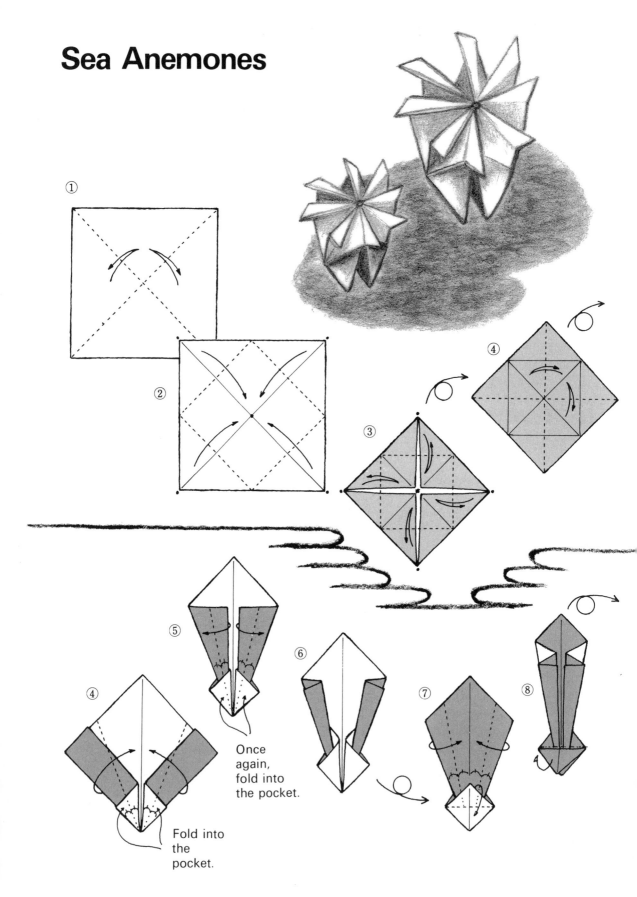

①

②

③

④

④

⑤

⑥

⑦

⑧

Fold into the pocket.

Once again, fold into the pocket.

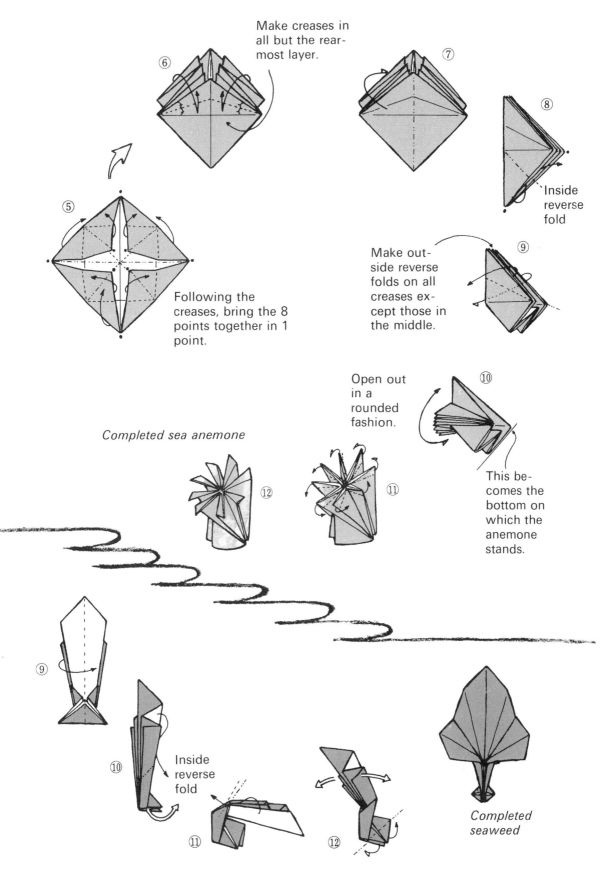

Make creases in
all but the rear-
most layer.

⑥

⑦

⑧

Inside
reverse
fold

⑤

Following the
creases, bring the 8
points together in 1
point.

Make out-
side reverse
folds on all
creases ex-
cept those in
the middle.

⑨

Open out
in a
rounded
fashion.

⑩

This be-
comes the
bottom on
which the
anemone
stands.

Completed sea anemone

⑫

⑪

⑨

⑩

Inside
reverse
fold

⑪

⑫

*Completed
seaweed*

273

Blintz fold

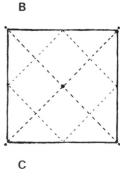

A

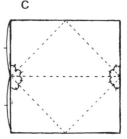

B

Bringing the four corners of a square piece of paper together in the center in the way shown in *A* is a characteristic origami technique producing what is called the blintz fold (the *zabuton*, or cushion, fold in Japanese). In making this essential, basic form, most people use the method shown in *B*; that is, they first establish the center of the paper by folding two diagonal lines. If the paper is a reasonably accurately square, however, it may be produced —as shown in *C*—by a single line bisecting one side.

C

The *C* method is not necessarily superior to the *B* method. But I hope you will remember that there is usually more than one way to produce a desired form. The best method is the one that produces the desired effect in the finished work.

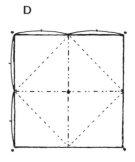

D

Incidentally, a reexamination of the *masu* (measuring-box) fold on pp. 106–107, in Chapter 2, should make it apparent that it is in the form shown in *D*. Although this proposal, made by Hisashi Abè, seems insignificant, it actually represents a tremendous improvement.

The perfectly fitting lid

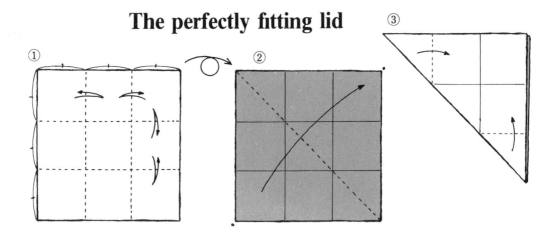

① ② ③

To fold a traditional measuring-box and lid that fit perfectly, the lengths of *a* and *b* may be calculated as follows:

$$a = 4/3 = 1.333\cdots\cdots\cdots$$
$$b = \sqrt{2} = 1.41421\cdots\cdots\cdots$$

Although both *a* and *b* are endlessly repeating numbers, the slight difference existing between them apparently accounts for the fit.

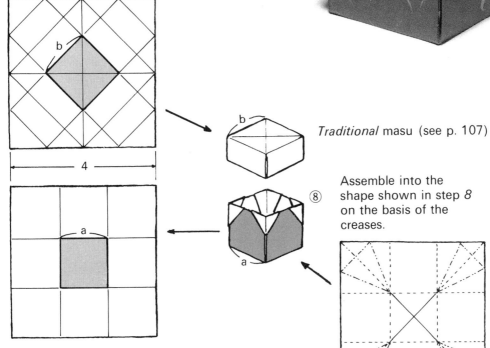

Traditional masu (see p. 107)

⑧ Assemble into the shape shown in step *8* on the basis of the creases.

⑦

From this point, fold again as in steps *3–5*.

④

⑤

⑥

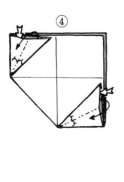

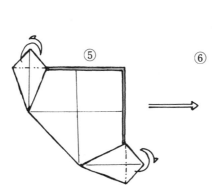

Improvements on Traditional Works

Nest
of boxes

I have already shown one modern improvement in a traditional work by demonstrating how the *masu* can be produced by making mountain folds (seen from the underside) that bisect and run along the sides of the paper. Another such improvement is this way of folding the old-fashioned nest of boxes all from one size of paper, instead of using various sizes as is done in the traditional version.

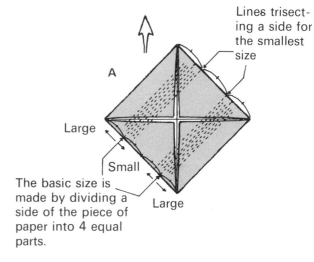

A

Lines trisecting a side for the smallest size

Large

Small

The basic size is made by dividing a side of the piece of paper into 4 equal parts.

Large

Decorative Lid

The grip is the decoration added to this *masu* lid.

①

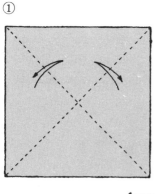

②

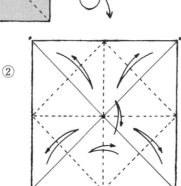

③

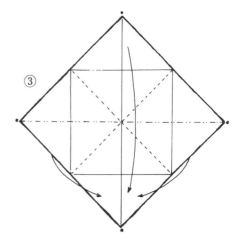

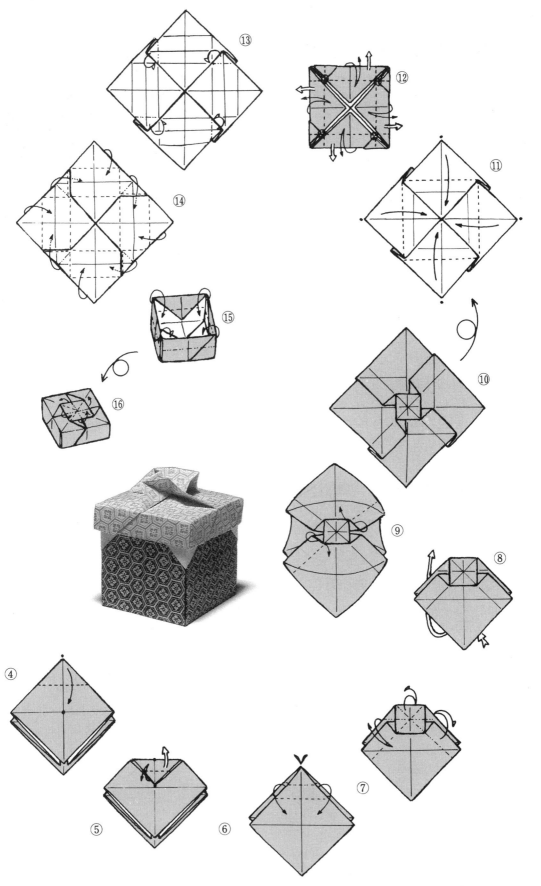

Cube Box

After having considered the traditional *masu* from various angles, I came up with this inverted version of the one on the preceding page. With this, I shall conclude my series illustrating the Great Development of the *Masu*.

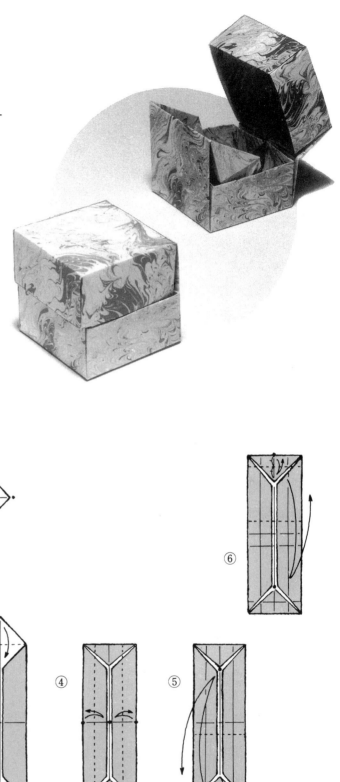

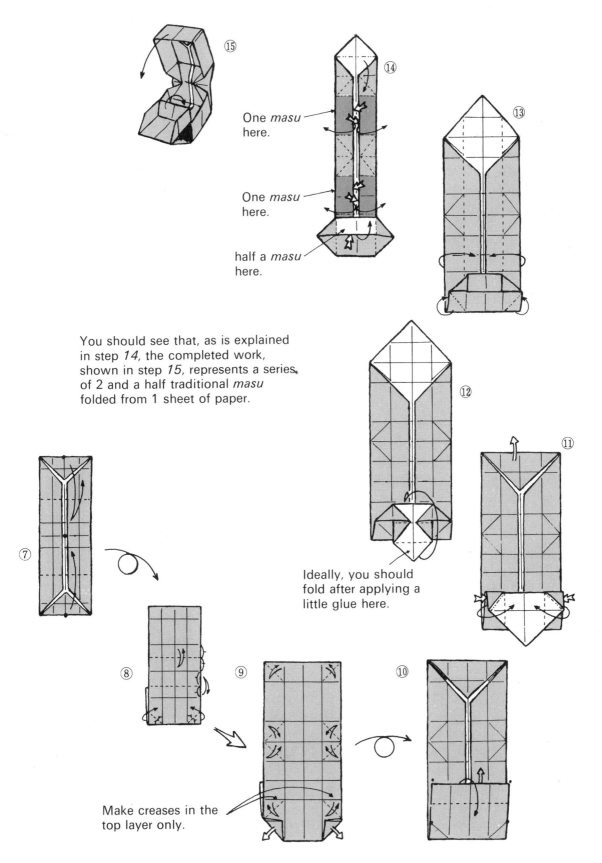

⑮

⑭

One *masu* here.

One *masu* here.

half a *masu* here.

⑬

You should see that, as is explained in step *14*, the completed work, shown in step *15*, represents a series of 2 and a half traditional *masu* folded from 1 sheet of paper.

⑫

⑪

Ideally, you should fold after applying a little glue here.

⑦

⑧

⑨

⑩

Make creases in the top layer only.

Four-dimensional (?) Box

First make the body and lid of the box by producing two *masu* of a fairly large size. Next, from twenty or twenty-four sheets of paper about one centimeter smaller to a side than the ones used in making the *masu*, make ten or twelve of the crushed cubes shown here. Put them in the box. The photograph should show the meaning of the title and the fun that can be had with this origami work.

Use 2 sheets of paper for each cube.

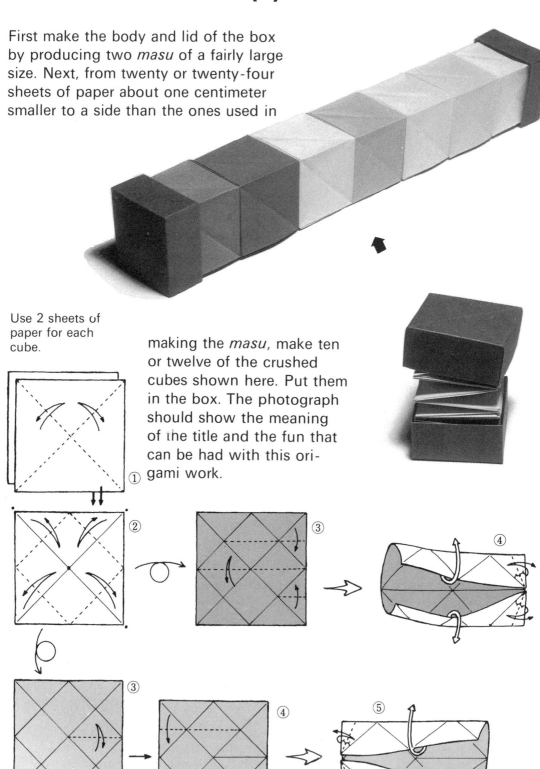

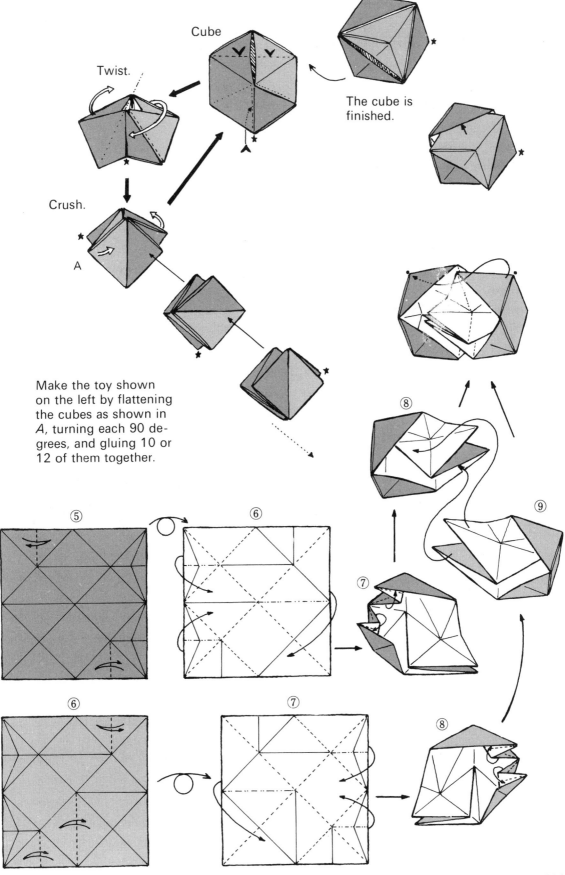

Cube

Twist.

The cube is finished.

Crush.

A

Make the toy shown on the left by flattening the cubes as shown in A, turning each 90 degrees, and gluing 10 or 12 of them together.

⑤

⑥

⑥

⑦

⑦

⑧

⑧

⑨

281

Book (Paperback)

The idea of making a book using origami techniques is fascinating. The one presented here in photographs is my eclectic paperback version of the excellent hard-cover books produced by Martin Wall and David Brill. In theory, this version can be used to produce books with many more pages. Actually, however, the practical limit is sixteen pages with front and back covers. On pp. 284–285 is a twelve-page, hard-cover version made with compound techniques in which a separate piece of paper is used for the cover.

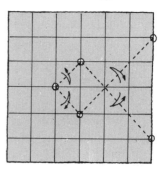

Martin Wall's easy 4-page book

16-page paperback

10-page paperback

David Brill's excellent 10-page book

10-page book

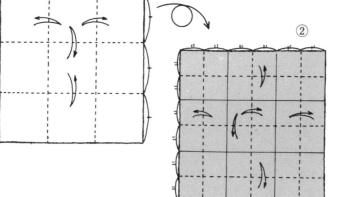

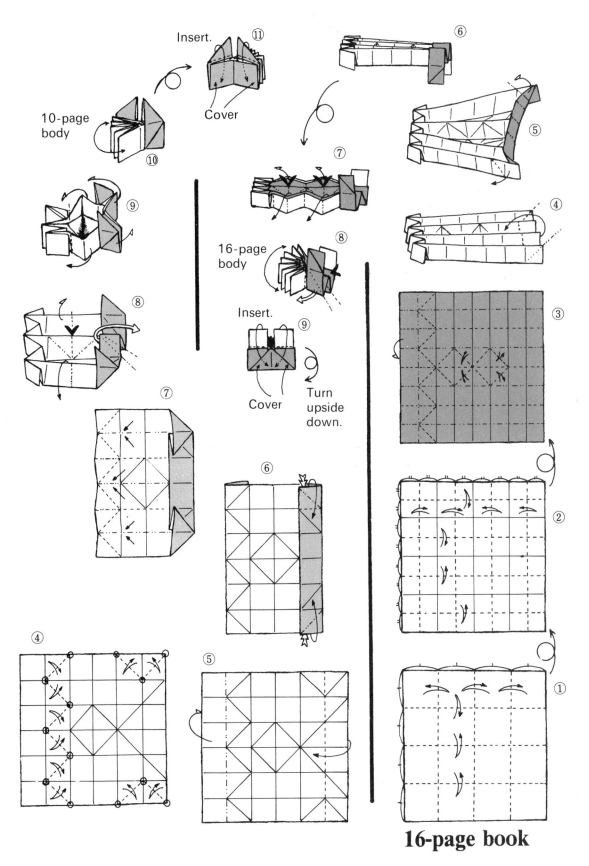

Insert.

⑪

⑥

Cover

10-page
body

⑩

⑤

⑨

④

16-page
body

⑦

⑧

⑧

Insert.

⑨

④

Cover

Turn
upside
down.

⑦

③

⑥

②

④

⑤

①

16-page book

Hard-cover Book with Case

This is easier to fold than the paperback on the preceding pages.

Minibook

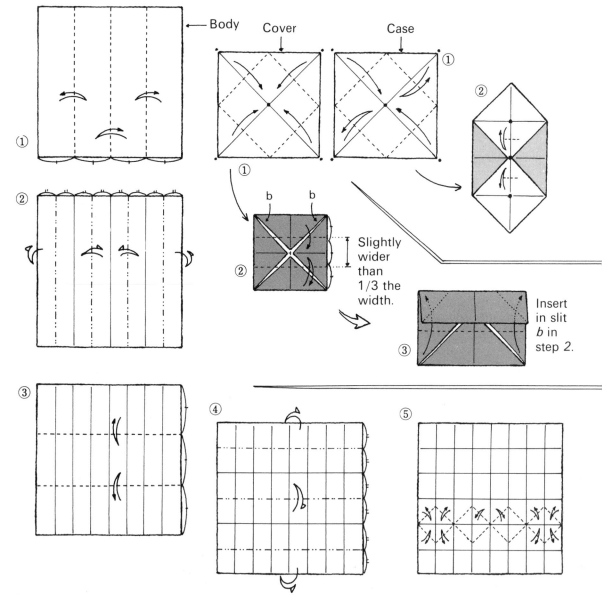

Body ← ① ②

Cover ①

Case ①

②

b b

② Slightly wider than 1/3 the width.

③ Insert in slit *b* in step *2*.

③

④

⑤

284

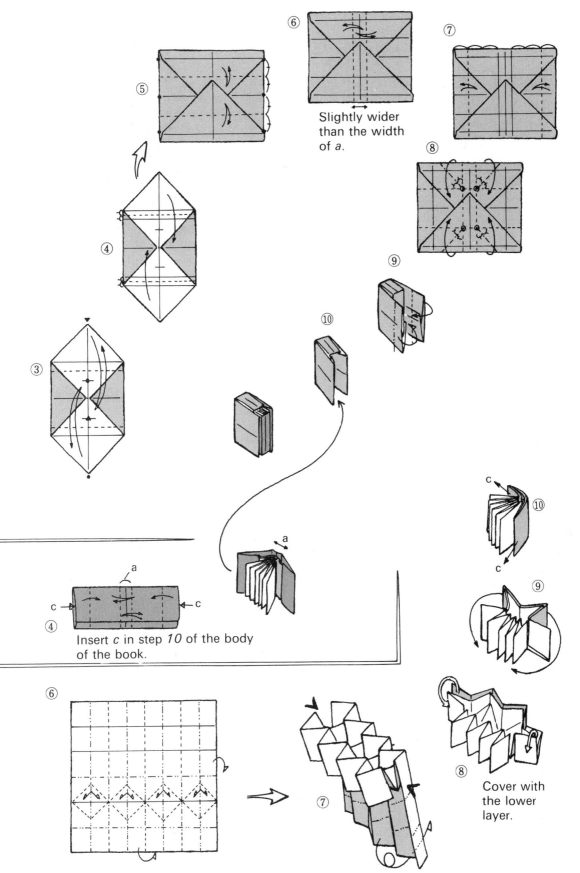

⑥ Slightly wider than the width of *a*.

Insert *c* in step *10* of the body of the book.

⑧ Cover with the lower layer.

285

Bookcase

Now that you have some books,
you need a bookcase to keep them
in. As the diagrams make clear,
both books and case have been
produced at the very limits of
ingenuity and therefore represent a
sample of the fusion of theory and
representation. Paperback books
made from paper one-fourth the
size of that used for the case will
be a perfect fit.

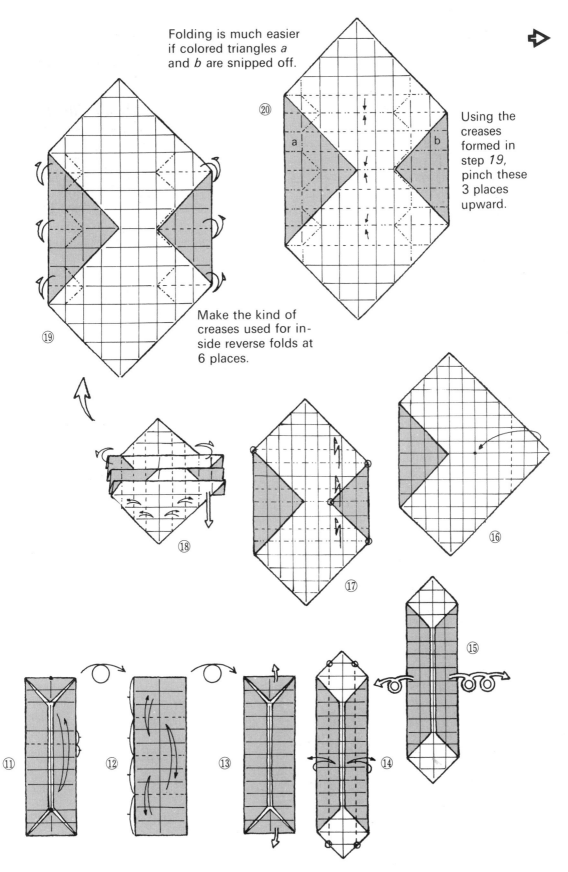

Folding is much easier if colored triangles *a* and *b* are snipped off.

Using the creases formed in step *19*, pinch these 3 places upward.

Make the kind of creases used for inside reverse folds at 6 places.

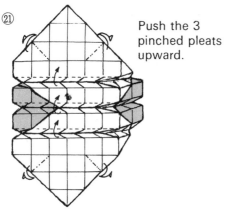

㉑ Push the 3 pinched pleats upward.

Making enough books to fill this case is a big task.

For a perfect match, make 10-page paperback books (p. 282) from paper 1/4 the size of the paper used to make the bookcase.

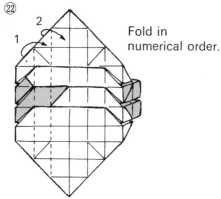

㉒ Fold in numerical order.

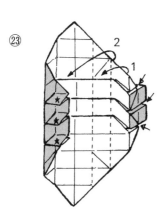

㉓ Insert pleats into the slots marked with arrows.

㉖

The finished bookcase will be sturdier if you put a very small dab of glue on the points marked ★.

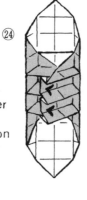

㉔

㉕

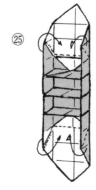

Chair and Sofa

①

It is time to amplify the interior decor by adding chairs, a sofa, and a coffee table to the bookcase and books. Since the coffee table is merely the traditional raised tray (*ozen*) made from rectangular paper (side proportion of 1:2), I have included no diagrammatic explanation. Ultimately a human figure will be added to the room. Paper-size ratios are given later.

② Do no more than make a mark.

③

④

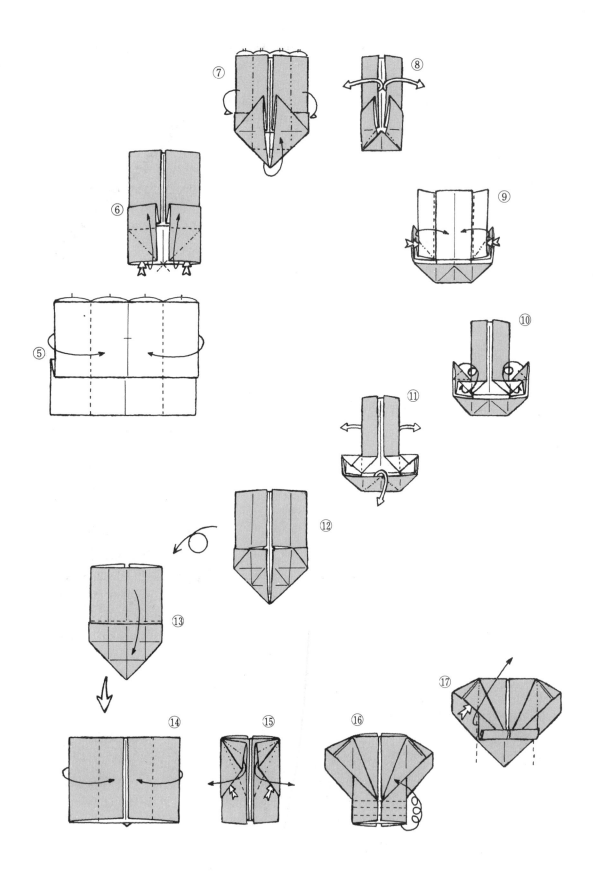

Furnishings made from traditional folds

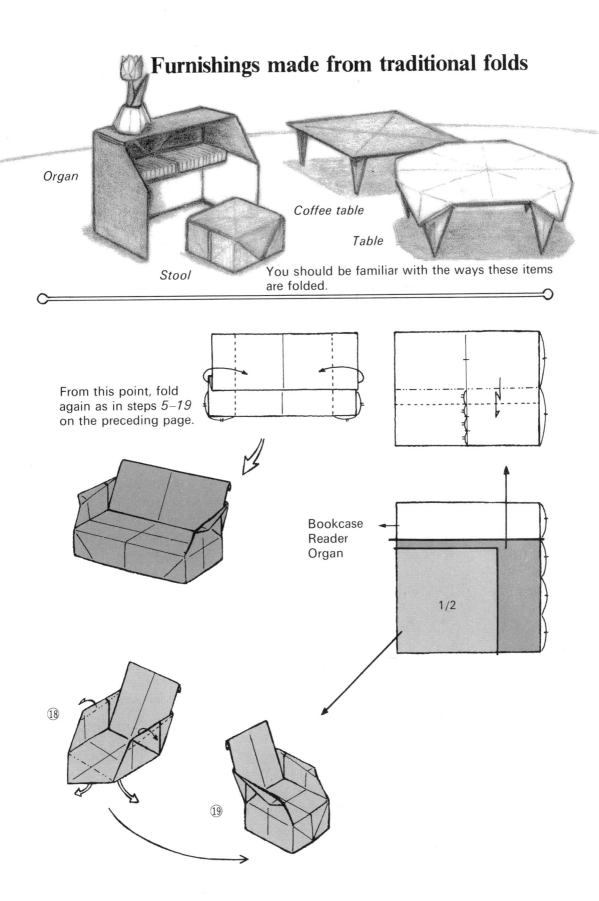

Organ

Coffee table

Table

Stool

You should be familiar with the ways these items are folded.

From this point, fold again as in steps *5–19* on the preceding page.

Bookcase
Reader
Organ

1/2

⑱

⑲

The Reader

The folding method developed by the famous American origamian Neal Elias is the basis for this work.

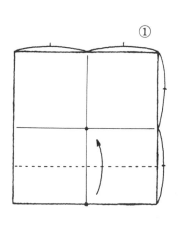

① ②

③

Make 4 inside reverse folds to create elbows and knees.

⑱

c

a b

④

c ⟵ ⟶ d

⑤

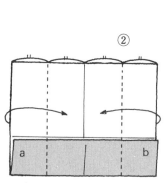

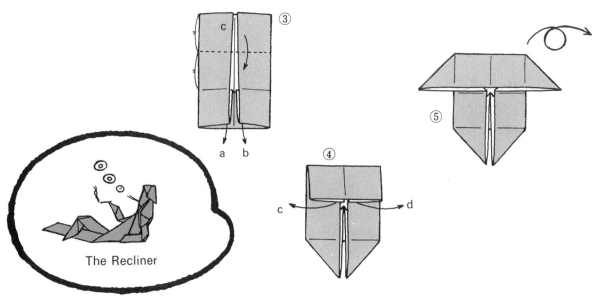

The Recliner

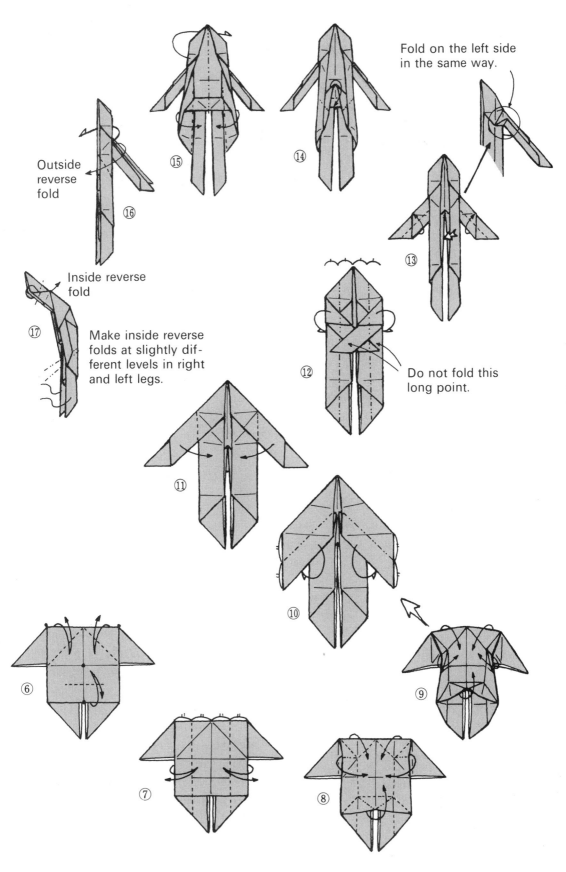

Fold on the left side
in the same way.

Outside
reverse
fold

⑯

⑮

⑭

⑬

Inside reverse
fold

⑰

Make inside reverse
folds at slightly dif-
ferent levels in right
and left legs.

⑫

Do not fold this
long point.

⑪

⑩

⑥

⑨

⑦

⑧

Tricorn Hat and Tree I

This Tricorn Hat and Tree I are made from the equilateral triangle the sixty-degree fold, shown on p. 71. Made from a square of newspaper fifty-five centimeters to a side, the hat will fit a child's head.

Made from a square of newspaper taken as shown below, the hat will fit a child.

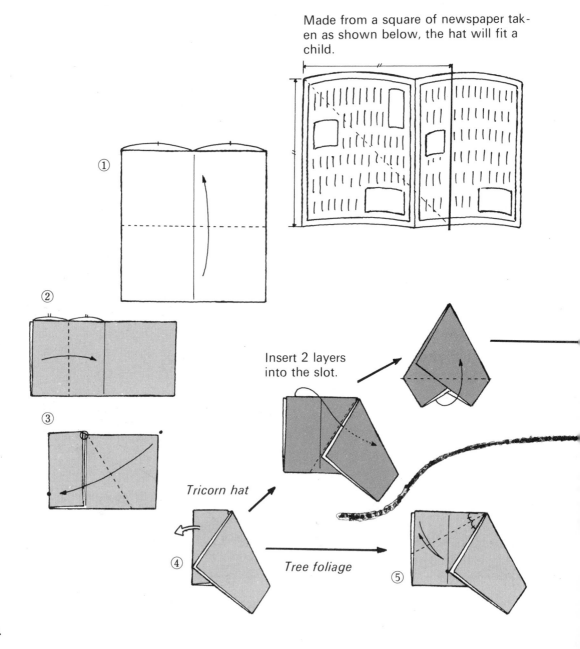

Insert 2 layers into the slot.

Tricorn hat

④

Tree foliage

⑤

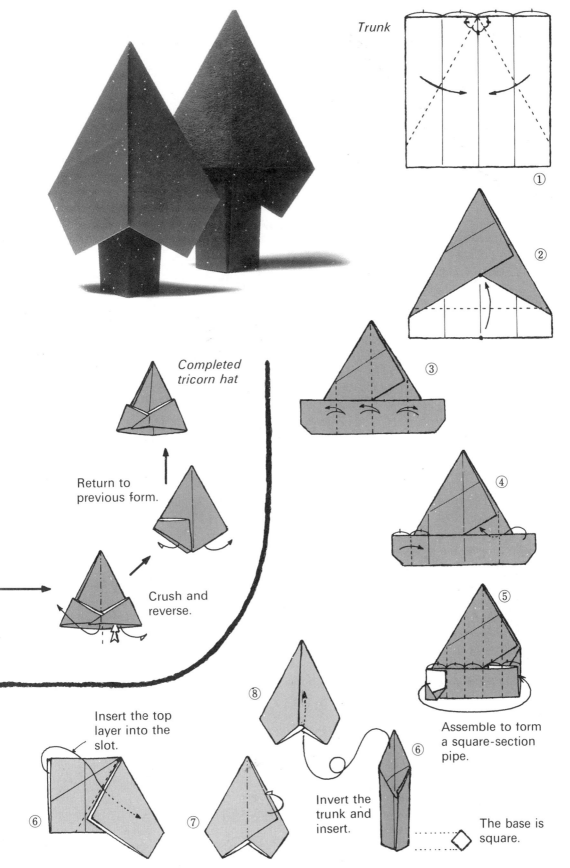

Trunk

①

②

③

Completed
tricorn hat

Return to
previous form.

Crush and
reverse.

④

⑤

Assemble to form
a square-section
pipe.

⑧

Insert the top
layer into the
slot.

Invert the
trunk and
insert.

⑥

The base is
square.

⑥

⑦

Trees II and III

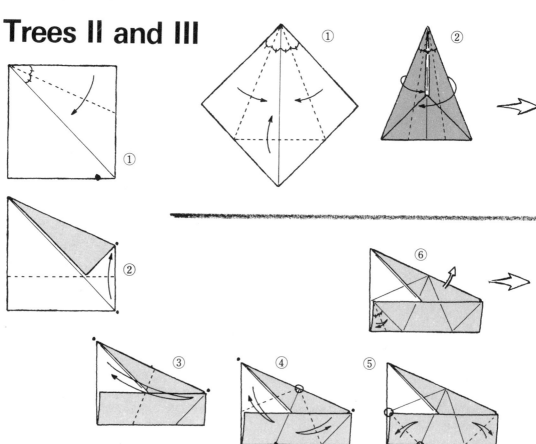

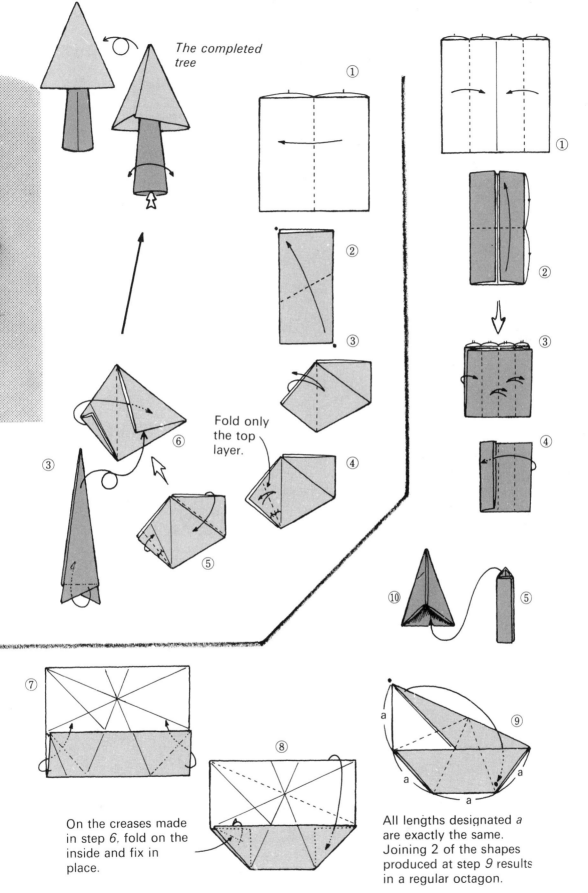

The completed tree

① ② ③

Fold only the top layer.

④ ⑤ ⑥

On the creases made in step *6*, fold on the inside and fix in place.

All lengths designated *a* are exactly the same. Joining 2 of the shapes produced at step *9* results in a regular octagon.

① ② ③ ④ ⑤ ⑩

For the Sake of the Numbers

Amost all of the trees in the preceding series have been
geometrical forms. I include this
fourth solely because the area in
step *9* of the foliage is half that
of the original piece of paper.
Making it from four sheets of
paper produces a much larger
tree.

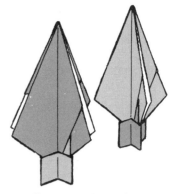

Completed tree IV

Tree IV

Trunk

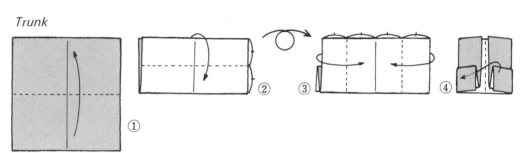

Foliage

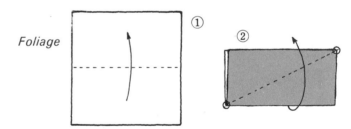

Tree V

Trunk

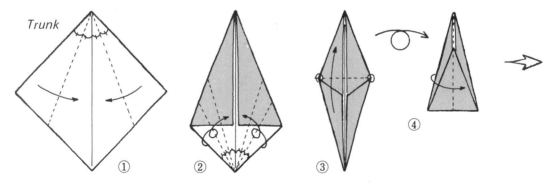

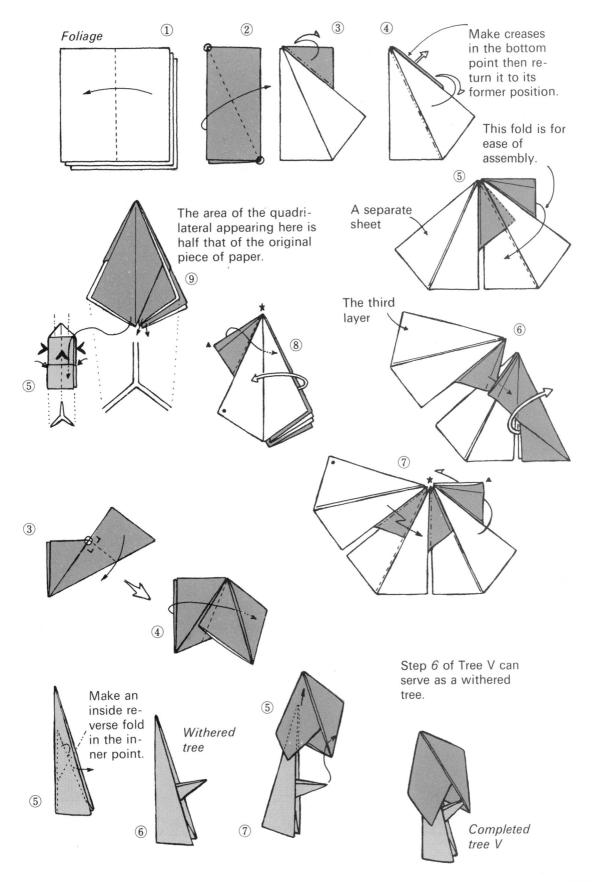

Foliage ①

② ③ ④

Make creases in the bottom point then return it to its former position.

This fold is for ease of assembly.

⑤

A separate sheet

The area of the quadrilateral appearing here is half that of the original piece of paper.

⑨

The third layer

⑥

⑤

⑧

⑦

③

④

Step *6* of Tree V can serve as a withered tree.

Make an inside reverse fold in the inner point.

⑤

Withered tree

⑥

⑤

⑦

Completed tree V

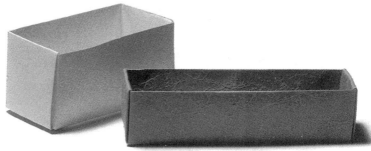

Long rectangular box

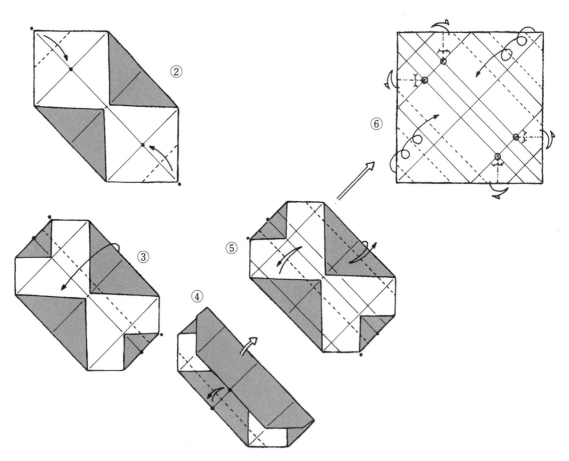

Try devising lids by using the folding methods employed in these two different kinds of boxes. The method found in the traditional nest of boxes (p. 276) will work well.

Rectangular box

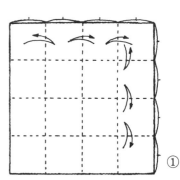

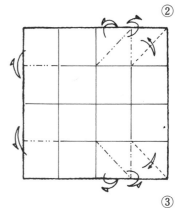

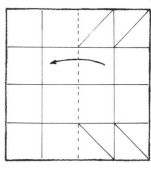

With a peaked roof, this rectangular box produces a houselike appearance. But it looks more like a tool shed or a barn than a dwelling for humans. Fine houses with sloping roofs are forthcoming in later pages.

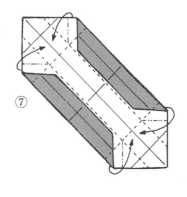

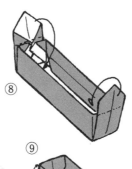

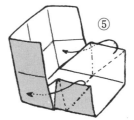

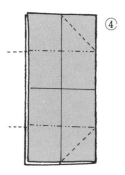

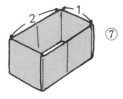

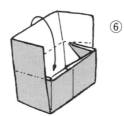

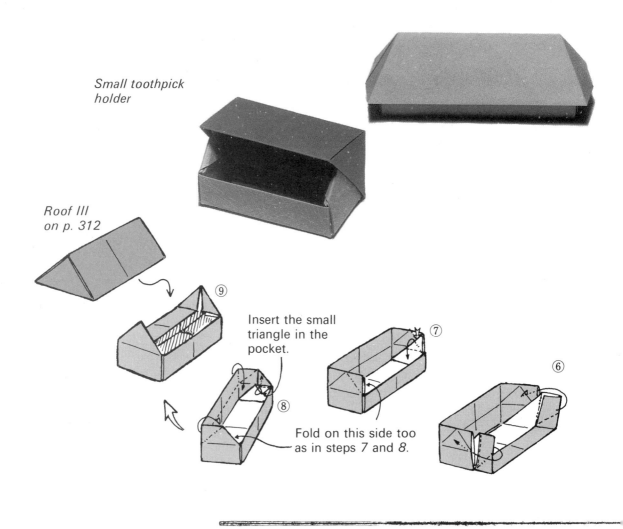

Small toothpick holder

Roof III on p. 312

⑨

Insert the small triangle in the pocket.

⑦

⑥

⑧

Fold on this side too as in steps 7 and 8.

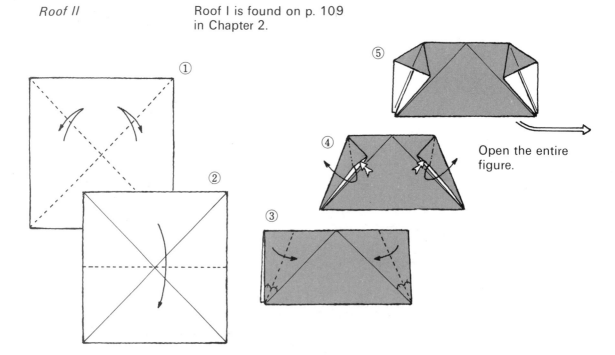

Roof II

Roof I is found on p. 109 in Chapter 2.

⑤

①

②

④

Open the entire figure.

③

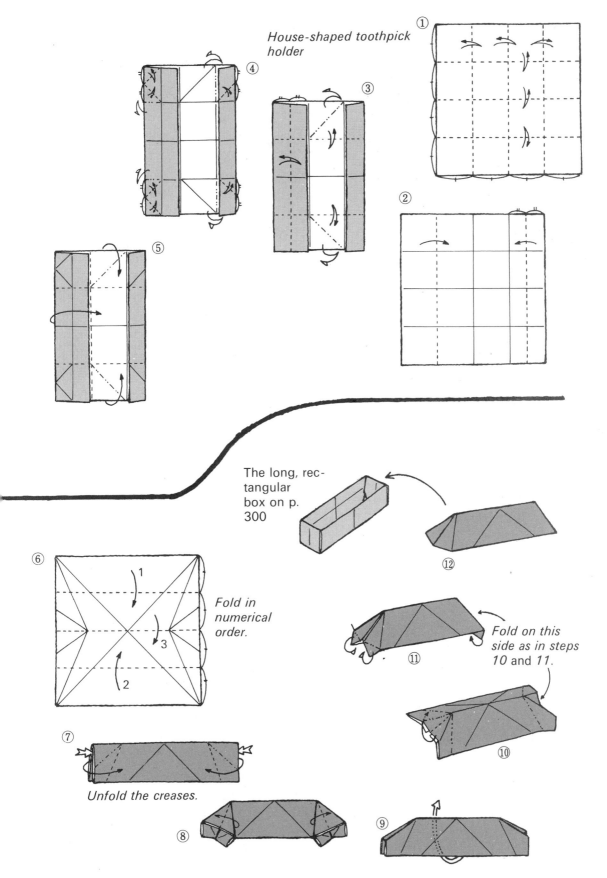

House-shaped toothpick
holder

The long, rec-
tangular
box on p.
300

Fold in
numerical
order.

Unfold the creases.

Fold on this
side as in steps
10 and *11*.

Friedrich Froebel

The German educator and originator of the kindergarten system Friedrich Froebel (1782–1852) was the first person to value origami highly as educational material. The house on the next page is one of the origami used in his times; the nature of many of the works he employed has recently been revealed. The house presented here is a sturdier, improved version.

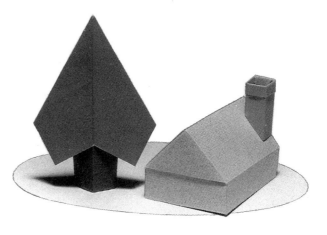

House   ## Chimney

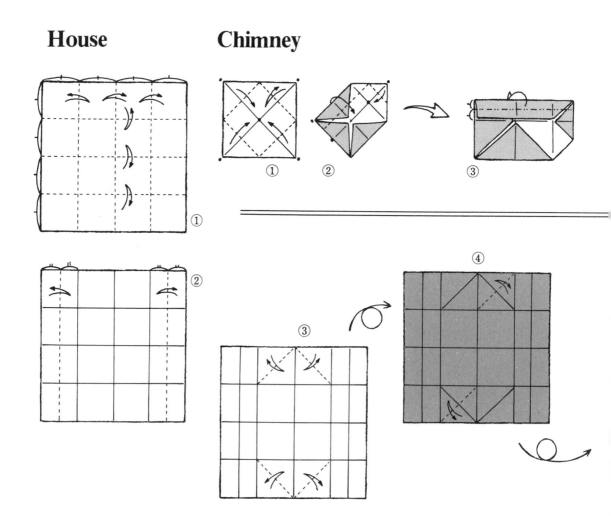

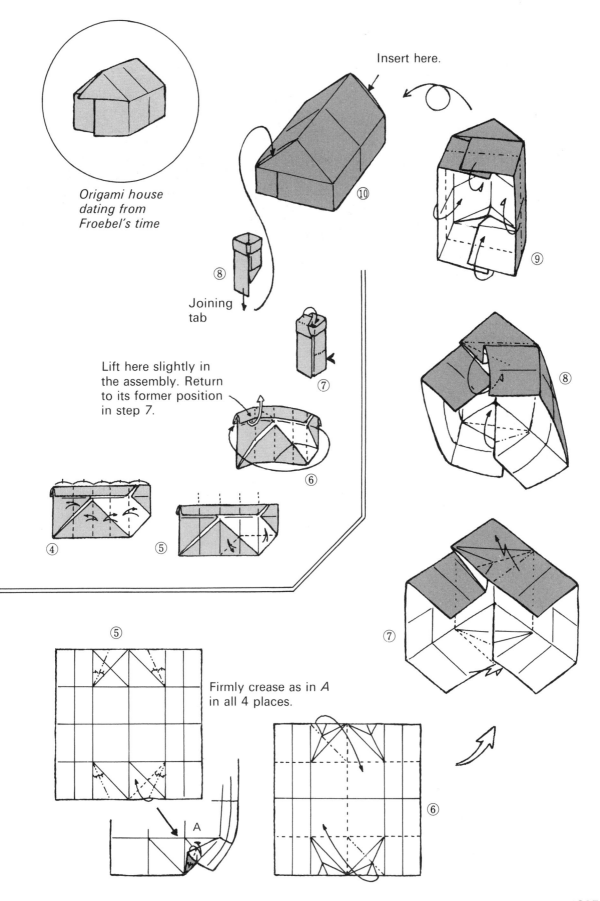

Origami house dating from Froebel's time

Insert here.

⑩

⑧

Joining tab

Lift here slightly in the assembly. Return to its former position in step 7.

⑦

⑥

④

⑤

⑨

⑧

⑦

⑤

Firmly crease as in A in all 4 places.

A

⑥

Church

The church is com-
posed of five different
forms made from five
sheets of paper.

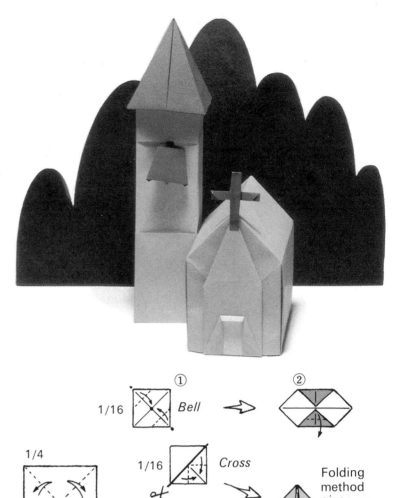

Chapel

Directions for
folding given on
pp. 308–309

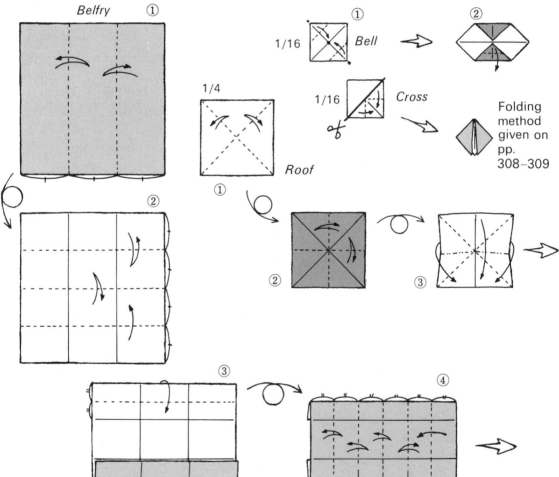

Belfry ①

②

③

Roof
①

1/4

②

③

Bell
1/16 ①

②

Cross
1/16

Folding
method
given on
pp.
308–309

④

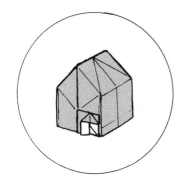

Learning from others

As I said, I made a revised version of the house (p. 305) from Froebel's time, but I was never completely satisfied with it. One day, after adding a belfry and converting it to a church, I showed it to my small daughter Minako, who said, "But church doors are always in the middle." And right she was. I revised the origami into the form shown on the next page.

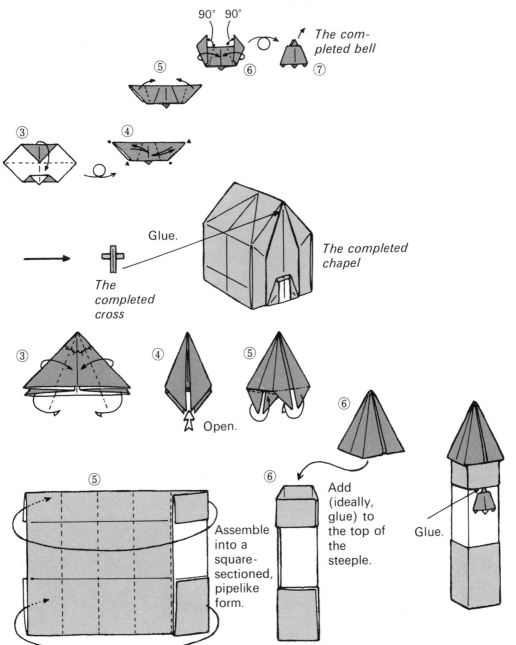

90° 90°

⑤ ⑥ ⑦ The completed bell

③ ④

③ ④ ⑤ Open.

The completed cross

Glue.

The completed chapel

⑤ Assemble into a square-sectioned, pipelike form.

⑥ Add (ideally, glue) to the top of the steeple.

Glue.

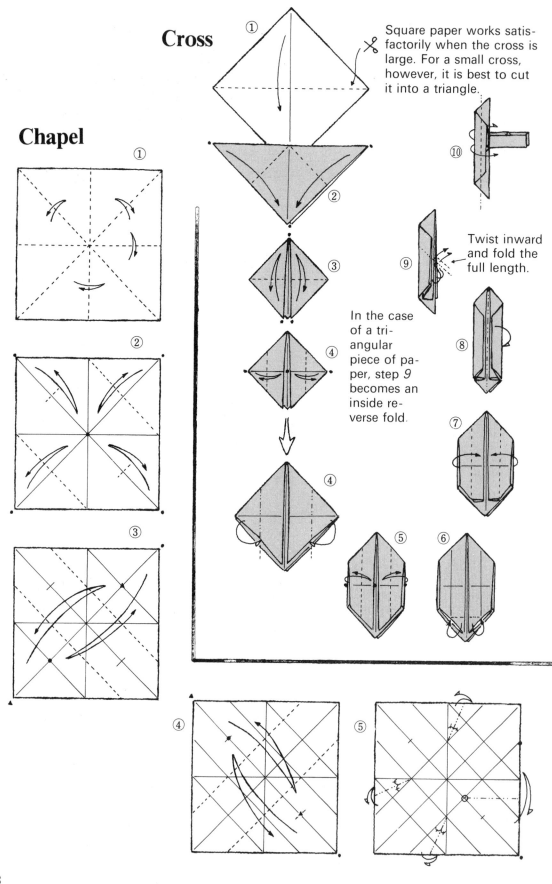

Cross

Chapel

Square paper works satisfactorily when the cross is large. For a small cross, however, it is best to cut it into a triangle.

In the case of a triangular piece of paper, step 9 becomes an inside reverse fold.

Twist inward and fold the full length.

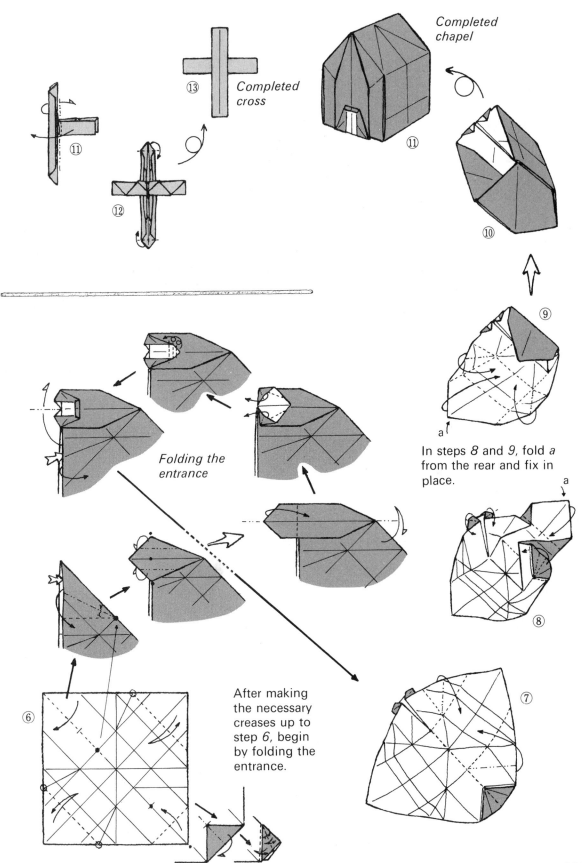

⑬ Completed cross

⑪

⑫

Completed chapel

⑪

⑩

⑨

In steps *8* and *9*, fold *a* from the rear and fix in place.

a

⑧

a

⑦

Folding the entrance

After making the necessary creases up to step *6*, begin by folding the entrance.

⑥

I am very proud
of the peaked
roof, which rep-
resents very
high-class de-
sign. The reason
why shall appear
hereafter.

Tree VI

The foliage is
made from the
equilateral triangle
on p. 202 in
Chapter 5.

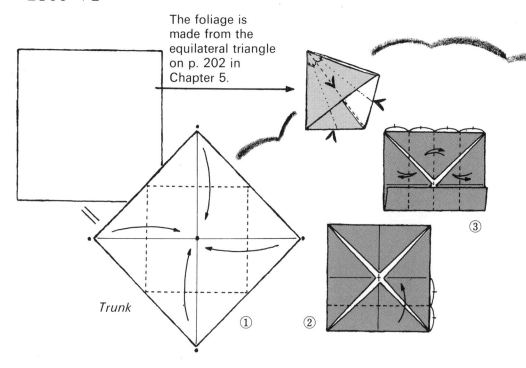

Trunk

①　②　③

Why the design is high-class?
House (rectangular box)

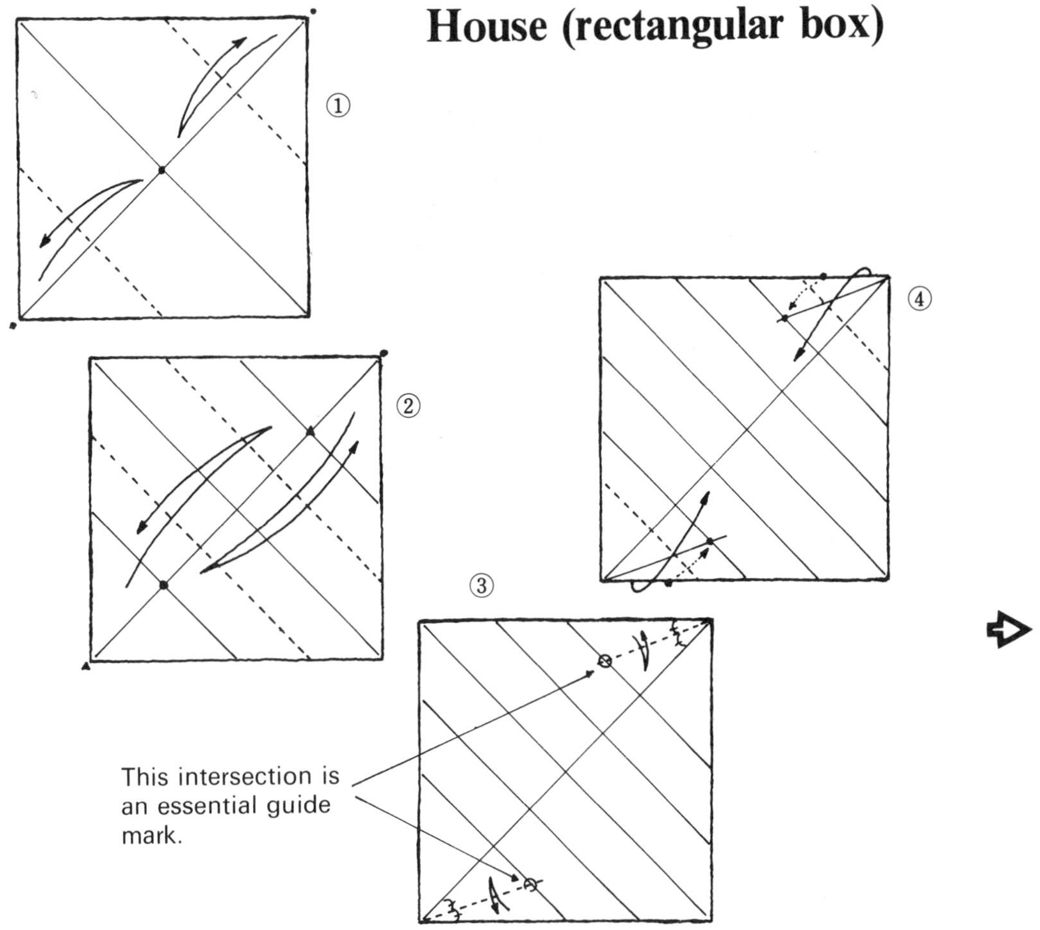

①

②

③

This intersection is
an essential guide
mark.

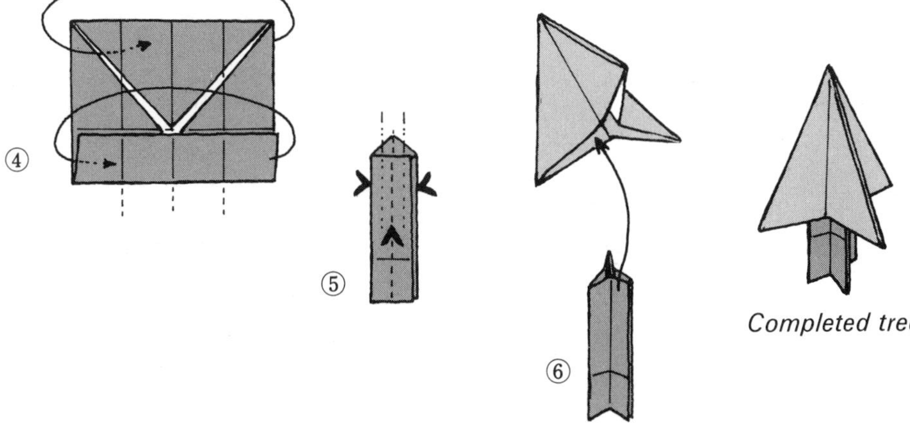

④

④

⑤

⑥

Completed tree

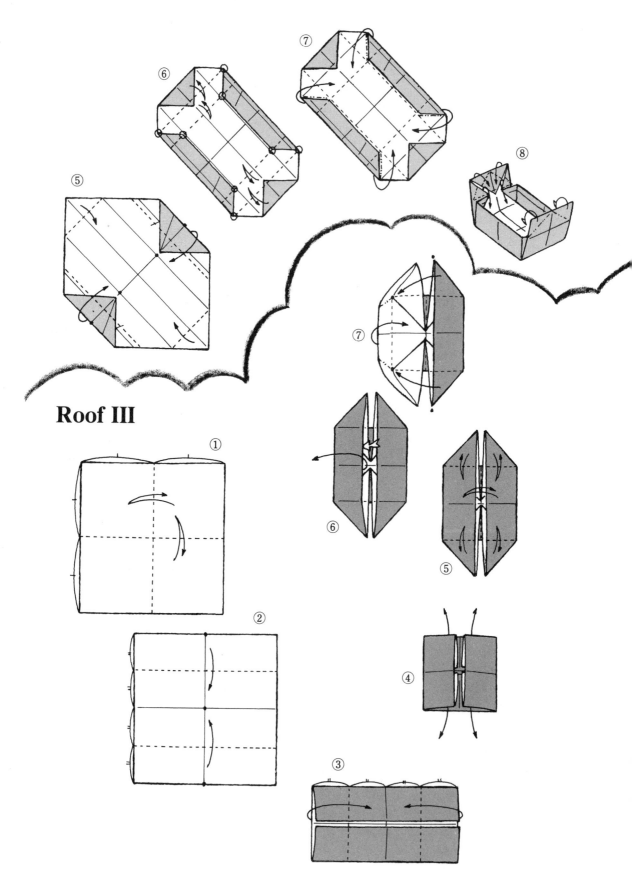

Roof III

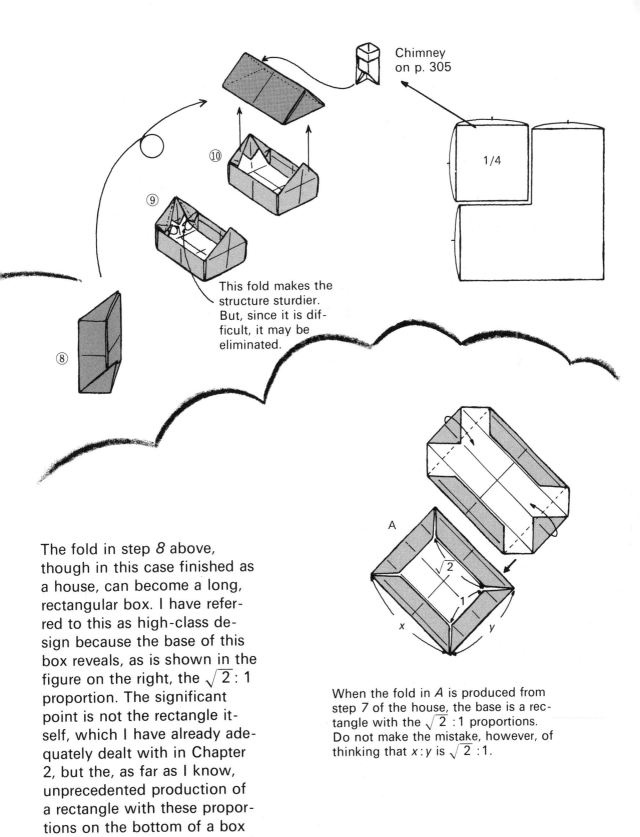

Chimney on p. 305

1/4

⑩

⑨

This fold makes the structure sturdier. But, since it is difficult, it may be eliminated.

⑧

A

$\sqrt{2}$

1

x

y

The fold in step *8* above, though in this case finished as a house, can become a long, rectangular box. I have referred to this as high-class design because the base of this box reveals, as is shown in the figure on the right, the $\sqrt{2}:1$ proportion. The significant point is not the rectangle itself, which I have already adequately dealt with in Chapter 2, but the, as far as I know, unprecedented production of a rectangle with these proportions on the bottom of a box form.

When the fold in *A* is produced from step *7* of the house, the base is a rectangle with the $\sqrt{2}:1$ proportions. Do not make the mistake, however, of thinking that $x:y$ is $\sqrt{2}:1$.

Which House Is More Spacious?

The two houses in the photograph are both made from four pieces of paper of the same size. One is produced according to the diagrams on pp. 311–313; the other is house *A* made in the fashion shown below. A glance would seem to suggest to any eye that the house on the left (House *A*) is larger. In fact, however, they both have exactly the same floor area.

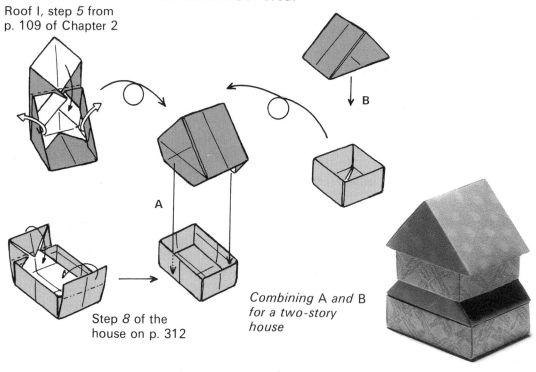

Roof I, step *5* from p. 109 of Chapter 2

A

B

Step *8* of the house on p. 312

Combining A *and* B *for a two-story house*

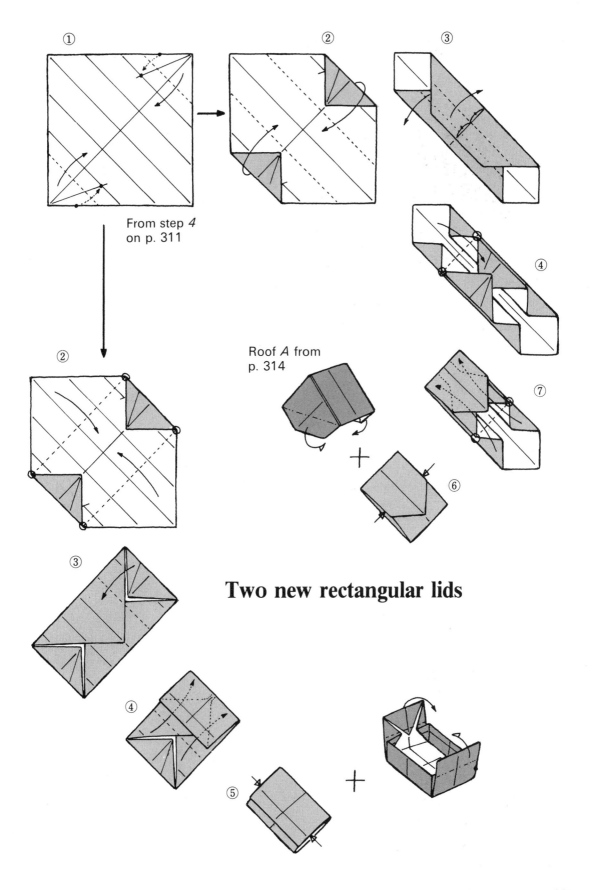

① ② ③

From step *4*
on p. 311

④

②

Roof *A* from
p. 314

⑦

⑥

③

Two new rectangular lids

④

⑤

+

Our Town

Why not
make some
houses for
use on
collage-type
pictures?

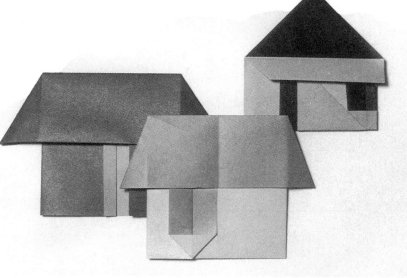

House A
with a window

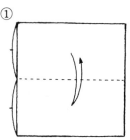
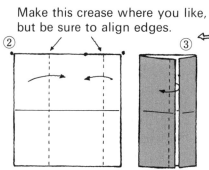
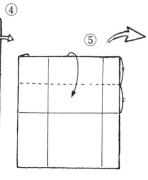

① ② ③ ④

House B with
an entrance

Make this crease where you like,
but be sure to align edges.

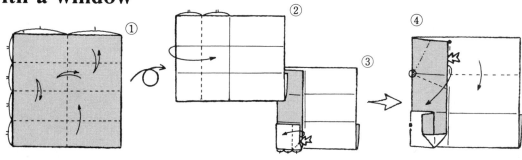

① ② ③ ④ ⑤

House C with a window
and an entrance

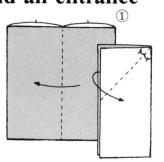
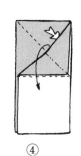
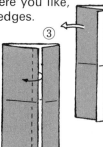
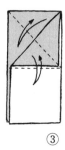
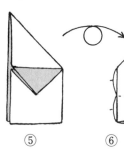

① ② ③ ④ ⑤ ⑥

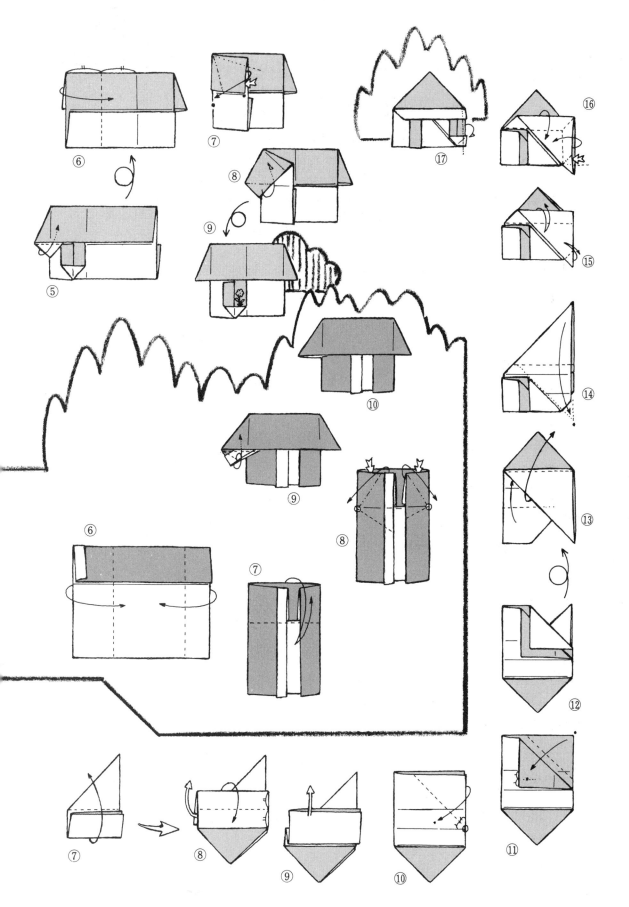

317

Fascinating Origami Aircraft

Origami aircraft—strictly speaking, gliders—are tremendously entertaining. Among them, the ones designed by Eiji Nakamura are especially well known. Mr. Nakamura agrees with the accepted idea that, in terms of gliding performance, rectangular sheets of paper are better than square ones because of their pronounced directionality.

Nonetheless, though my attitude may seem to contradict the ideals I have expressed throughout this book, I stubbornly prefer to go on using square paper as I make origami gliders for indoor pleasure. I am confident of the merit of the following two gliders.

Hang-glider I

Grain is beside the point when the paper is used in this way.

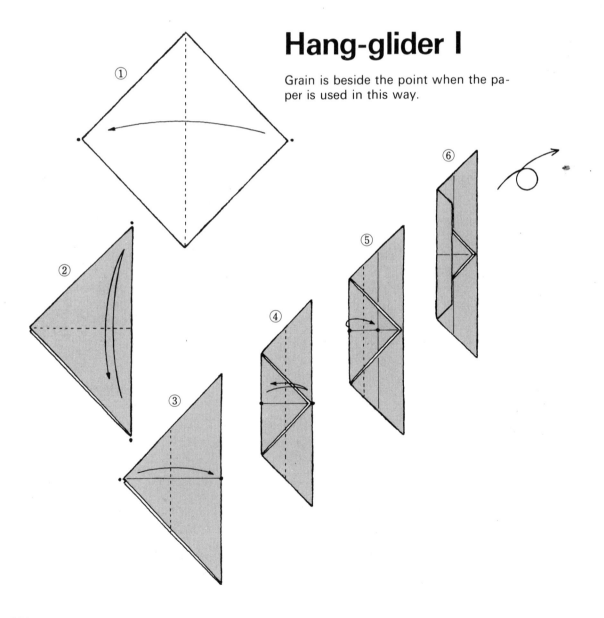

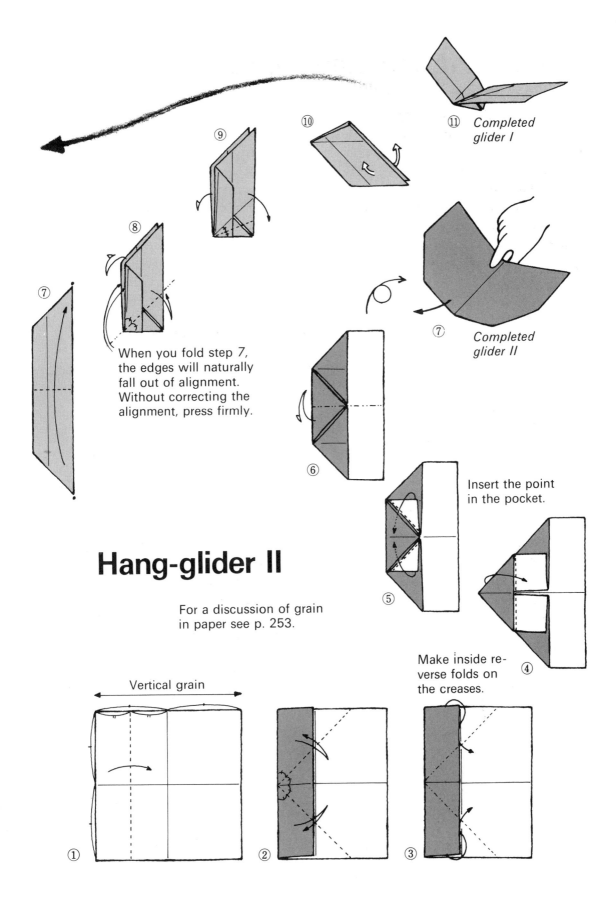

⑪ *Completed glider I*

⑦ *Completed glider II*

When you fold step 7, the edges will naturally fall out of alignment. Without correcting the alignment, press firmly.

Insert the point in the pocket.

Hang-glider II

For a discussion of grain in paper see p. 253.

Make inside reverse folds on the creases.

Vertical grain

Candle and Candlestick

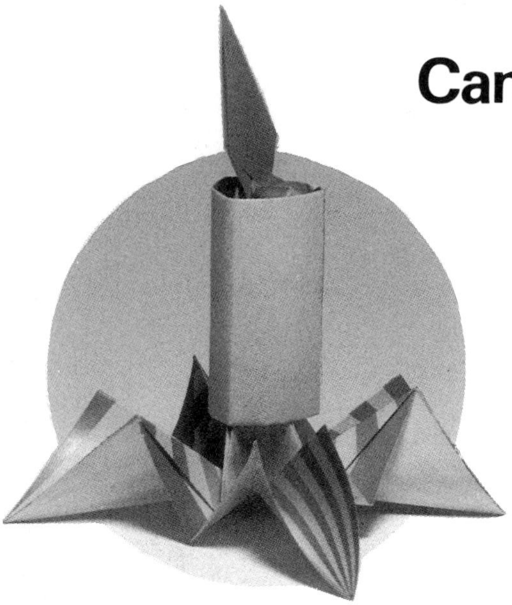

Candle

① The colored side should be up.

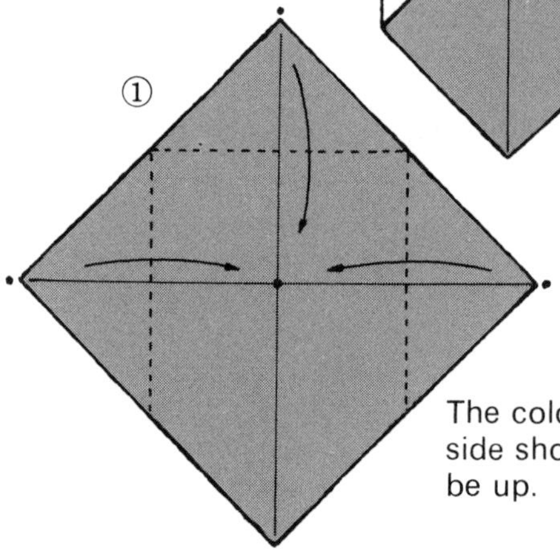

②

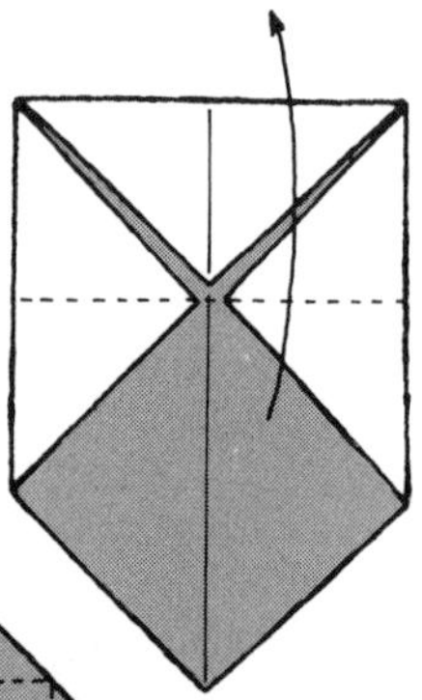

③

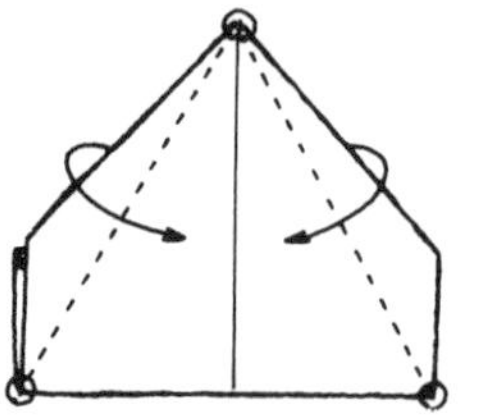

Candlestick

①

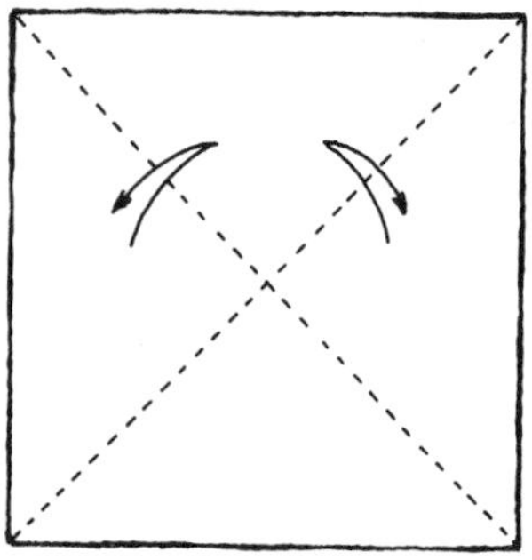

↻

②

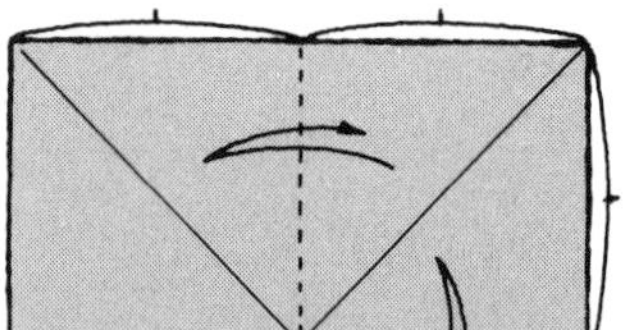

↻

③

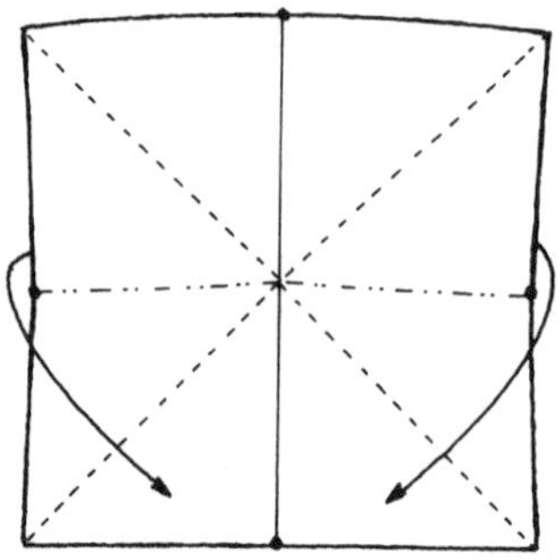

④

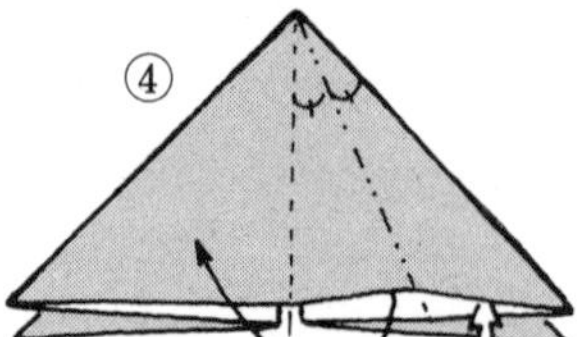

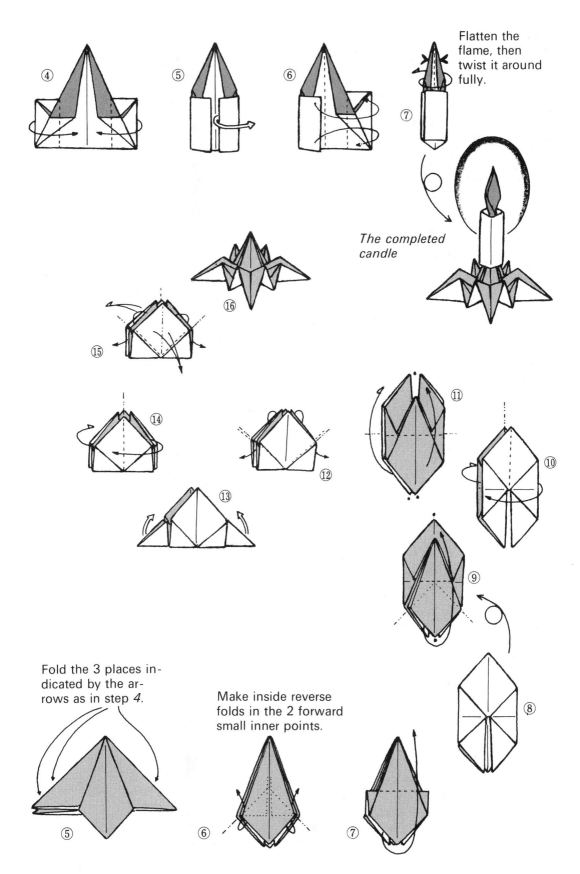

④

⑤

⑥

Flatten the flame, then twist it around fully.

⑦

The completed candle

⑯

⑮

⑭

⑫

⑬

⑪

⑩

⑨

⑧

Fold the 3 places indicated by the arrows as in step 4.

⑤

Make inside reverse folds in the 2 forward small inner points.

⑥

⑦

Sleigh

In place of Santa Claus, I have put Candle from p. 320 in this Sleigh, which is intended to serve as a Christmas decoration.

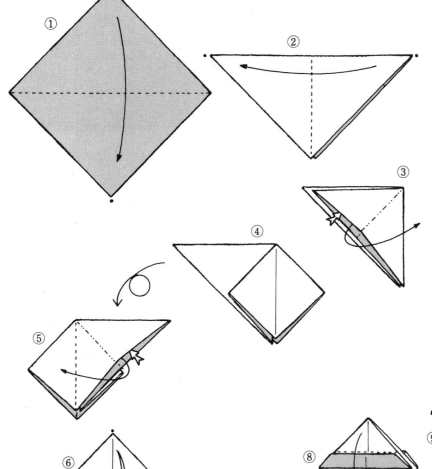

Divide the front and rear points into thirds and roll them upward.

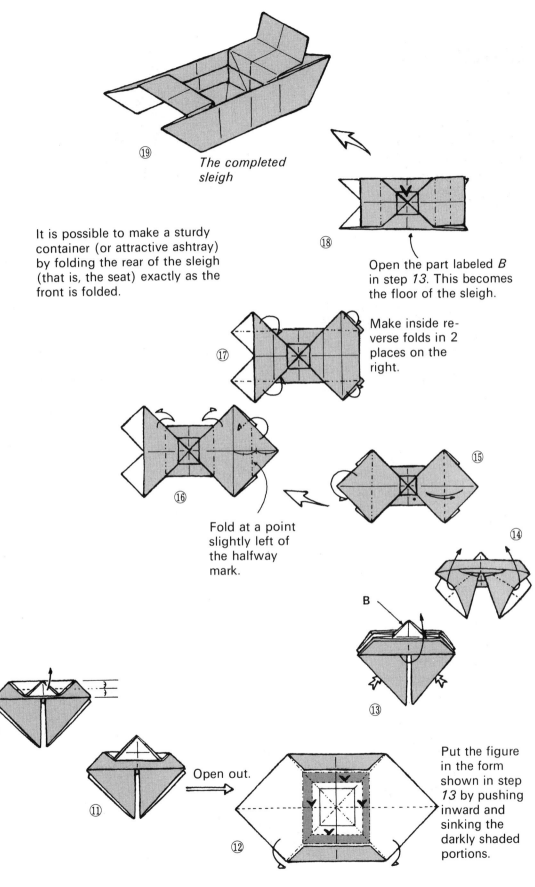

⑲

The completed sleigh

It is possible to make a sturdy container (or attractive ashtray) by folding the rear of the sleigh (that is, the seat) exactly as the front is folded.

⑱

Open the part labeled *B* in step *13*. This becomes the floor of the sleigh.

Make inside reverse folds in 2 places on the right.

⑰

⑯

⑮

Fold at a point slightly left of the halfway mark.

⑭

B

⑬

⑩

⑪

Open out.

⑫

Put the figure in the form shown in step *13* by pushing inward and sinking the darkly shaded portions.

Automobile

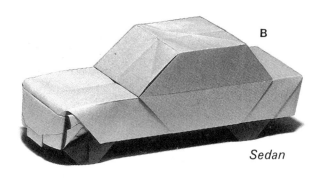

B

Sedan

This is a compound ori-
gami made from two
sheets of paper. The
folding of the roof is a
variation of the folding
of Sleigh on pp.
322–323.

A

Coupe

As a look at the photograph
makes clear, the license plate
can be folded from points *a*
and *b* in step *1* of the body.

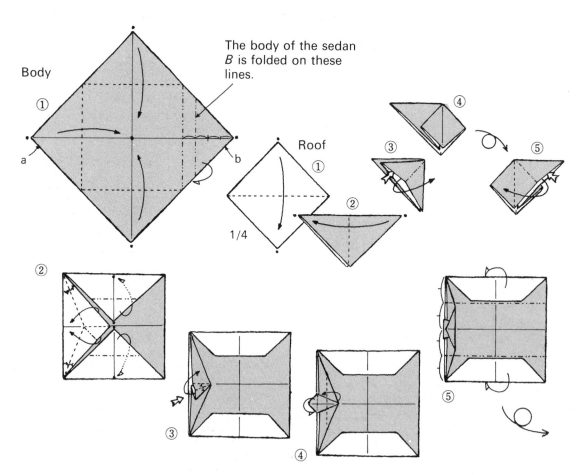

Body

The body of the sedan
B is folded on these
lines.

①

a

b

Roof

①

1/4

②

③

④

⑤

②

③

④

⑤

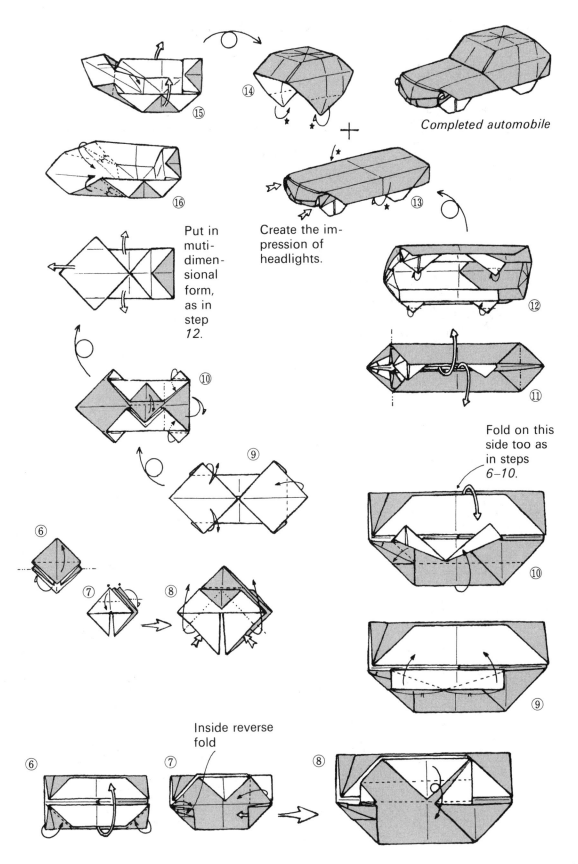

Completed automobile

Put in
muti-
dimen-
sional
form,
as in
step
12.

Create the im-
pression of
headlights.

Fold on this
side too as
in steps
6–10.

Inside reverse
fold

Pinwheel

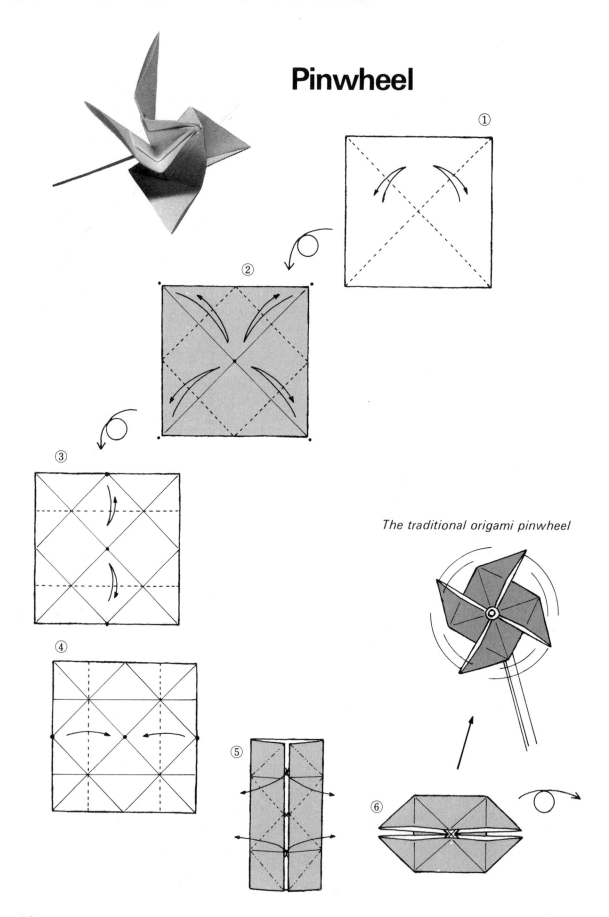

The traditional origami pinwheel

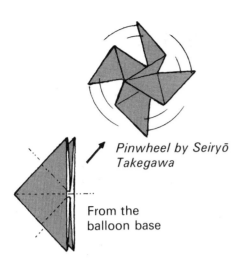

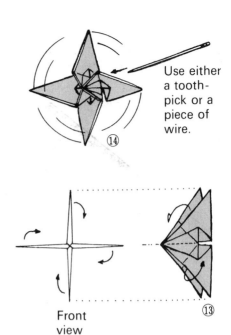

Use either a tooth-pick or a piece of wire.

⑭

Pinwheel by Seiryō Takegawa

From the balloon base

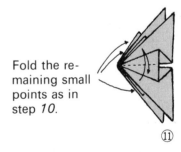

Front view

⑬

⑫

Although the traditional pin-wheel, taken up several times in Chapter 2, is beautiful, it cannot be saidalways to function as well as it ought.

The version by the late Mr. Seiryō Takegawa twirls beauti-fully and is made with a min-imum number of folds.

This version might be called a combination of the old and the new.

Fold the re-maining small points as in step *10*.

⑪

⑩

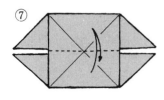

⑦ ⑧ ⑨

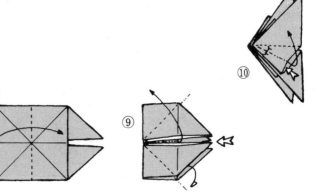

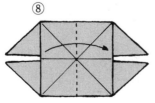

327

Mr. Chino's Sense of Humor

More than twenty years ago, when the American origami fan Nathan Lissac and his wife visited Japan, I took them to visit Toshio Chino, who was kind enough to show us color slides of a number of wonderful origami works. Perhaps the most impressive as an expression of Mr. Chino's artistic sense of humor was his leopard: two traditional boat origami, with a single marble in each, set on a piece of black-spotted yellow cloth.

In the next few pages, I begin by borrowing from his humorous works and go on to introduce various human facial features.

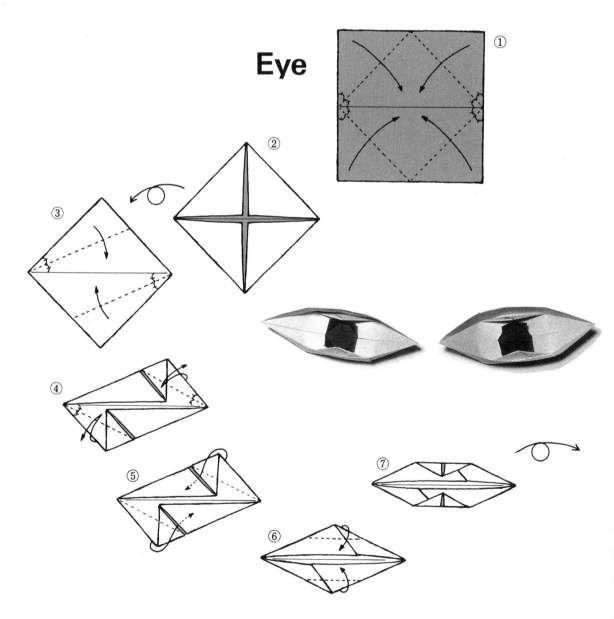

Eye

This fold is a boat. Adding a sail, as on the right, makes it a sailboat. (In such a case, the fold in step 7 is unnecessary.) But, since that is not very interesting, I have borrowed from Mr. Chino to give the origami a new twist.

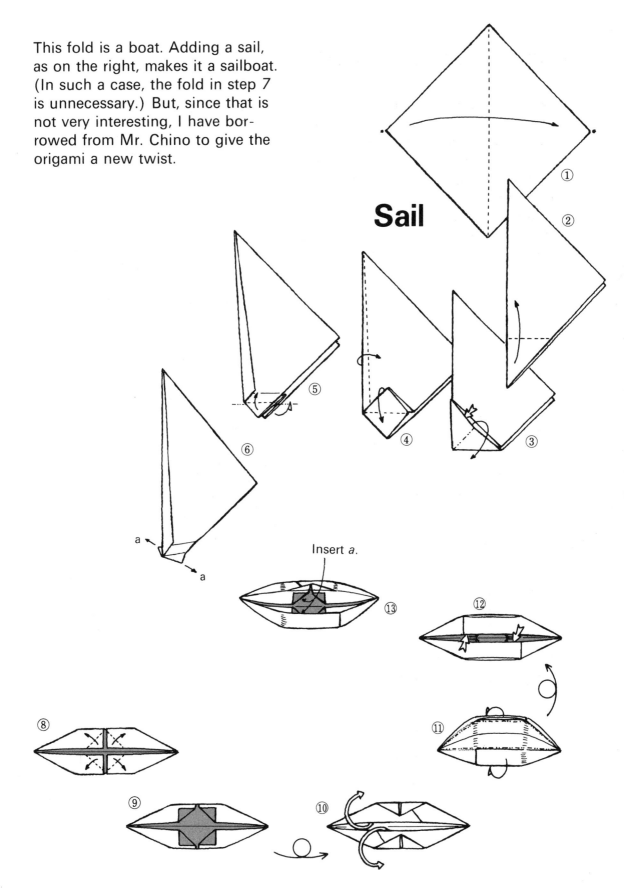

Sail

Insert *a*.

Lips

I was trying for the look of sexy female lips. In case I failed to produce the right impression, I have added some accessory elements—although some may think Dracula fangs and cigarettes out of place in an origami book.

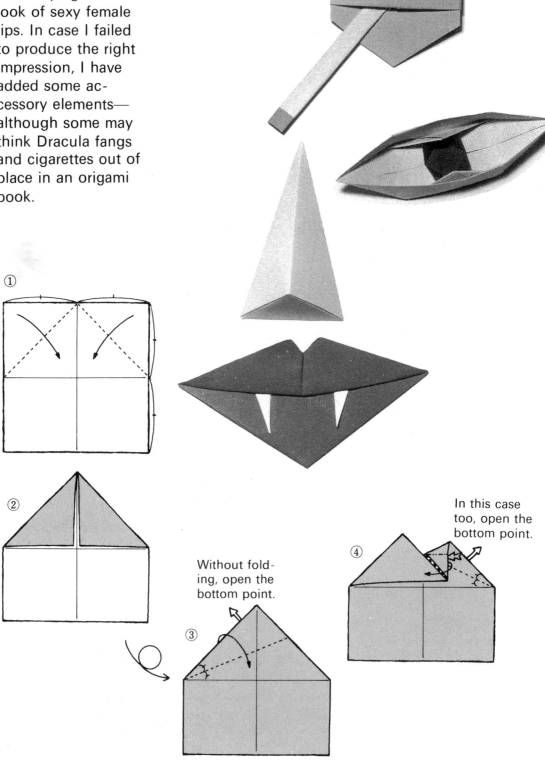

①

②

③ Without folding, open the bottom point.

④ In this case too, open the bottom point.

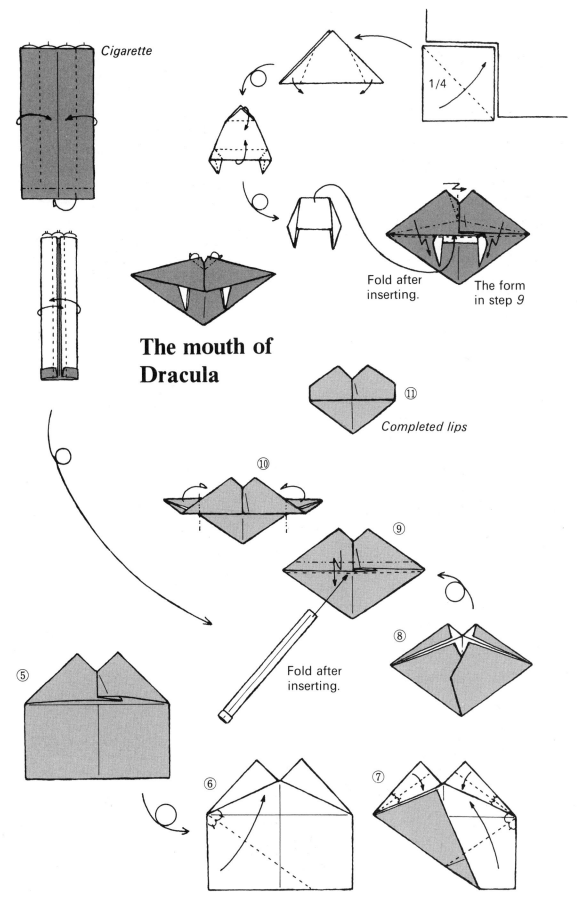

Cigarette

1/4

Fold after
inserting.

The form
in step 9

**The mouth of
Dracula**

⑪

Completed lips

⑩

⑨

⑧

⑤

Fold after
inserting.

⑥

⑦

Mustache

There is little meaning in mustaches and eyebrows without eyes and noses. In this section, I have attempted a multi-dimensional version of an old-fashioned Japanese New Years game in which eyes, noses, and mouths are cut out of heavy paper and arranged in amusing ways within a facial outline drawn on another sheet of paper.

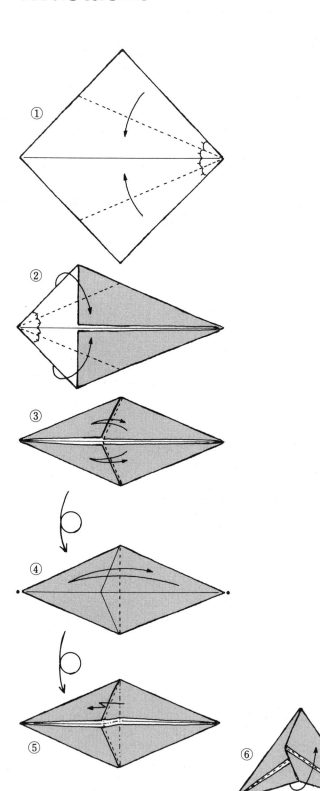

Eyebrow

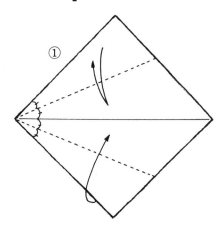

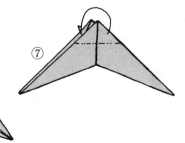

Witch Claws

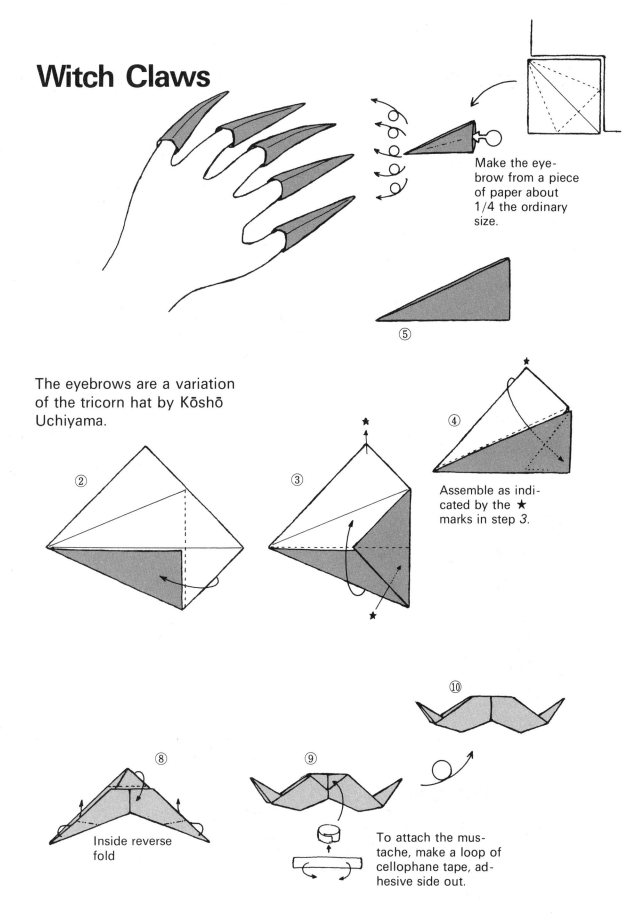

Make the eyebrow from a piece of paper about 1/4 the ordinary size.

⑤

The eyebrows are a variation of the tricorn hat by Kōshō Uchiyama.

②

③

④

Assemble as indicated by the ★ marks in step 3.

⑧
Inside reverse fold

⑨
To attach the mustache, make a loop of cellophane tape, adhesive side out.

⑩

Nose

With the completion of the eyes, lips, mustache, eyebrows, and nose, all the parts of the face are ready.

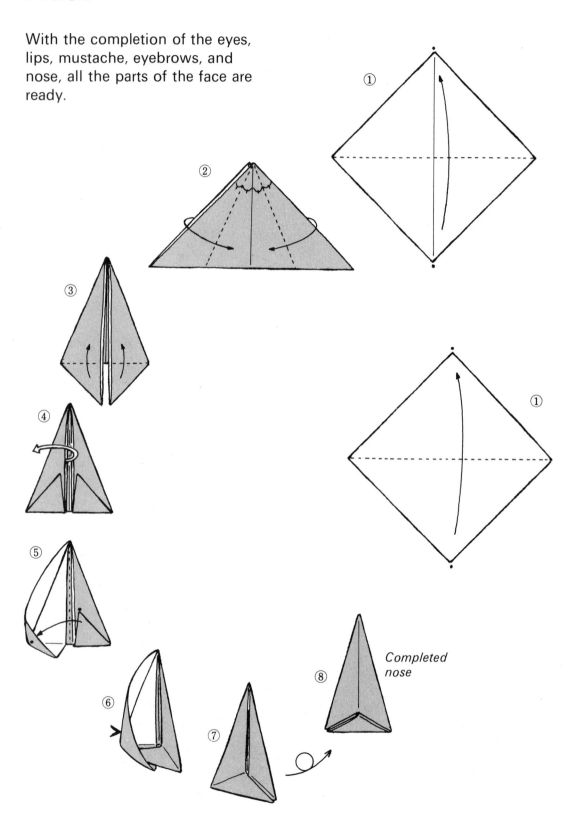

Completed nose

Pinocchio Nose (or Bird Beak)

Since there is little humor in a perfectly regular nose, I have presented this other one. Attach it to your own nose for a Pinocchio look. Or hold it against your mouth like a bird beak and, sucking in, see how long you can hold it on.

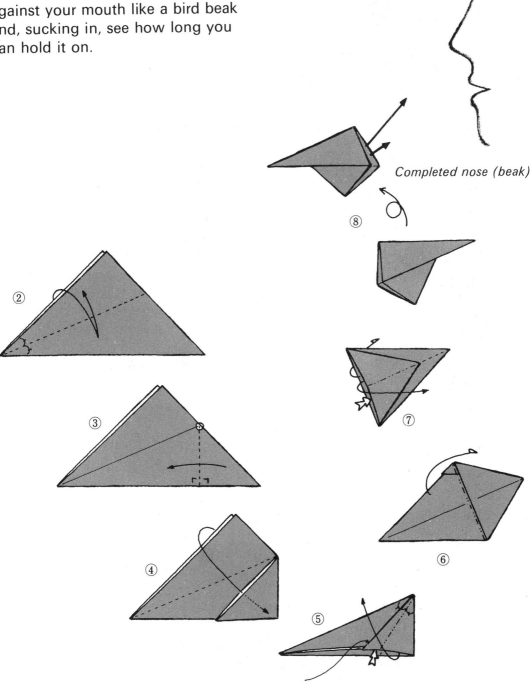

Completed nose (beak)

Open, taking care that this does not slip from the pocket.

Cattleya

To show how random this selection of themes is, I move from faces to flowers.

The folding method of the cattleya is extremely easy, though you may be confused by the reassembly process beginning at step *11*. All will be well, however, if you simply assemble as the creases indicate.

Like the conversion of the rouge container into a cube, the cup into a spinning top, the measruring box into a cube, the crane into a pheasant, and the *hakama* into a dinosaur, this is an adaptation of a traditional fold.

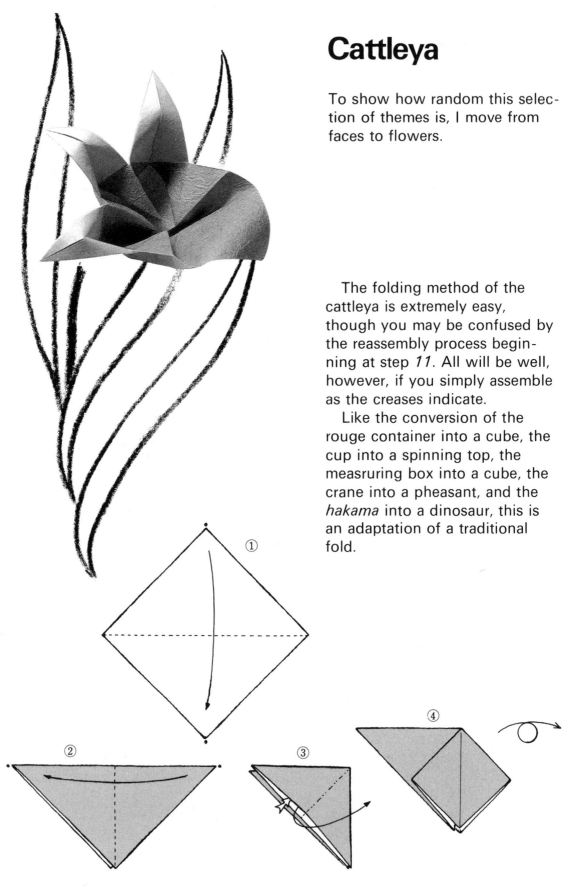

Curl the petals as shown in the photograph on p. 336.

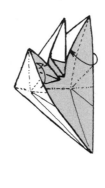

Fold here as in step *11*.

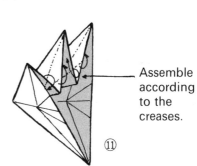

Assemble according to the creases.

No new creases are made after step *8*. Assemble on the basis of creases already made.

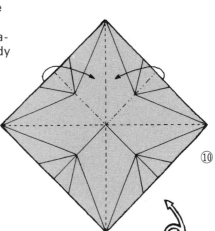

Traditional fold: incense container

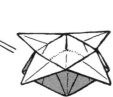

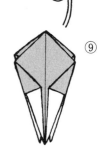

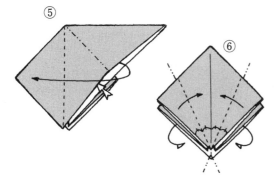

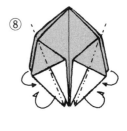

Rose

The folding diagrams
look exactly like a
puzzle.

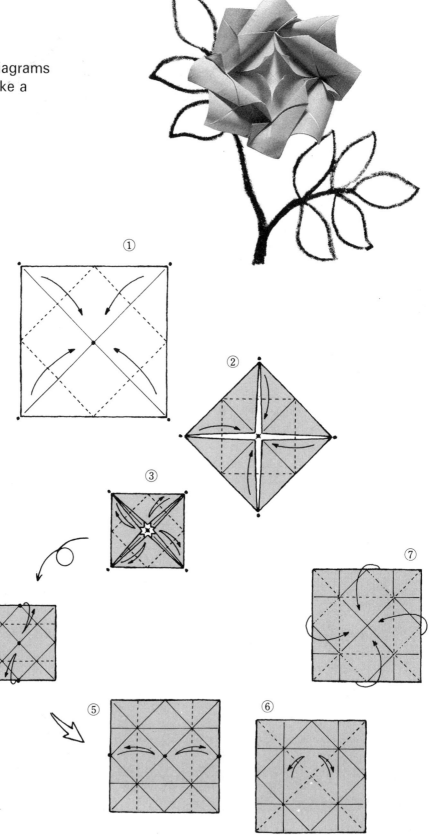

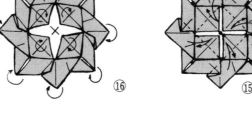

⑯

⑮

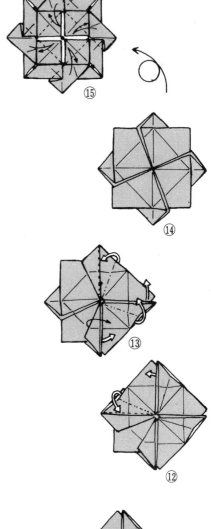

⑭

⑬

⑫

⑪

Though the folding of steps *10–14* may seem confusing, a close examination of the diagrams shows that it is not actually very difficult.

The impression of the finished origami is closer to that of a wild rose. Try varying it to suit your own ideas; for instance, you might convert it into a dahlia.

⑧

Open out all the lower points.

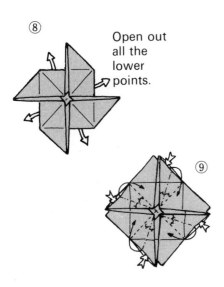

⑨

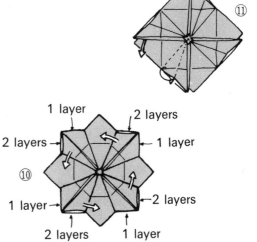

1 layer

2 layers

2 layers →

← 1 layer

⑩

→ 2 layers

1 layer →

2 layers

1 layer

Sparrow

Now I move from flowers to birds. You may have to fold it several times to get this sparrow looking the way you want it to. In other words, it is fairly difficult.

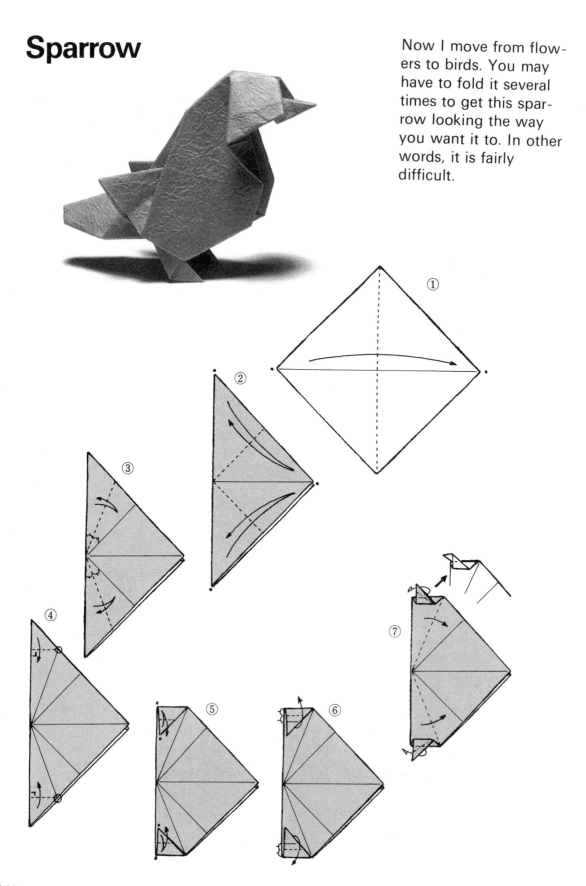

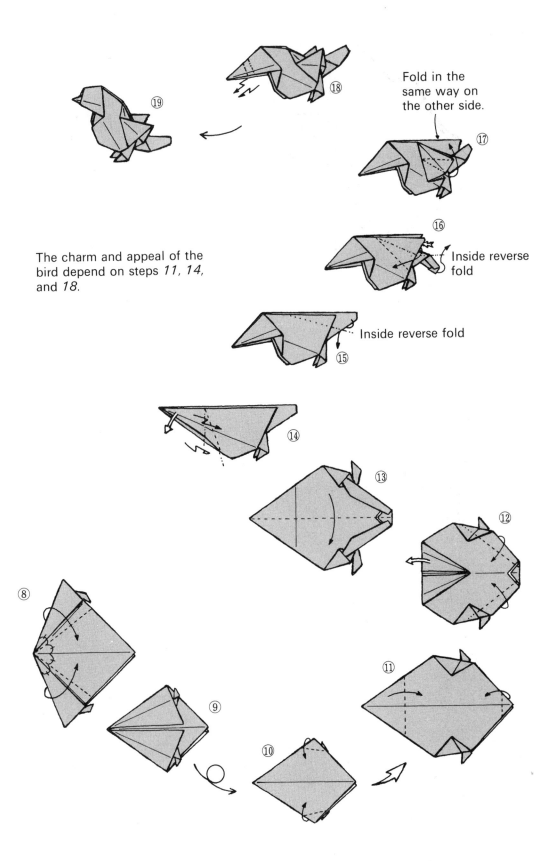

Fold in the same way on the other side.

Inside reverse fold

Inside reverse fold

The charm and appeal of the bird depend on steps *11, 14,* and *18*.

Duck

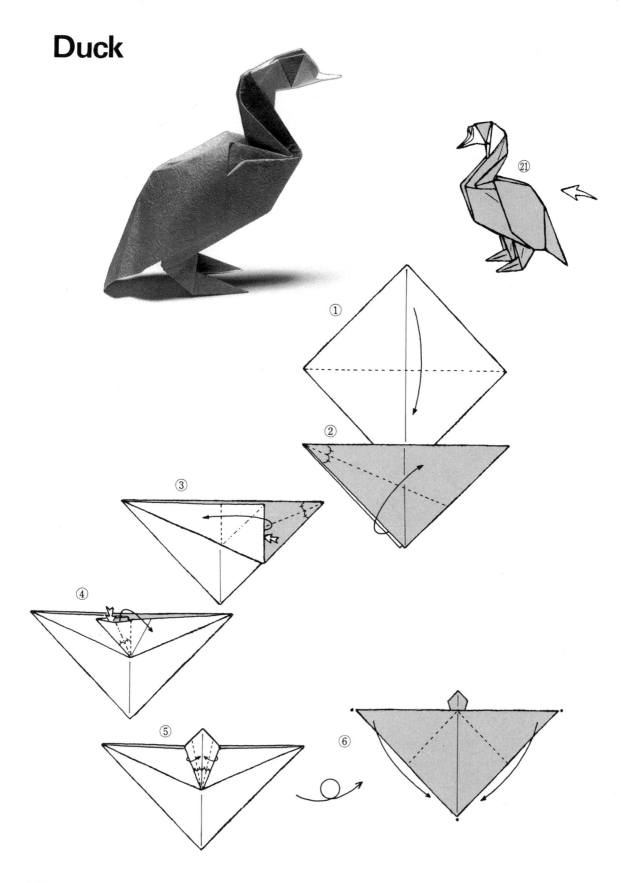

343

Swallow

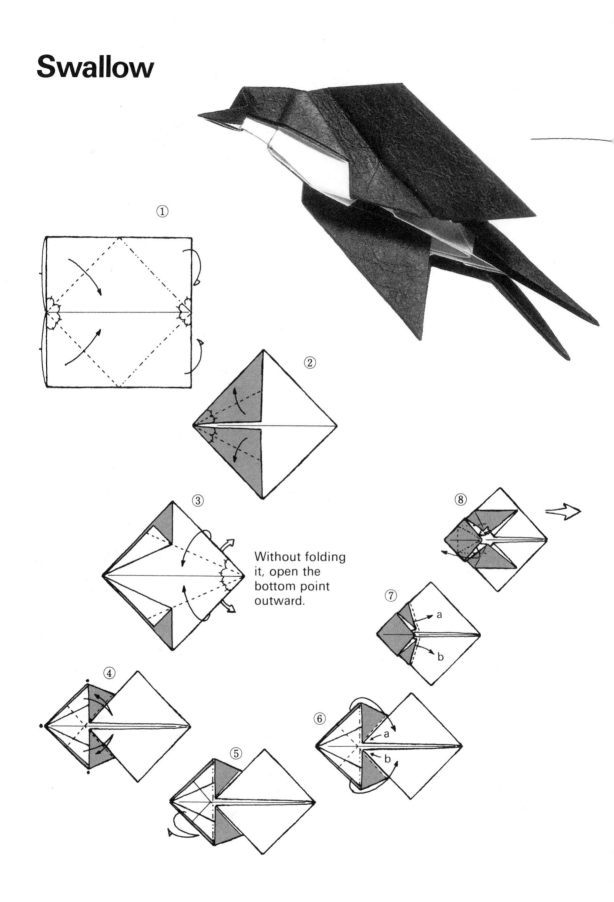

① ② ③

Without folding
it, open the
bottom point
outward.

④ ⑤ ⑥

⑦ ⑧

a
b

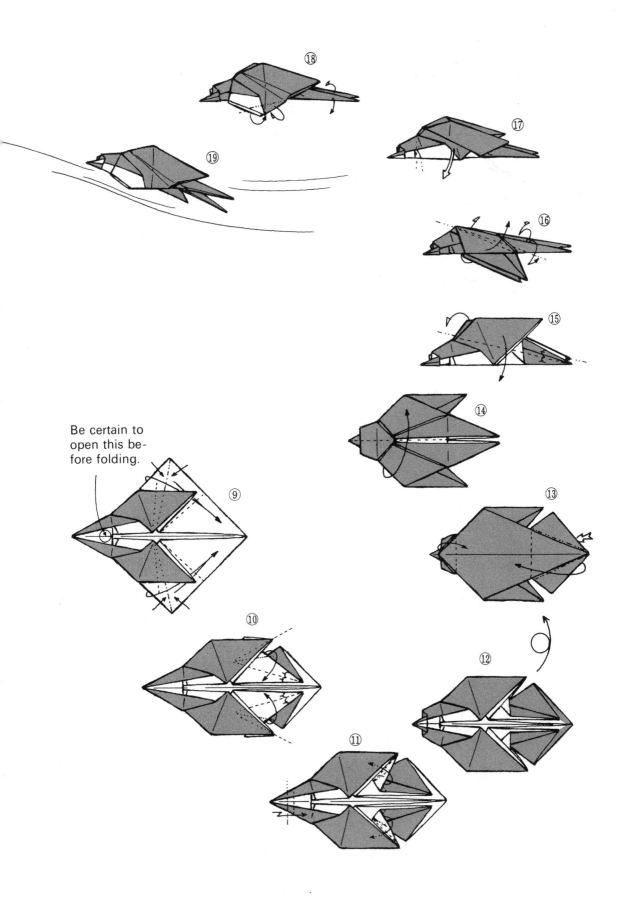

Be certain to
open this be-
fore folding.

Cormorant with Outstretched Wings

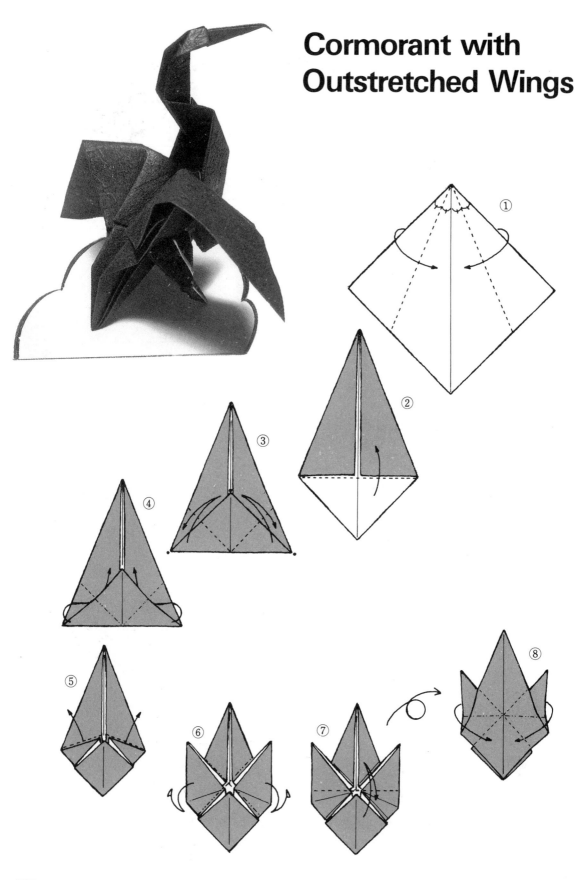

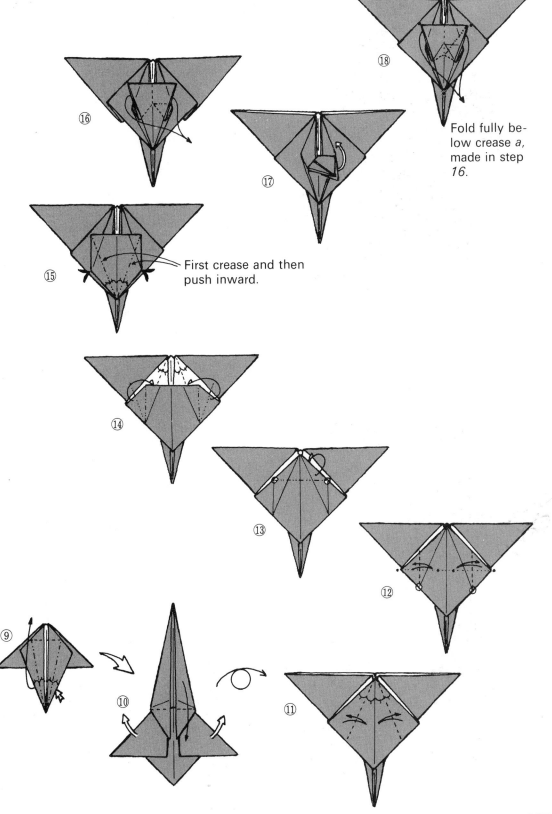

Fold fully below crease *a*, made in step *16*.

First crease and then push inward.

347

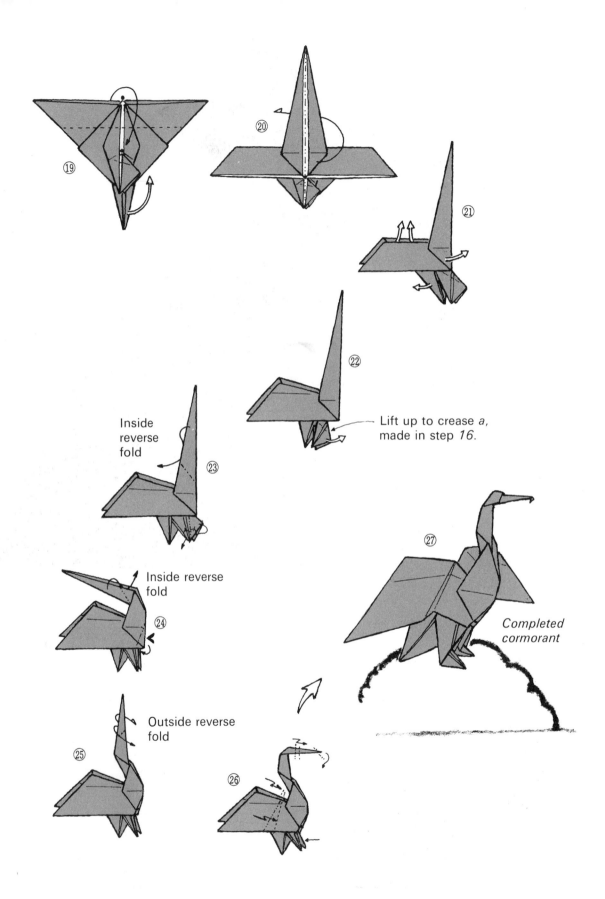

⑲

⑳

㉑

㉒ Lift up to crease *a*, made in step *16*.

Inside reverse fold ㉓

Inside reverse fold ㉔

Outside reverse fold

㉕

㉖

㉗ Completed cormorant

Eagle

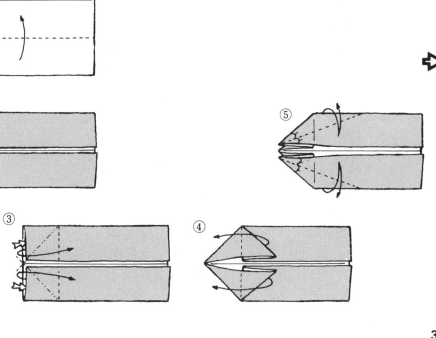

①

②

③

④

⑤

➾

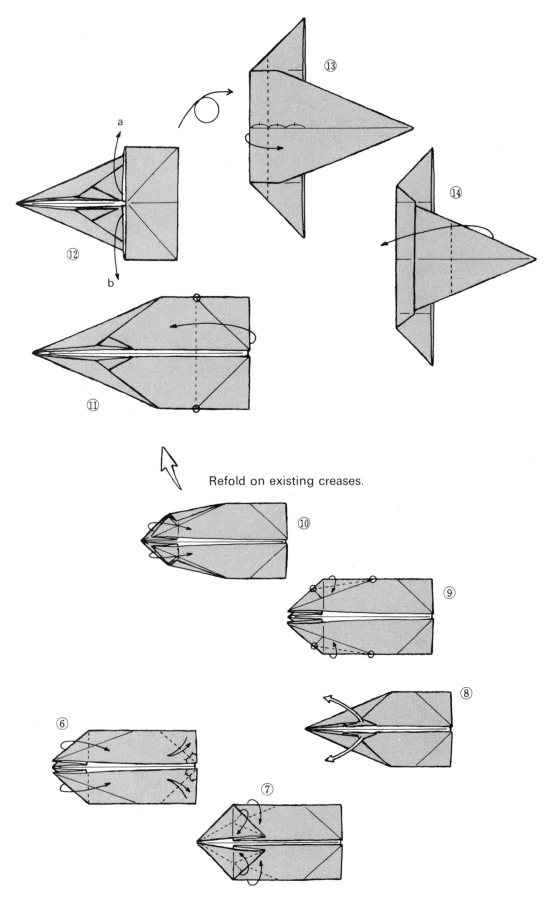

Refold on existing creases.

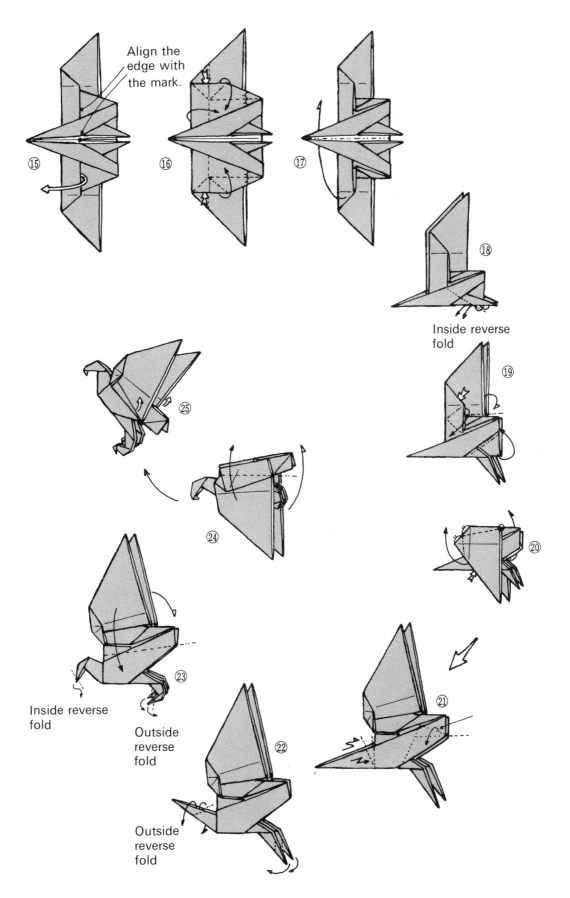

Align the edge with the mark.

⑮

⑯

⑰

⑱

Inside reverse fold

⑲

⑳

㉑

㉒

Outside reverse fold

㉓

Inside reverse fold

Outside reverse fold

㉔

㉕

Swan

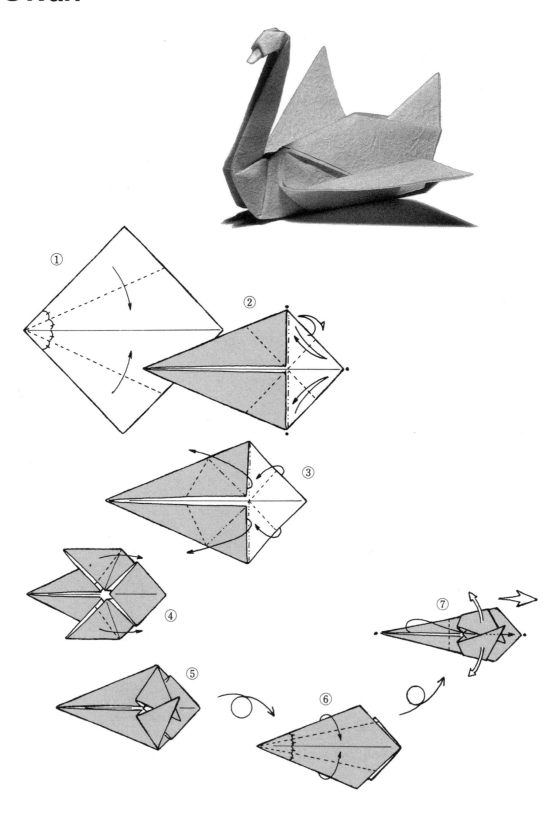

The five preceding origami birds have been representational; the ones on the next pages are more symbolic. Comparing them will show you how origami can take various approaches to the same theme. I like all of them.

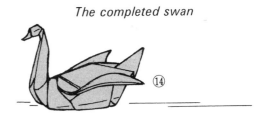

The completed swan

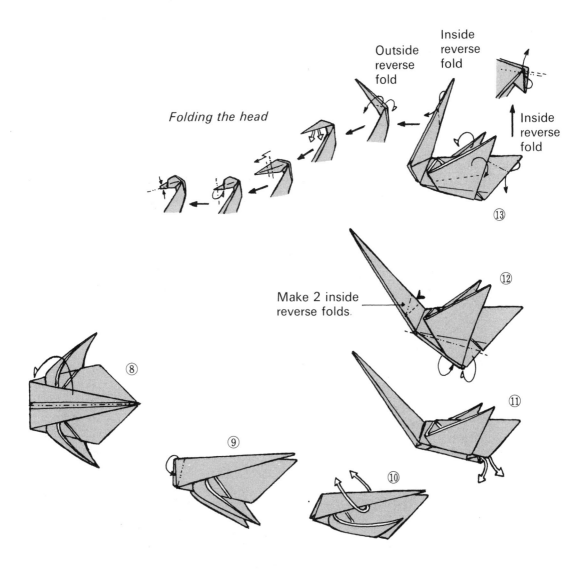

Folding the head

Outside reverse fold

Inside reverse fold

Inside reverse fold

Make 2 inside reverse folds.

The Simple Splendor of Symbolic Forms

As I have pointed out, origami may be either representational or symbolic. In general symbolic origami are simple to fold and are therefore easily reproduced.

Swan II

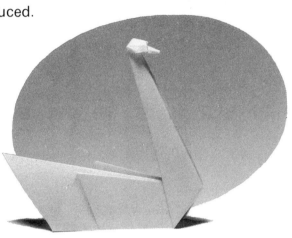

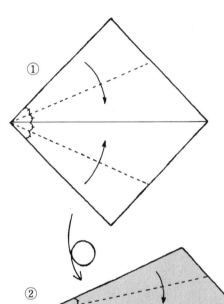

The folding method of this virtually legendary form can be varied in many ways. I am especially fond of it.

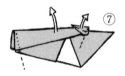

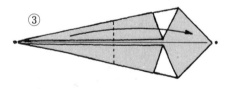

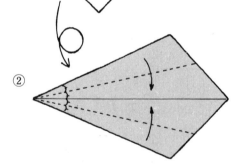

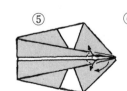

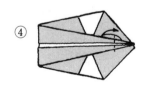

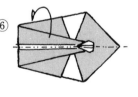

Dove

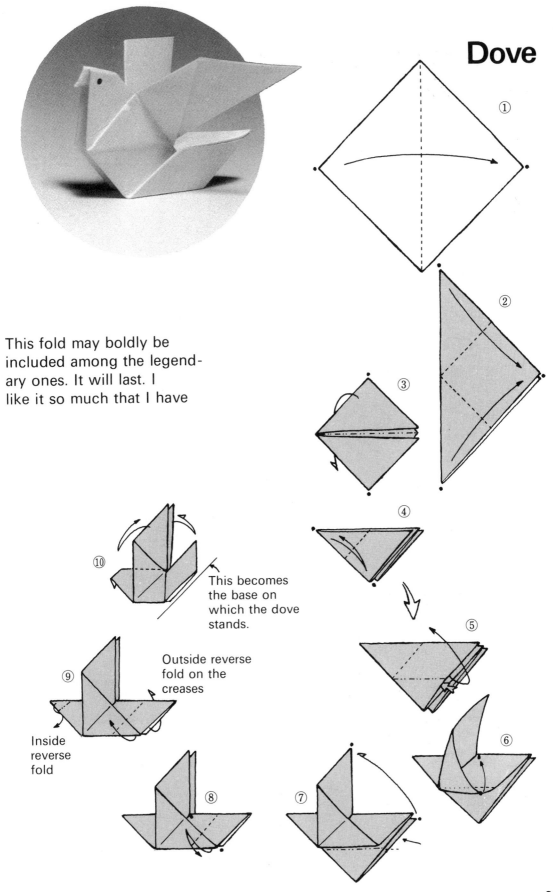

This fold may boldly be included among the legendary ones. It will last. I like it so much that I have

This becomes the base on which the dove stands.

Outside reverse fold on the creases

Inside reverse fold

Peacock

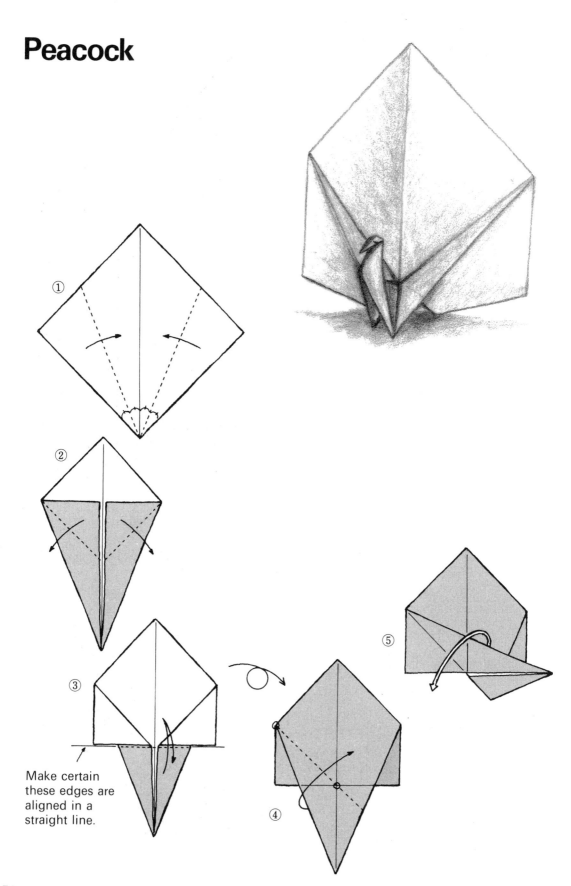

①

②

③ Make certain these edges are aligned in a straight line.

④

⑤

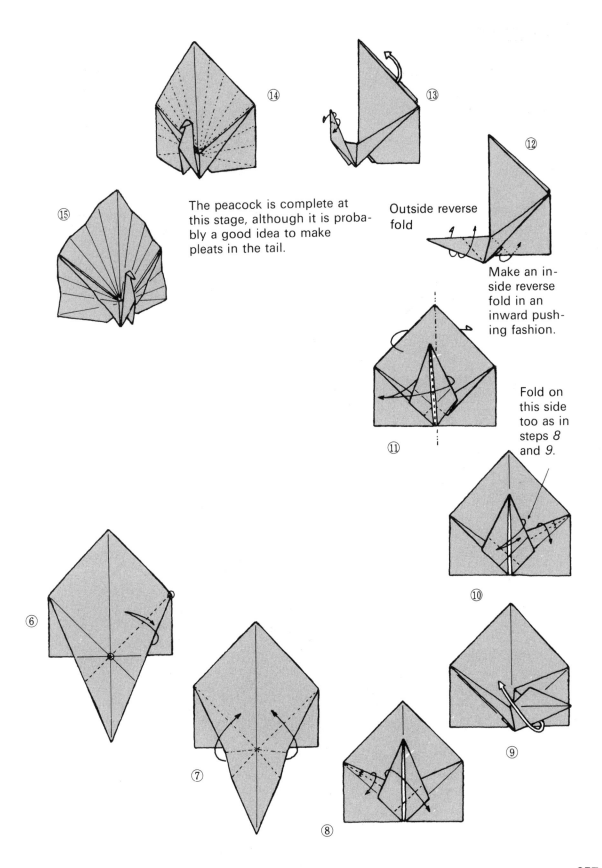

The peacock is complete at this stage, although it is probably a good idea to make pleats in the tail.

Outside reverse fold

Make an inside reverse fold in an inward pushing fashion.

Fold on this side too as in steps 8 and 9.

Chicken

This is my favorite of the
more than ten chicken
origami I have developed.

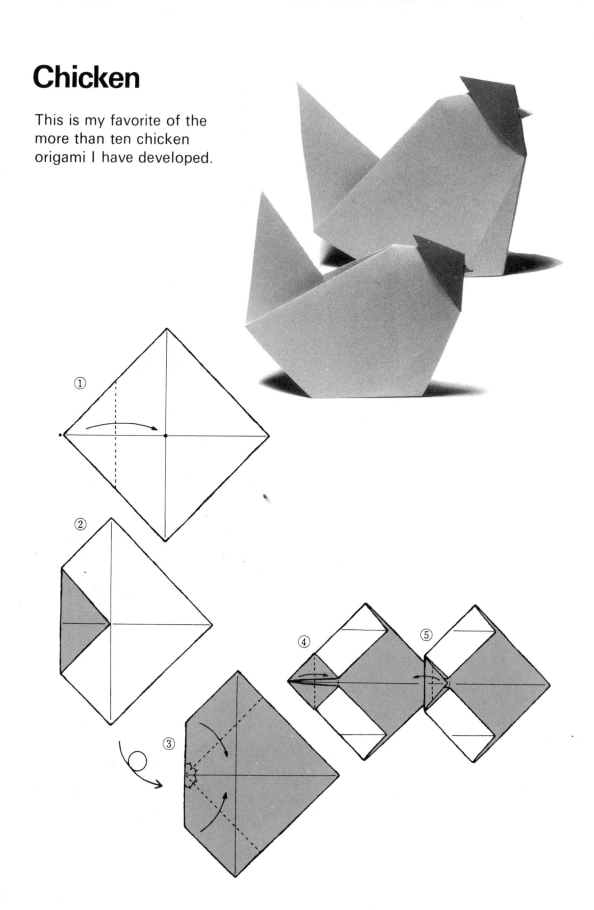

① ② ③ ④ ⑤

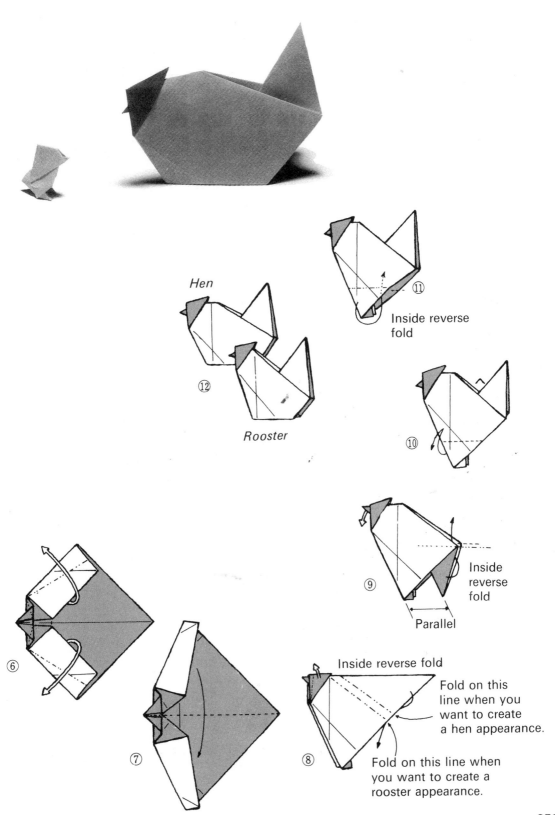

Hen

⑫

Rooster

⑪ Inside reverse fold

⑩

⑨ Inside reverse fold

Parallel

⑥

⑦

Inside reverse fold

⑧ Fold on this line when you want to create a hen appearance.

Fold on this line when you want to create a rooster appearance.

Fluttering Pheasant

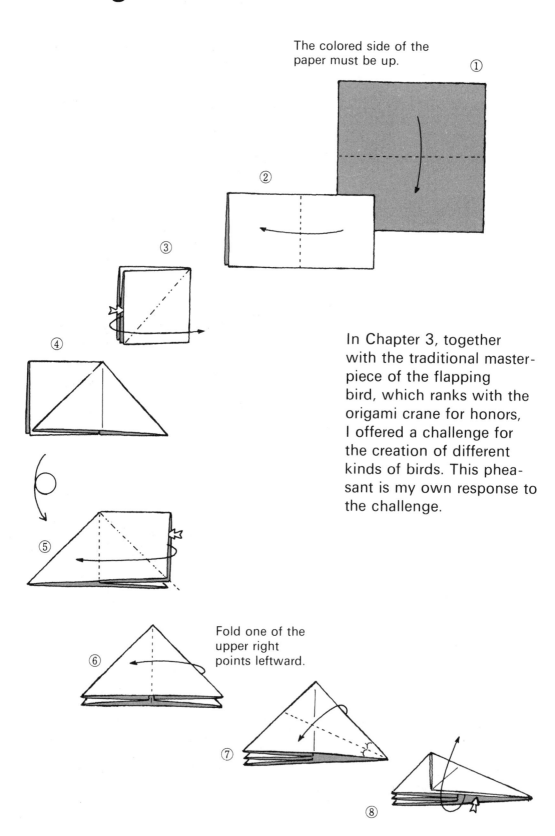

The colored side of the paper must be up.

In Chapter 3, together with the traditional master-piece of the flapping bird, which ranks with the origami crane for honors, I offered a challenge for the creation of different kinds of birds. This pheasant is my own response to the challenge.

Fold one of the upper right points leftward.

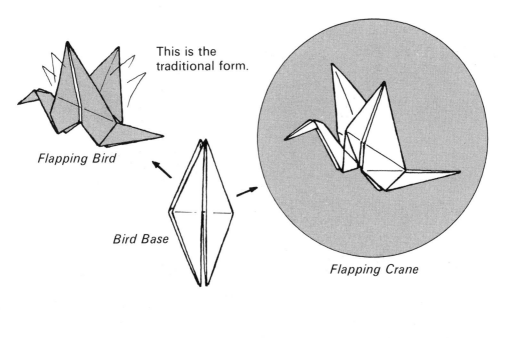

This is the traditional form.

Flapping Bird

Bird Base

Flapping Crane

Outside reverse fold

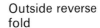

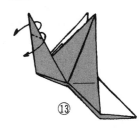

⑬

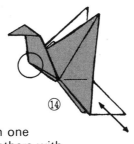

⑭

Holding the breast in one hand, pull the tail feathers with the other to make the wings flap.

After opening this, make an outside reverse fold.

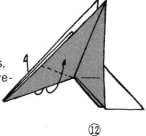

⑫

⑪

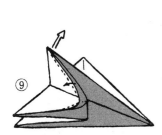

⑨

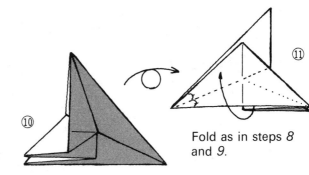

⑩

Fold as in steps *8* and *9*.

361

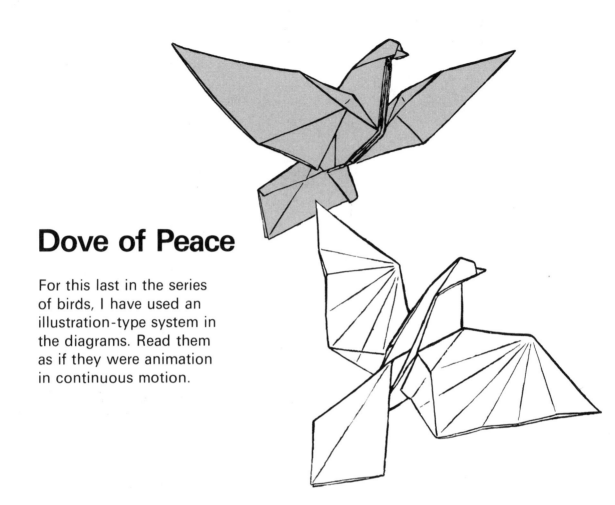

Dove of Peace

For this last in the series of birds, I have used an illustration-type system in the diagrams. Read them as if they were animation in continuous motion.

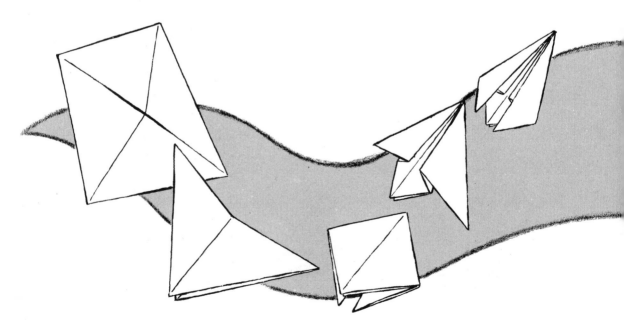

Angel

I still cannot forget the impression Toshio Chino's angel made on me when I first saw it, more than twenty years ago. This is one of the four origami that I have developed using his angel as a model. I have used something similar for the constellation Virgo as well.

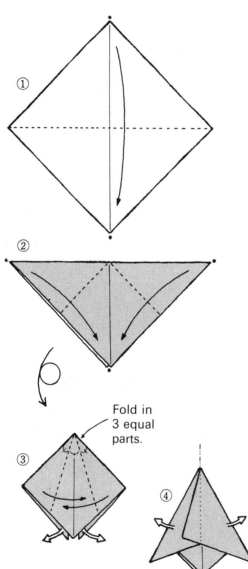

①

②

③ Fold in 3 equal parts.

④

⑤

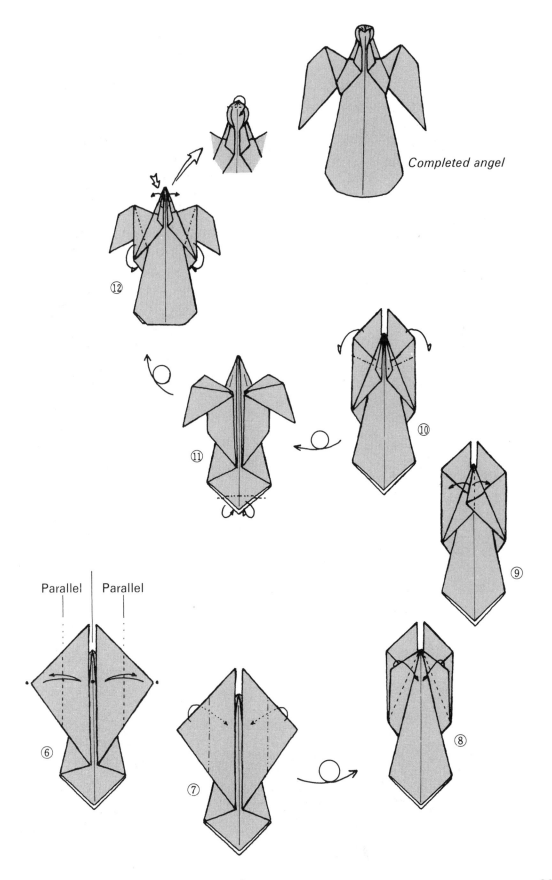

Completed angel

Parallel | Parallel

⑥ ⑦ ⑧ ⑨ ⑩ ⑪ ⑫

Adam and Eve

This long book is now drawing to a close. As my readers will have noticed from the frequency with which other people's names appear in its pages, during my twenty-five years of origami experience, I have been influenced directly and indirectly by many people. The greatest influence has certainly been that of Kōshō Uchiyama, whose book *Junsui Origami* (Pure origami; May, 1979, Kokudo-sha) has been a constant source of challenge for me. I feel that, in the present book, I have risen to that challenge.

Furthermore, I do not feel it disrespectful to attempt to challenge a person I regard as a teacher. Indeed, Mr. Uchiyama would no doubt welcome such a challenge.

In fact, I have included the naked figures of Adam and Eve here—fully aware of the attractive female nude origami that he has already made public.

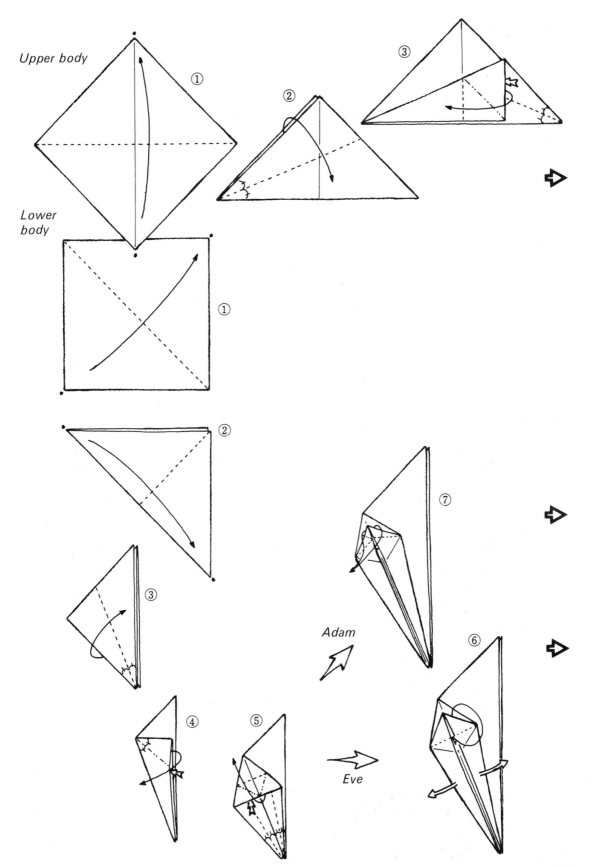

Upper body

Lower
body

Adam

Eve

367

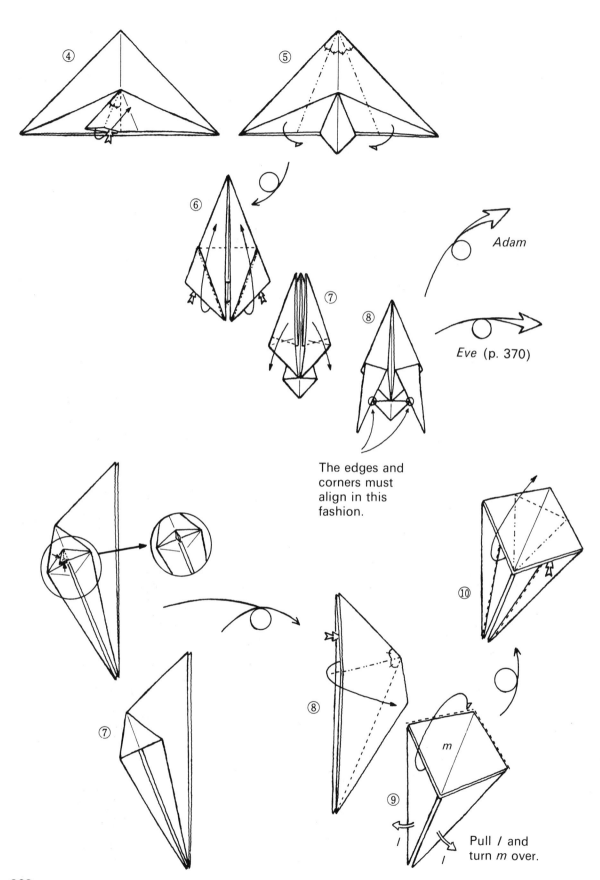

④

⑤

⑥

⑦

⑧

Adam

Eve (p. 370)

The edges and
corners must
align in this
fashion.

⑦

⑧

⑨

⑩

m

l

l

Pull *l* and
turn *m* over.

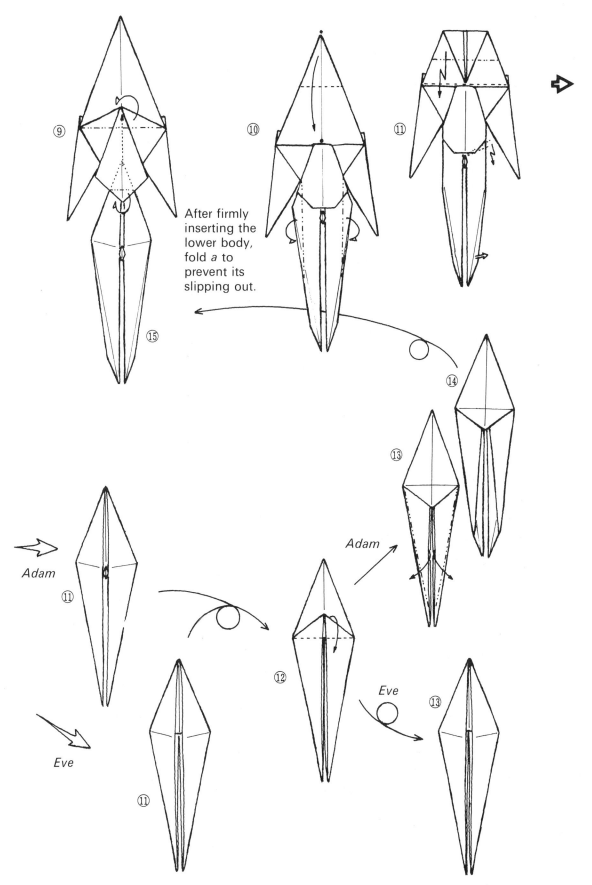

⑨

⑩

After firmly
inserting the
lower body,
fold *a* to
prevent its
slipping out.

⑮

⑪

⑭

⑬

Adam

⑪

Eve

⑪

⑫

Adam

Eve

⑬

Fold in
numerical
order.

⑫

⑬

⑭

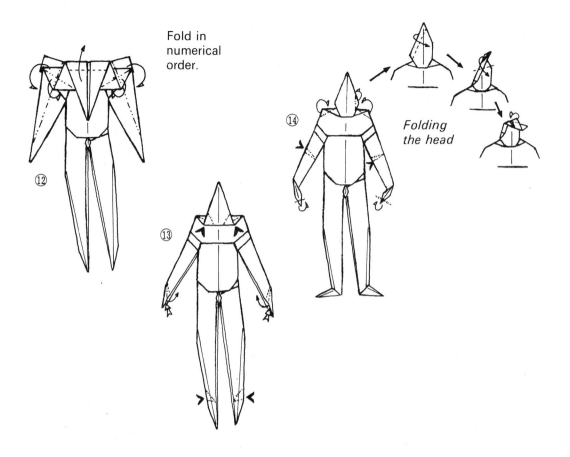

*Folding
the head*

⑨

⑭

Following a
process similar
to the one used
in Adam, insert
the lower body
well; then fold
b to prevent its
slipping out.

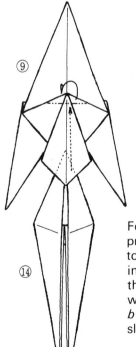

⑩

Folding *c* pro-
duces slack that
can be taken up
by adjusting the
pleat *s*.

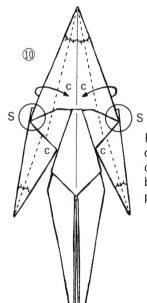

The final poses
and positioning
of the heads
shown here are
only possibilities.
Work out the
ones you like
best.

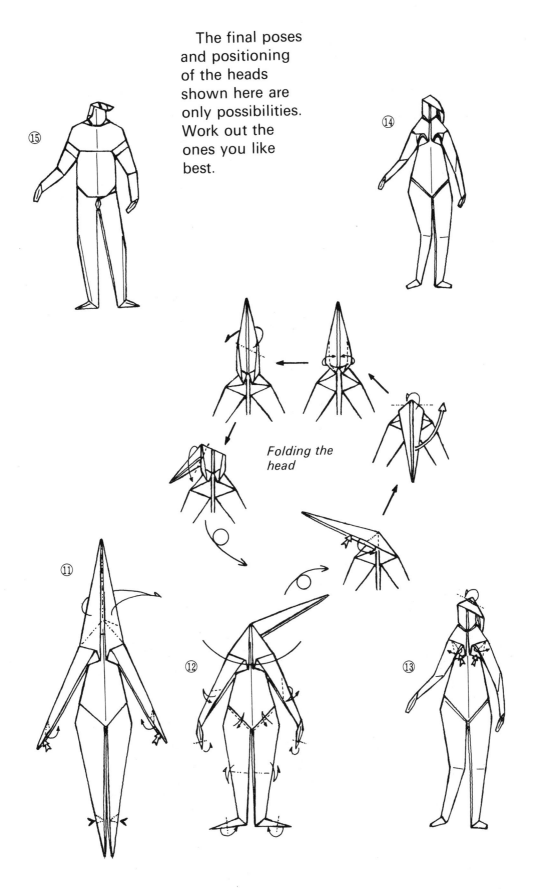

Folding the head

Old Sol

Sun (or sunflower) to end
the book on a sunny note.

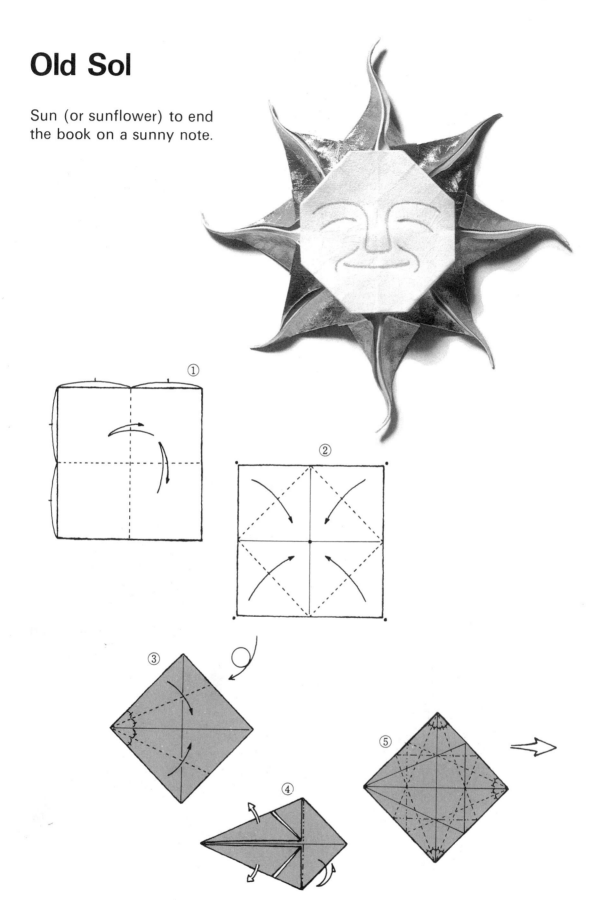

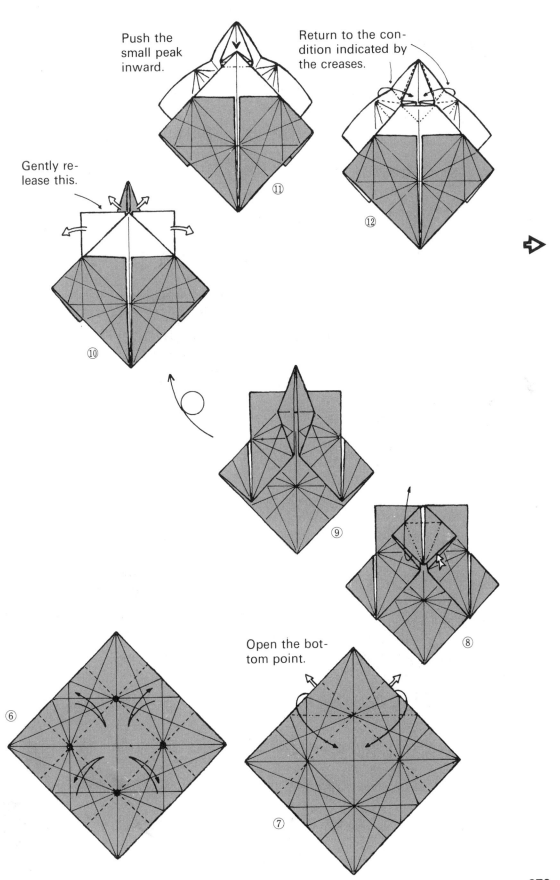

Push the
small peak
inward.

Return to the con-
dition indicated by
the creases.

⑪

⑫

Gently re-
lease this.

⑩

⑨

⑧

Open the bot-
tom point.

⑥

⑦

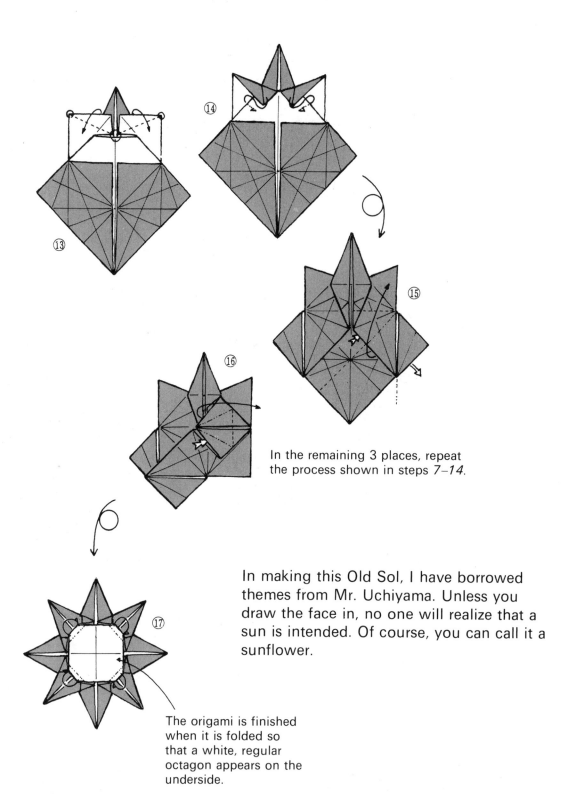

In the remaining 3 places, repeat the process shown in steps *7–14*.

In making this Old Sol, I have borrowed themes from Mr. Uchiyama. Unless you draw the face in, no one will realize that a sun is intended. Of course, you can call it a sunflower.

The origami is finished when it is folded so that a white, regular octagon appears on the underside.

Appendix

Production Guide for the Panorama Cubes

(see frontispieces on pp. 9–15)

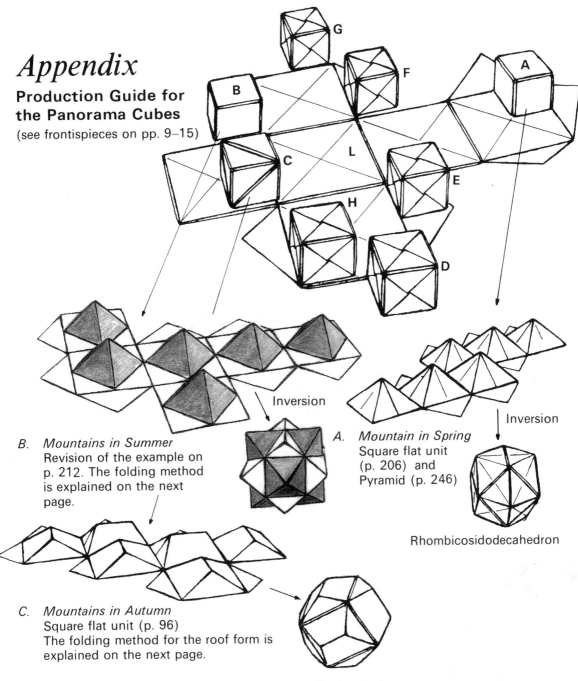

Inversion

B. *Mountains in Summer*
Revision of the example on p. 212. The folding method is explained on the next page.

Inversion

A. *Mountain in Spring*
Square flat unit (p. 206) and Pyramid (p. 246)

Rhombicosidodecahedron

C. *Mountains in Autumn*
Square flat unit (p. 96)
The folding method for the roof form is explained on the next page.

Dodecahedron

Note: Paper sizes (for the origami in the frontispieces):
  A–N = 15 cm to a side
  K = 35 cm to a side
  Small items = 1/16 and 1/16×1/4 of 15 cm paper
  Exceptions: Starfish (Five-pointed star) 1/16×1/3; Univalve shell 1/16×1/2. Both are rectangular.
Joining tabs: 14 each of A–C and 13 each of D–H. Glue the square units.

Reference: The 2 of the 11 possible developments of the cube not used in this work.

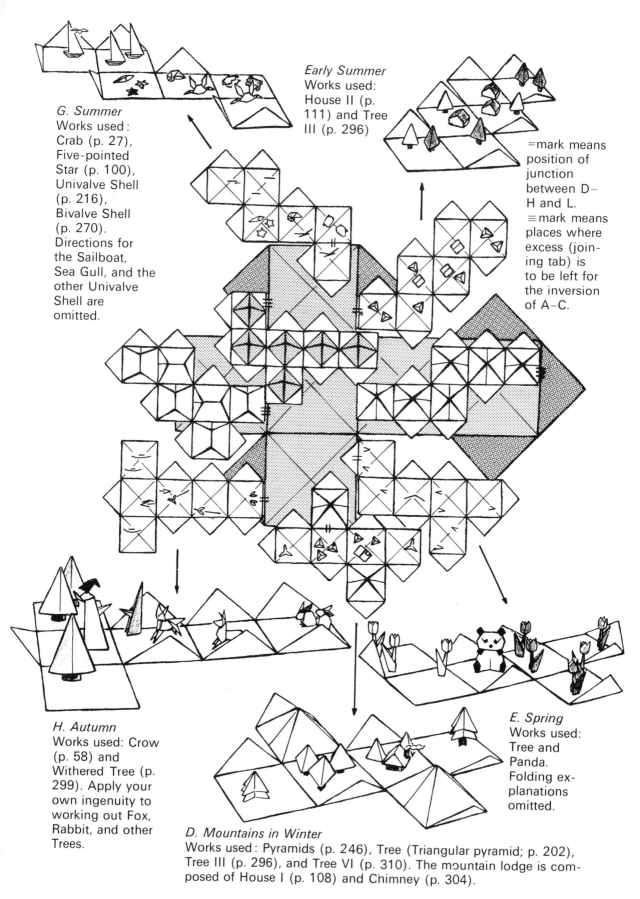

G. Summer
Works used:
Crab (p. 27),
Five-pointed
Star (p. 100),
Univalve Shell
(p. 216),
Bivalve Shell
(p. 270).
Directions for
the Sailboat,
Sea Gull, and the
other Univalve
Shell are
omitted.

Early Summer
Works used:
House II (p.
111) and Tree
III (p. 296)

=mark means
position of
junction
between D–
H and L.
≡mark means
places where
excess (join-
ing tab) is
to be left for
the inversion
of A–C.

H. Autumn
Works used: Crow
(p. 58) and
Withered Tree (p.
299). Apply your
own ingenuity to
working out Fox,
Rabbit, and other
Trees.

D. Mountains in Winter
Works used: Pyramids (p. 246), Tree (Triangular pyramid; p. 202),
Tree III (p. 296), and Tree VI (p. 310). The mountain lodge is com-
posed of House I (p. 108) and Chimney (p. 304).

E. Spring
Works used:
Tree and
Panda.
Folding ex-
planations
omitted.

You will need 6 full sheets of paper,
6 half sheets of paper, and 1 extra
full sheet for joining tabs. From 6
full sheets make square flat units according to the directions on p. 96.

Completed figure

This example should make the
relations between the cube and
the regular dodecahedron clear.

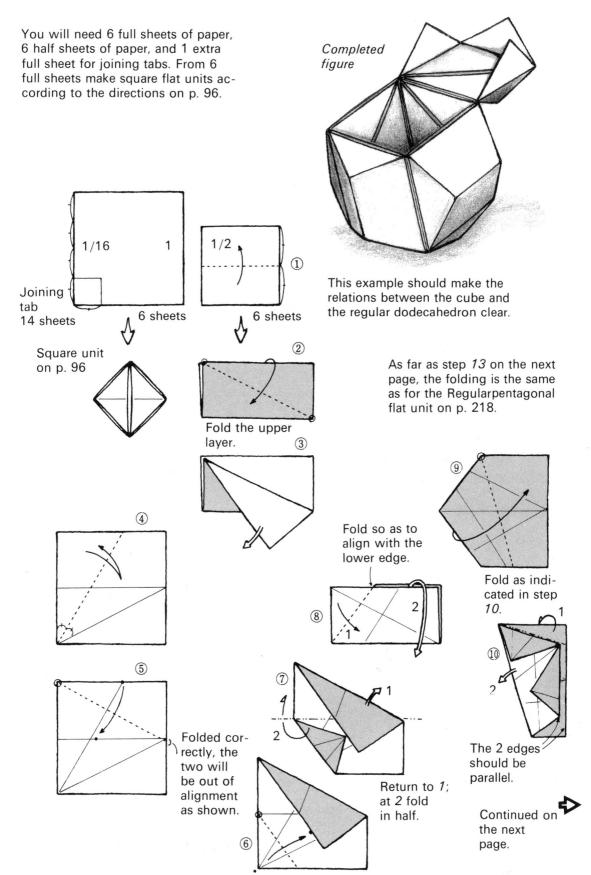

Joining tab
14 sheets

6 sheets

1/16   1

1/2   ①

6 sheets

Square unit
on p. 96

②

Fold the upper
layer.

③

As far as step *13* on the next
page, the folding is the same
as for the Regularpentagonal
flat unit on p. 218.

④

⑨

Fold as indi-
cated in step
10.

Fold so as to
align with the
lower edge.

⑧   1   2

①

⑩

2

⑤

⑦

4   1

2

The 2 edges
should be
parallel.

Folded cor-
rectly, the
two will
be out of
alignment
as shown.

Return to *1*;
at *2* fold
in half.

⑥

Continued on
the next
page.

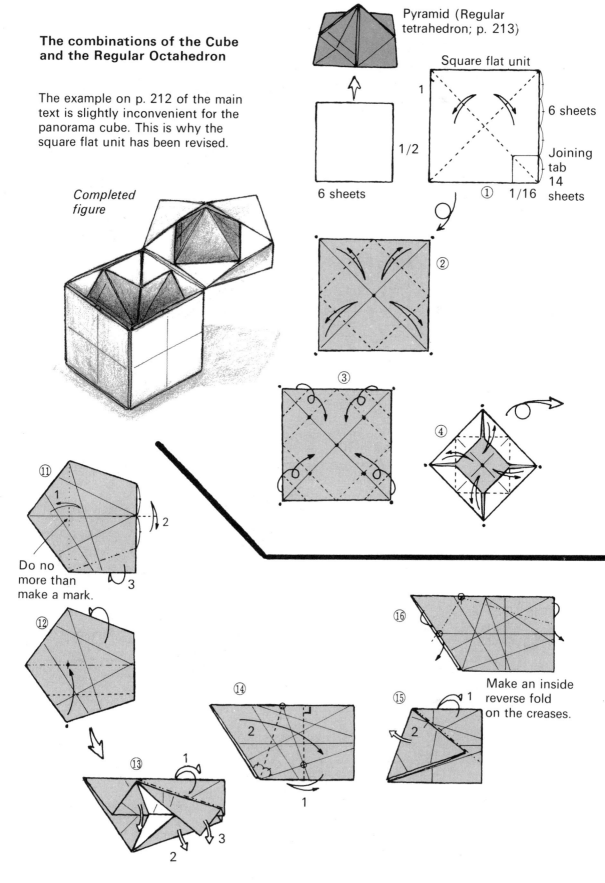

The combinations of the Cube and the Regular Octahedron

The example on p. 212 of the main text is slightly inconvenient for the panorama cube. This is why the square flat unit has been revised.

Pyramid (Regular tetrahedron; p. 213)

Square flat unit

1

1/2

6 sheets

6 sheets

6 sheets

Joining tab 14 sheets

① 1/16

②

③

④

Completed figure

⑪

1

2

3

Do no more than make a mark.

⑫

⑬

1

2

3

⑭

2

1

1

⑮

1

2

⑯

Make an inside reverse fold on the creases.

378

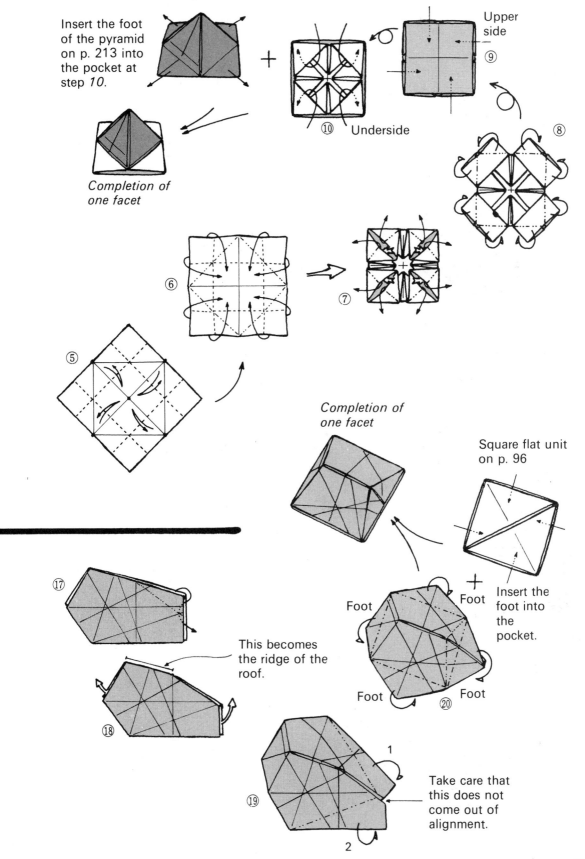

Insert the foot of the pyramid on p. 213 into the pocket at step *10*.

Completion of one facet

Upper side

⑨

⑩ Underside

⑧

⑥

⑦

⑤

Completion of one facet

Square flat unit on p. 96

Insert the foot into the pocket.

⑰

This becomes the ridge of the roof.

⑱

Foot   Foot

Foot   Foot
⑳

⑲

1

2

Take care that this does not come out of alignment.

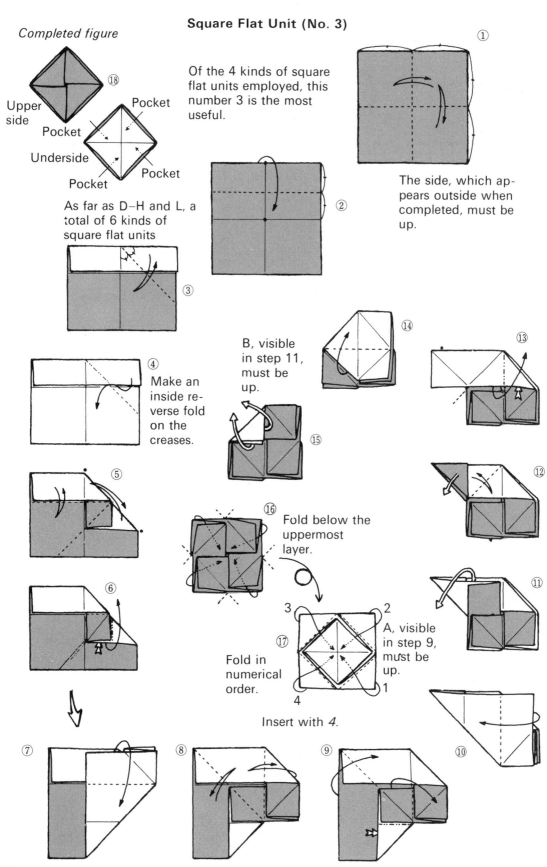

Completed figure

Square Flat Unit (No. 3)

① The side, which appears outside when completed, must be up.

Of the 4 kinds of square flat units employed, this number 3 is the most useful.

Upper side
Pocket
Pocket
Underside
Pocket
Pocket

⑱

As far as D–H and L, a total of 6 kinds of square flat units

②

③

④ Make an inside reverse fold on the creases.

⑤

⑥

⑦

⑧

⑨

⑩

⑪

⑫

⑬

⑭

⑮ B, visible in step 11, must be up.

⑯ Fold below the uppermost layer.

⑰ Fold in numerical order.

3 2
A, visible in step 9, must be up.
4 1

Insert with *4*.

Index